DECENTRALIZATION AND RECENTRALIZATION IN THE DEVELOPING WORLD

DECENTRALIZATION AND RECENTRALIZATION IN THE DEVELOPING WORLD

~~~

COMPARATIVE STUDIES FROM AFRICA AND LATIN AMERICA

J. Tyler Dickovick

THE PENNSYLVANIA STATE UNIVERSITY PRESS
UNIVERSITY PARK, PENNSYLVANIA

Library of Congress Cataloging-in-Publication Data

Dickovick, James Tyler, 1973–
Decentralization and recentralization in the developing
world : comparative studies from Africa and Latin
America / J. Tyler Dickovick
        p.   cm.
Includes bibliographical references and iindex.
Summary: "Examines decentralization and
recentralization in the developing world, focusing on a
comparison of Brazil and South Africa in the 1990s.
Argues that decentralization follows declines in executive
power, while subsequent recentralization in contigent
    upon presidents gaining exceptional governing
opportunities, especially by resolving economic crises"—
Privided by publisher.
ISBN 978-0-271-03790-5
ISBN 978-0-271-03791-2 (pbk. : alk. paper)
1. Central-local government relations—Developing
countries—Case studies
2. Decentralization in government—Developing
countries—Case studies.
3. Central-local government relations—Brazil.
4. Decentralization in government—South Africa.
5. Central-local government relations—Brazil.
6. Decentralization in government—South Africa.
7. Brazil—Politics and government—1985–2002.
8. South Africa—Politics and government—1994–.
9. Comparative government.
I. Title.

JF60.D49 2011
320.809172'4—dc22
2010041984

It is the policy of The Pennsylvania State University Press to
use acid-free paper. Publications on uncoated stock satisfy
the minimum requirements of American National Standard
for Information Sciences—Permanence of Paper for
Printed Library Material, ANSI Z39.48–1992.

CONTENTS

FIGURES AND TABLES

FIGURE

TABLES

ACKNOWLEDGMENTS

This book owes a debt of gratitude first to the faculty at Princeton University who made it possible. Three faculty members in particular supported this project in its original incarnation. First and foremost, Kent Eaton is a colleague who first made political science accessible for me as a pre-dissertation student, then outdid himself with timely encouragement and insightful critiques in subsequent years. His work has made my own possible, and I am eternally grateful. Deborah Yashar's insights and convictions have inspired me in many ways. Her unflagging commitment to "the human side" of politics and her profound understandings of social change are something I can only hope to approximate in coming years. Finally, Jeffrey Herbst served as my dissertation chair and was supportive from the outset, helping me to define this research, conduct fieldwork, and improve the final result. His interventions were always timely, thoughtful, and appreciated.

Others at Princeton also encouraged and supported me immensely. I would especially like to thank Stan Katz and Evan Lieberman for volunteering so much of their time and energy. I will always appreciate having had the chance to learn from many others as well, including Jeremy Adelman, Nancy Bermeo, Joanne Gowa, Atul Kohli, Kathryn Stoner-Weiss, Joshua Tucker, and Lynn White. Among my graduate cohort, I want to thank Conor Healy and Steve Tibbets first, as well as Jose Aleman, Will Barndt, Marc Berenson, Jason Brownlee, Sarah Chartock, Jennifer Dowd, Matt Fouse, Antoinette Handley, Eszter Hargittai, Julia de Kadt, Jaime Kirzner-Roberts, Luda Krytynskaia, José Antonio Lucero, Rani Mullen, Rachel Beatty Riedl, Marty Stein, and Maya Tudor.

I am immensely grateful for the support and critiques I have received from colleagues. (And I offer the disclaimer here that any remaining errors are my own.) Along with Kent Eaton, Al Montero went further than anyone to help me improve this work. Others who have helped me greatly on this and related work include Katrina Burgess, Mark Carey, Ed Connerley, Alberto Diaz-Cayeros, Jonathan Eastwood, Tulia Falleti, Tracy Beck Fenwick, Eduardo Gómez, Jim Kahn, Jesse Ribot, David Samuels, Andrew Selee, Paul Smoke, and Erik Wibbels, among many others.

Sandy Thatcher deserves especially warm thanks for all his efforts during his time at Penn State Press to bring this project to fruition. I am also very thankful for the help of Penn State Press editor Laura Reed-Morrisson and the exceptional work of copyeditor Sue Breckenridge.

Several programs at Princeton and at Washington and Lee University have been central in supporting this research. The Woodrow Wilson School graduate program sponsored me in many ways, and I am thankful to Carmen Ambar and Ann Lengyel in particular, though the list continues on to many others. The Fellowship of Woodrow Wilson Scholars, run by Stan Katz (and Sandy Paroly), enabled me to complete far more than I might have otherwise. The Graduate School and the Program in Latin American Studies supported summer research, as did the Center for International Studies and Center for Regional Studies, now merged into the Princeton Institute for International and Regional Studies (PIIRS).

At Washington and Lee, I am thankful to the Politics Department (chaired by Mark Rush, and filled with colleagues who have supported me in so many ways) and to the Williams School, led by Dean Larry Peppers. I am thankful for the support of the Lenfest Grant and Glenn Grant funds, and for research assistance from a NASDAQ/SunTrust grant. Among research assistants, I was very pleased to have the help of Tom Brower on this project, along with Fernanda Caldas, Monica Magnusson, and Christine Sprow.

Fieldwork and writing were also facilitated by numerous institutions beyond my university homes. Howard Wolpe and Nicole Rumeau at the Woodrow Wilson International Center in Washington generously arranged a summer's support and invaluable access to the resources of the WWIC. Overseas, Peter Spink at the Fundação Getúlio Vargas–São Paulo and Annette Seegers at the University of Cape Town generously offered institutional bases that are the envy of any researcher in Brazil or South Africa, respectively. I much appreciate their help. In Peru, I owe thanks to Prom-Perú, INDECOPI, and the Instituto de Estudios Peruanos. The United Nations Capital Development Fund jumpstarted my research in Senegal; thanks especially to Christian Fournier and Boubacar Fall, among others in New York and Dakar.

I am also thankful for the support of my family over the time I have worked on this project, beginning with my mom, Deborah Dickovick, and sister, Kathryn Dickovick Lambert, as well as Bob Twiss and Adam and Steele and Will Lambert. I also owe special thanks to the São Paulo side of my family for their support. My *sogra*, Nélida Giovannetti Del Conte, is extraordinary: she housed me in Brazil, taught me Portuguese over *telenovelas*, and made me *feijoada vegetariana*. Cristy and Ruy Zardetto and Adriana and Marcelo Paulo (and their children) have made me feel welcome in their homes and in their family. My father-in-law, Franco Del Conte, sadly passed away as this book neared completion. He was a man who taught me incredible amounts about the Latin American experience. I was honored to have had the opportunity to get to know him.

Most of all, of course, I want to express my love and appreciation for my wife, Alessandra Del Conte, and our daughters, Carolina and Gabriela. These last few years with them have been the best of my life. In this case, correlation is causation. Counting on their sympathy and kindness, I know they will understand that if I am to dedicate this book to anyone, it must be to my father, J. Gary Dickovick. I still miss him, and will continue to try to be something close to the husband and father he was.

ABBREVIATIONS

ANC	African National Congress (South Africa)
AP	Acción Popular (Peru)
APRA	Alianza Popular Revolucionária Americana (Peru); American Popular Revolutionary Alliance
BLA	Black Local Authorities (South Africa)
BNDES	Banco Nacional de Desenvolvimento Econômico e Social (Brazil); National Bank for Economic and Social Development
CNA	Constituent National Assembly
CNCL	Conférence National des Collectivités Locales (Senegal); National Conference for Local Collectivities
COSATU	Council of South African Trade Unions
CTAR	Consejos Transitorios de Administración Regional (Peru); Transitional Councils for Regional Administration
DCL	Direction des Collectivités Locales (Senegal); Office for Local Collectivities
DPLG	Department of Provincial and Local Government (South Africa)
FDD	Fonds de Dotation de la Décentralization (Senegal); Decentralization Fund
FECL	Fonds d'Equipement des Collectivités locales (Senegal); Local Government Capital Fund
FEF	Fundo de Estabilização Fiscal (Brazil); Fiscal Stability Fund
FFC	Financial and Fiscal Commission (South Africa)
FONCODES	Fondo Nacional de la Compensación y del Desarrollo Social (Peru); National Fund for Compensation and Social Development
FONCOMUN	Fondo de Compensación Municipal (Peru); Municipal Compensation Fund
FPE	Fundo de Participação dos Estados (Brazil); State Participation Fund

FPM	Fundo de Participação dos Municípios (Brazil); Municipal Participation Fund
FSE	Fundo Social de Emergência (Brazil); Social Emergency Fund
FUNDEF	Fundo de Manutenção e Desenvolvimento do Ensino Fundamental e da Valorização do Magistério (Brazil); Fund for Basic Education and Teacher Enhancement
ICMS	Imposto sobre a Circulação de Mercadorias e Serviços (Brazil); Value-added Tax on Goods and Services.
IFP	Inkatha Freedom Party (South Africa)
IGR	intergovernmental relations
IGT	intergovernmental transfer
IMF	International Monetary Fund
INAMPS	Instituto Nacional de Assistência Médica da Previdência Social (Brazil); National Institute for Medical Assistance and Social Protection
IPI	Imposto sobre Produtos Industrializados (Brazil); Tax on Industrial Products
LRF	Lei de Responsabilidade Fiscal (Brazil); Fiscal Responsibility Law
MARE	Ministério da Administração Federal e Reforma do Estado (Brazil); Ministry of Administration and State Reform
MEC	Member of the Executive Council (South Africa)
MinMEC	Ministers and Members of the Executive Council (South Africa)
MTEF	Medium-Term Expenditure Framework (South Africa)
NCOP	National Council of Provinces (South Africa)
NP	National Party (South Africa)
PAC	Pan-Africanist Congress (South Africa)
PADMIR	Programme d'Appui à la Décentralisation en Milieu Rural (Senegal); Rural Decentralization Support Program
PDS	Parti Démocratique Sénégalais (Senegal); Senegalese Democratic Party
PFL	Partido da Frente Liberal (Brazil); Liberal Front
PFMA	Public Finance Management Act (South Africa)
PMDB	Partido do Movimento Democrático Brasileiro (Brazil); Brazilian Democratic Movement Party
PS	Parti Socialiste (Senegal); Socialist Party

PSDB	Partido da Social Democracia Brasileira (Brazil); Brazilian Social Democratic Party
PT	Partido dos Trabalhadores (Brazil); Workers' Party
RSA	Republic of South Africa
SADTU	South African Democratic Teachers' Union (South Africa)
SAMWU	South African Municipal Workers Union (South Africa)
SNG	subnational government
SUS	Sistema Único de Saúde (Brazil); Single Health Plan
UNDP	United Nations Development Program
USAID	United States Agency for International Development
WLA	White Local Authorities (South Africa)

1

—⟨⟨⟨⟩⟩⟩—

DECENTRALIZATION AND RECENTRALIZATION
IN DEVELOPING COUNTRIES

In the 1980s and 1990s, a wave of decentralization swept across much of the developing world. Along with democratization and economic liberalization, decentralization became a major theme in the relocation of political and economic power. The wave affected a wide range of states: historically centralized command economies and federal countries; developed and undeveloped economies; and in regions around the world, from Eastern Europe to East Asia to South America to sub-Saharan Africa. This impressive sweep of decentralization has increasingly captured the attention of scholars. In the developing world, the literature is on the front burner in Latin America, where major federations such as Brazil, Argentina, and Mexico decentralized significantly as they democratized in the 1980s and 1990s. In Africa too, democratically inclined governments in small, unitary states have increasingly looked to decentralize power to overcome the pathologies of centralized rule. Political scientists have long recognized that the power to govern depends on the control of fiscal resources, and increasingly we have needed to emphasize that this is true of both central and subnational governments: questions about which level of government controls fiscal resources have profound implications for our most fundamental theories about where power lies.

For all the recent excitement, the wave of devolution has crested in some countries, and indeed in others it has reversed. Increasingly in recent years, decentralization processes have been overturned by newly powerful central governments. This demands explanation as well. Literature on decentralization and federalism, which necessarily focus on the devolution of power to subnational levels, has not given these processes sufficient attention. Only in very recent work have scholars begun to address the pressing issues of recentralization and the consolidation of central power in the period after decentralizing reforms. We need to examine the processes of decentralization and recentralization in a single framework. It is crucial that studies of decentralization address not only when, in the words of W. B. Yeats, "the center cannot hold," but also when the center can hold or regain political power, fiscal resources, and administrative control.

Brazil and South Africa are two countries that illustrate the phenomena of decentralization and recentralization in different ways. This study explains when and why central governments decentralize and centralize fiscal power, with a central comparison based on Brazil, a robust federal country, and South Africa, a country with a much weaker form of federalism. Both initiated political and fiscal decentralization processes as they democratized in the 1980s and 1990s, respectively. By 1996 subnational governments in both countries were run by newly empowered elected officials whose tax revenues and expenditures totaled nearly 60 percent of national totals. Subnational governments (SNGs) received constitutionally guaranteed transfers and gained the right to contract debt in capital markets. The extent of decentralization in the two countries is well documented, even if arguments about causes and consequences remain contentious. These were, in short, two of the most astonishing cases of decentralization in the developing world in the 1980s and 1990s.

Yet both countries have also experienced significant limitations on decentralization. In Brazil, overt recentralization has occurred, following economic crises that gave presidents unique opportunities to reduce subnational power. This has defied the expectations of many Brazilianists who view the country as a case of decentralism run amok, a federation where the states (*estados*) dominate politics and the central government is chronically weak. By contrast, South Africa's recentralization has been more limited, but the central government there has consolidated several institutions that call into question the very significance of the decentralization process. Whereas the country's provinces continue to manage a very high percentage of revenues, the center has held onto and reinforced its control over SNGs through tight monitoring and control of spending and borrowing. In both countries, then, central governments have succeeded in limiting and reducing the fiscal powers of subnational governments: they have trimmed borrowing powers, reduced abilities to provide patronage, managed expenditures with increasing technocratic efficiency, and passed increasingly strict statutes that criminalize subnational fiscal irresponsibility.

The importance of these questions extends far beyond these two cases, however, and even to countries with unitary systems of governance. Accordingly,

I also examine two unitary countries—Peru and Senegal—in order to show that a common set of dynamics informs both federal and unitary states; I examine the period from the wave of decentralization in the 1980s to the present. Answering these questions about decentralization and recentralization gives insight into broader issues of public finance and state power by shining a light on moments when fiscal resources are redistributed.

I organize this opening chapter as follows. First, I explain how electoral decline and economic crisis alter executive power relative to actors representing subnational interests. The weakening of executives' partisan powers drives decentralizing change. Arguments linking decentralization to partisan decline have been formulated by Kathleen O'Neill (2003, 2005) as a largely top-down process, and while O'Neill's work underpins part of the analysis here, I also account for decentralization processes that occur "from below" in federal states. The *resolution* of economic crisis, on the other hand, serves as an impetus for recentralizing change, as I illustrate in a subsequent section. I show thereafter how presidential power plays out in three institutional arenas to shape subnational governments' autonomy over their revenues, their expenditures, and their ability to set and enforce contracts. After a brief examination of alternative arguments, I discuss how historical-institutional and rational-institutional arguments must be combined to account for the various forms of subnational fiscal autonomy in each country case.

Explaining Subnational Fiscal Autonomy

As is clear from the outset, I do not deem decentralization to be an adequate analytical outcome but also seek explanations for its converse: (re)centralization. This means exploring when SNG autonomy is increased, when it is decreased, and when it remains the same. I thus conceptualize the dependent variable as *subnational fiscal autonomy,* or *the set of fiscal relationships between the autonomous levels of government in a single country.* This includes various elements of intergovernmental fiscal relations, such as revenue and tax distribution, expenditure responsibilities, and the independence of the different levels of government with respect to contracting in labor and capital markets. In the simplest terms: which levels of government control tax revenues, who is responsible for which policies, and who can borrow and hire and fire at will? In federal states, fiscal relationships will arise among three levels of government: the national (federal) government, local governments, and intermediate-level (i.e., state or provincial) governments. In unitary states, fiscal relations are usually between only two levels—the national and the local—though changes in the political and fiscal importance of regional governments also occur. This study is not about relationships between the different vertical layers of a single central state bureaucracy.

To understand subnational fiscal autonomy better, I consider three components, of which revenue autonomy is the first and most prominent. Revenue autonomy refers to how independent SNGs are from national governments for their revenues. One source of revenues for SNGs is intergovernmental transfers (IGTs). We can measure SNG autonomy by assessing whether these transfers are "automatic" or not. Do central governments have the right to impose conditions on the SNG receiving transfers? If so, this means lower revenue autonomy. On the other hand, where substantial unconditional transfers are guaranteed in the constitution, a country would have higher subnational revenue autonomy. SNGs also procure revenues from own-sources, that is, from their own taxation. Here, we can measure what taxes SNGs are allowed to collect. Can domineering central governments ensure subnational dependence by refusing to devolve tax authority? Or might SNGs have the right to collect valuable income or value-added taxes? Together, the degree of "automaticity" of IGTs and the independence over taxation give a reasonable estimate of how much revenue autonomy an SNG possesses.

Expenditure autonomy is the second element. Provincial and local governments are deemed to have greater autonomy where they have control over their spending. If provinces and municipalities have the freedom to spend their revenues on whatever they want (including patronage), they are more autonomous than their counterparts in other countries with no such discretion. Are SNGs legally assigned specific responsibilities, and are these assignments enforced? Are SNGs required to assume public goods responsibilities de jure, and do they de facto? I focus in particular on two major policy areas—education and health care—where decentralization has proved salient, thereby ensuring variation on the dependent variable. SNGs that have high expenditure autonomy are less compelled by the central government to spend their resources on specific policy areas. The measure of expenditure autonomy, then, will be taken by looking at the rules in place governing expenditures by SNGs. As discussed in chapter 4, this contrasts with the use of aggregate spending figures to measure expenditure decentralization; the reason for this is that subnational spending will correlate strongly (though not perfectly) with subnational revenues. Given a certain extent of devolution in revenues/expenditures, the question becomes how subnational spending is controlled.

Table 1.1 Measuring subnational fiscal autonomy

Type of autonomy	Measurement
Revenue autonomy	• SNGs have taxation authority? • SNGs receive guaranteed transfers from center? • SNGs revenue guarantees are constitutionally protected?
Expenditure autonomy	• SNGs operate free of spending mandates? • SNGs set independent budgets? • SNGs spending is free of monitoring by national ministries?
Contractual autonomy	• SNGs are legally autonomous from central governments? • SNGs can contract debt in capital markets? • SNGs can negotiate labor costs with civil service?

As we shall see, this choice becomes especially important in the context of the Brazil–South Africa comparison.

The third and final component of SNG autonomy may be termed contractual autonomy. In this category, the constitutional or legal independence of SNGs is the *sine qua non* for other forms of autonomy. Beyond this, there are two main types of contractual authority: capital market autonomy and labor market autonomy. SNGs can reasonably be said to have more authority over fiscal matters if they are empowered to enter into independent contracts with employees and creditors, without the explicit oversight of national governments. SNGs that control their own wage bills and debt burdens are more autonomous than those who must look to central governments to set these parameters. Can SNGs borrow on the open market? Do they have their own banks that make soft loans? Can they hire and fire, and change wages, at will? Each of these rights would be indicative of greater subnational contractual autonomy. Those with constitutional guarantees of authority in their jurisdiction are less susceptible to being dissolved or otherwise disbanded by national governments; their contractual autonomy is obviously higher in this case. Table 1.1 encapsulates several of the key questions that may be asked in assessing the measures of subnational autonomy.

The conceptual framework of subnational autonomy allows me to capture the essence of both decentralization and recentralization in a single dependent variable by highlighting increases and decreases in SNG autonomy over time. Decentralization and (re)centralization are not simply questions of cross-national comparative statics, but rather involve calculations and bargains between several sets of actors, including executives and legislators at both the national and subnational levels, with political parties and party systems playing important mediating roles and shaping the calculations of actors in the intergovernmental fiscal system. Taken together, these two sides of the coin constitute the ebb and flow of fiscal power in an intergovernmental system.

The Argument: Decline, Crisis, and the Exercise of Executive Power

Why do central governments choose to decentralize power, and under what conditions can central governments reverse the decentralization of power? I argue that subnational autonomy varies inversely with the power of chief executives, since presidents (or chief executives representing heads of state in parliamentary systems) typically wish to limit subnational autonomy, while SNGs wish to increase their own autonomy. Causally, this presidential power in turn depends on changes in the national political economy, at least in the short run where political institutions such as electoral rules and party systems remain relatively stable. Shifts in executive power occur specifically at moments of electoral decline and economic crisis. The national electoral decline of the chief executive's party reduces presidential power; building on O'Neill's (2005) argument, this often forces presidents to increase subnational autonomy by decentralizing resources and powers. Presidents can reverse these increases and centralize only under extraordinary circumstances. Economic crisis—specifically, the resolution of crisis—creates such an opportunity, strengthening the hands of presidents and enabling centralization efforts that would not otherwise succeed.

Presidents typically prefer not to decentralize power.[1] In the area of intergovernmental relations, they prefer to limit subnational actors and maximize their own power and discretion over national resources. This is true in both presidential systems (such as in much of Latin America and Africa) as well as parliamentary systems (of which South Africa is a representative case here).[2] While history suggests presidents (especially in countries such as Brazil) respond to the needs of their subnational bases of support, we may make the initial assumption that presidents by virtue of their political position prefer to limit SNG autonomy on fiscal questions. Under this assumption, decentralization is seen as a presidential initiative only in the sense that presidents act in accordance with institutionally generated outcomes.

1. While this assumption will not hold true in all cases, I follow the logic of Levi (1988).
2. I use the term "presidents" throughout the empirical cases to refer to chief executives, including those in parliamentary systems. This is because the head of government in South Africa's parliamentary system is called—somewhat confusingly for scholars of parliamentarism—the president. In general, I refer to heads of state.

Presidents decentralize when under political duress, and even top-down decentralization must be seen as a form of constrained optimization, not a reflection of underlying presidential preferences. Presidents are more often eager to recentralize, but their ability to do so is contingent on relatively uncommon governing opportunities, as noted below. In short, I argue that decline leads to decentralization and crisis to centralization. I consider these two independent variables—electoral decline and macroeconomic crisis— and their consequences in turn.

Executive Partisan Decline and Decentralization

Governments decentralize power, and increase subnational autonomy, when presidential partisan powers weaken. This is true when presidents face national electoral defeat or require subnational support to hold together a governing coalition. At these moments of weakness, presidents are vulnerable to bottom-up pressures from subnational actors within their own governing coalitions, where these subnational interests are institutionally powerful, as in Brazil (see Eaton 2004a; Samuels 2003). Decline of the president's national party strength also increases the attractiveness of top-down solutions whereby presidents strengthen SNGs in order to develop or strengthen regional bases for the future (cf. O'Neill 2005). From O'Neill's perspective, presidential partisan weakness is especially salient when subnational copartisans are well positioned to win elections and have strong representation in national legislatures. That is, national governing parties decentralize when they are waning nationally, but are strong subnationally.

Democratization may be seen as a special case of governmental decline— wherein regimes themselves decline—and democratization is thus likely to bring decentralization in its wake.[3] This may occur because "democrats are decentralizers" or because there is some "elective affinity" between democratization and decentralization, insofar as both are predicated on dispersing rather than concentrating power. While many decentralizing processes occur alongside transitions from authoritarian rule, I do not argue that democratization alone causes decentralization. I show that declining regimes facing Constituent National Assemblies (CNAs) are likely to increase SNG autonomy,

---

3. Eaton (2000, 2004a) treats the connections between democratization and decentralization and finds that decentralization indeed follows on the heels of democratization. My analysis supports this finding and suggests that the logic can be extended more broadly to democracies and is not specific to moments of regime change.

just like declining governments awaiting elections. In the unitary cases (Peru and Senegal), decentralization occurred when parties anticipated defeat in regularly scheduled national elections, while in federal Brazil and South Africa, decentralization occurred during regime changes at CNAs. Decline drove decentralization in all four case countries, despite these variations in regime politics. Taking as given that the likelihood of decentralized governance increases with democracy and decreases with authoritarianism, I conduct my analysis by looking principally at variation within nominally democratic regimes and at moments of transition.[4]

Cases where governing parties decentralized from the top down before losing national elections support a rational expectations model of intergovernmental relations. In such cases, to include South Africa and Peru in the late 1980s, decentralization not only preceded national electoral defeat, but also became increasingly salient in direct relation to the certainty of that defeat. The National Party in South Africa and the Alianza Popular Revolucionária Americana in Peru in particular sought aggressive decentralization at an increasing pace as their electoral defeats at the national level became increasingly certain.

Central governments may have electoral reasons to decentralize in the face of decline even when they are not strongest at the subnational level, however. Victoria Rodriguez argues that decentralization in Mexico was a scheme concocted out of tactical decisions to raise public support of the regime and to enhance the government's legitimacy (Rodriguez 1997).[5] The benefits to governments of decentralization may thus outweigh the costs, even if the national party stands to lose regional elections. Admitting this possibility means we retain the analytical emphasis on the calculations of central government actors, while relaxing the assumption that the center devolves power only when the governing party is strong subnationally. The Senegalese case examined in chapter 6 seems to blend the two top-down motives outlined by O'Neill and Rodriguez, respectively: the Parti Socialiste in the 1990s sought to strengthen its subnational political base while also engaging in a popular reform; the combination may be

4. I deal subsequently with the obviously problematic fate of democracy in 1990s Peru.

5. Arguments by O'Neill and Rodriguez thus both rely on electoral logic, but have quite different implications. In the former, the decentralizing parties are all but resigned to losing national power, while they are clinging desperately to national power in the latter. For O'Neill, decentralization brings only benefits to the current governing party or coalition. For Rodriguez, decentralization is a costly concession for the current governing party, but one accepted in order to raise the probability of winning the next national election. For Rodriguez, decentralization can be manipulated by national elites to ensure the maintenance of regime power.

seen as the party "diversifying its portfolio of holdings" as electoral uncertainty increased.

Also of great import to the study here, however, are processes of decentralization that do not conform to top-down, electoralist models, but rather depend on deeply entrenched political institutions that shape calculations by political players. Kent Eaton's (2004a) analyses of decentralization "from below" blend rational-institutional and historical-institutional arguments to evaluate decentralization across different time periods. Brazil, for instance, is best viewed as a country whose decentralization processes have been driven by powerful subnational actors, with shifts in the political economy triggering changes in subnational autonomy; political parties, legislatures, and states serve as mediating factors or intervening variables in such processes. In chapter 2, I discuss at length the historical trajectories that give rise to top-down dynamics in unitary and weakly federal countries, and the bottom-up dynamics that prevail in robustly federal states; this highlights the need to offer rationalist accounts that are historically informed rather than ahistorical.

Crisis Resolution and Recentralization

Centralization and recentralization (or, more generally, reductions in subnational autonomy) have received less attention than decentralization processes in recent years. There are good reasons for this. The greater emphasis on decentralization is due to several asymmetries. Recentralization is conditional upon some prior instance of decentralized governance, whereas decentralization processes are conditional upon prior centralized governance; given the nature of the centralized state in the developing world, it is understandable that decentralization would take precedence. Moreover, decentralization is examined in a variety of issue areas, including fiscal decentralization, administrative decentralization, and political decentralization (cf. Falleti 2005), whereas studies of recentralization generally focus on central control of revenue authority. Related to both of these facts, and perhaps most importantly, recentralization is likely to be quite contested. Decentralization invests power and authority in subnational officials, and these officials once empowered are likely to strongly resist recentralization with the resources at their disposal (O'Neill 2005, 60).

Yet the political-economic approach that offers explanations of decentralization "from above" and "from below" leaves several questions unanswered. Most importantly, why would incoming governments not reverse decentralization? If declining parties can decentralize without friction at the end of their mandates, why can't newly inaugurated governments (often at the peak of their legitimacy, unlike their "outgoing" predecessors) simply reverse the legislation? Why does decentralization "stick" in some countries, but get reversed elsewhere?

The comparative political economy literature on economic crisis provides guidance in understanding recentralizing changes. Economic crisis can shape important political changes, with some scholars finding that such a crisis leads to *less* central government control over a variety of decisions, at least at initial stages (Grindle 1996; Haggard and Kaufman 1995), while others highlight the leverage crises provide to central governments (e.g., Weyland 1998). The argument here modifies these two positions by arguing that *crisis resolution,* rather than the mere existence of crisis, drives the most significant processes of recentralization. Presidents that resolve crises have the political power to reduce subnational autonomy. Crisis actually triggers changes that favor the national executive in negotiations with subnational actors, by providing extraordinary governing opportunities for those presidents who succeed in stabilizing the economy. Whereas decline leads to decentralization, macroeconomic crisis—or more specifically, its resolution—leads to centralization.[6]

Two points must be elaborated with respect to the concept of economic crisis and its use as a variable. First is the question of conceptual precision, since crisis as a variable may be used sloppily to signify a range of economic phenomena of the analyst's choosing.[7] As recent work by Reinhart and Rogoff (2009) has shown, economic crises may be defined in several ways, ranging from crises based on quantitative macroeconomic indicators (such as inflation) to those understood as "events" (such as bank failures). Crises take a variety of forms, including fiscal crises (and government defaults), financial sector or banking collapses, exchange rate collapses, balance of payment crises, and inflationary crises. Each is associated with its own indicators, such as government deficits and indebtedness, asset price collapses, or inflation rates. Even more loosely, scholars have referred to economic "crises" in the developing world that are chronic rather than acute; these may include extended periods of no growth or slow growth (as in "lost decades" or "Africa's economic crisis"), dramatic slowdowns in real economic activity, or

6. The relationship between crisis and recentralization is noted in the literature, but merits more systematic treatment. For particular application to the Brazilian case, see especially Montero (2004) on the wake of the Real Plan. For further references to the relationship between crisis and decentralization, though not along the lines of the causal argument forwarded here, see Eaton (2004a), O'Neill (2005), Rodden (2006), and Wibbels (2005).

7. I am thankful to Erik Wibbels for his observations on this question.

simple economic contractions or reductions in capital investment. Without a firm grasp on the subset of crises purported to have causal impact, we are left with an analytical risk: observing the predicted outcome on a dependent variable, and inferring an impact of crisis whenever any of a number of economic conditions turns sour. We must define which crises matter for politics.

I expect significant effects on recentralization from economic crises that have a particular characteristic: they significantly affect purchasing power in the present. Crises in which citizens are seeing their purchasing power actively eroded will have distinct political consequences relative to other "crises" in which repercussions on the citizenry are still ambiguous or forthcoming. In open economies, the purchasing power of the money base can collapse in two principal ways: through inflation or through exchange rate collapse (i.e., the loss of purchasing power for imports).[8] Of course, where both inflationary crises and currency crises occur simultaneously, the anticipated effects would be even stronger. These crises in particular should matter because they shape citizens' willingness to allow dramatic market reform. Under the conditions of purchasing power crises, citizens operate "in the domain of losses," to use Weyland's (2002) term. From the perspective of prospect theory, an aversion to further losses—more simply, a desire to "just make it stop"—allows governments to implement strategies with higher risks and major implications for the institutional balance of power. This includes painful economic adjustments and—in the present case— recentralizing changes.

By the purchasing power criterion, many other forms of so-called crises should not lead to recentralization. Extreme fiscal imbalances, for instance, may constitute a "fiscal crisis," but these are not posited to have their political impact until purchasing power is affected. Fiscal deficits may of course eventually lead to collapses in purchasing power through the intervening variables of indebtedness, inflation, balance of payments crises, and exchange rate depreciation, but if these purchasing power declines have not yet been realized, then we would not anticipate a willingness to confer immediate authority to the central government executive on the basis of fiscal deficits alone. Similarly, trade deficits or imbalances in trade would not constitute a crisis for the purposes of the present argument until purchasing power was affected through a collapse in the exchange rate. Banking sector crises and

8. As a thought experiment, an economy with significant numbers of shareholders suffering from a major asset price collapse could witness a purchasing power crisis from a powerful negative wealth effect. In practical terms, this is unlikely to pertain to developing countries.

government defaults are also significant insofar as they engender actual purchasing power losses for the citizenry. Finally, the more chronic forms of crisis—especially long-term economic stagnation and underperformance— are not considered likely contributors here because they do not place citizens in risk-tolerant situations.

To a large extent, then, I follow Weyland's (1998, 2002) emphasis on hyperinflation, which is less susceptible to slipperiness than other indicators, although the exact threshold is debatable, often being defined at 100 per-cent per annum. Using this definition of hyperinflation has the advantage of conceptual clarity, but the choice is also informed by a theoretical choice, since hyperinflation may be seen as economic crisis in its most acute form, and as qualitatively different from other forms of economic crisis, in part because it gives citizens a greater propensity to accept risk; the psychological effect of hyperinflation on citizens and on politicians alike makes these crises ripe for bold policy prescription and offers the potential of extraordi-nary political leverage for those who tame it. In the cases examined here, hyperinflation was the key indicator of a crisis of purchasing power, though this was partially accompanied by collapses in exchange rates as well.[9] The *in extremis* nature of crisis also provides crucial political cover for centrali-zing reforms that might otherwise be construed as antidemocratic power grabs. Importantly, the South African case further shows the importance of a clear understanding of crisis: recentralization there was much more circum-scribed, due to the much more localized and limited nature of the crisis in government finances.

A second major issue with respect to the concept of crisis is the need to specify the path-dependent causal sequence linking crisis and recentralization. As noted above, crisis resolution (rather than crisis itself) is key to the com-plex chain of events that initiates and sustains recentralization. Crisis may be a necessary condition for presidents to initiate successful recentralization processes, but is not sufficient, since consummating a recentralization process depends on presidential leverage. The cases here leave clear that presidential administrations that take blame for causing an economic crisis will have great difficulty recentralizing; presidents who governed during the onset of crisis are likely to see declines in presidential leverage, which will have not a recentralizing impact, but rather the decentralizing impact noted above.

---

9. Collapses in exchange rates will matter most in countries where imports are significant for consumers. Hyperinflation would still be expected to have the greatest impact on the policy environment, given that its impact is generalized and not mediated through effects on imports.

Table 1.2 Inflation rates (annual % change in consumer prices)

	Brazil	Peru	Senegal	So. Africa
1985	226.0	163.4	13.0	16.2
1986	147.1	77.9	6.1	18.8
1987	228.3	85.8	-4.1	16.2
1988	629.1	667.0	-1.8	12.9
1989	1430.7	3398.3	0.4	14.5
1990	2947.7	7481.7	0.3	14.3
1991	477.4	409.5	-1.8	15.6
1992	1022.5	73.5	0.0	13.7
1993	1927.4	48.6	-0.7	9.9
1994	2075.8	23.7	32.1	8.8
1995	66.0	11.1	8.1	8.7
1996	16.0	11.6	2.8	7.3
1997	6.9	8.5	1.8	8.6
1998	3.2	7.3	1.0	6.9
1999	4.9	3.5	0.8	5.2
2000	7.1	3.8	0.7	5.4

SOURCE: IMF World Economic Outlook Database (2008)

By contrast, presidencies that can initiate and sustain a resolution to hyper-inflationary crises will increase their intergovernmental advantage and will have unique centralizing opportunities. Among the four case countries, two presidents (Fernando Henrique Cardoso in Brazil and Alberto Fujimori in Peru) resolved major hyperinflationary crises and used their resulting political leverage to engineer substantial reductions in SNG autonomy. Absent such a crisis, would-be centralizers in other cases (Thabo Mbeki in South Africa and Abdoulaye Wade in Senegal) had less scope to reverse decentralizing moves that had occurred to varying degrees in their countries, even though they had considerably greater partisan powers.

Recentralization processes were successfully initiated during a hyperinflationary moment in Brazil (1994–95), but these processes also had an even more significant path-dependent quality. The fiscal recentralization that occurred in Brazil built upon itself once initiated, with a presidential administration that was surprisingly successful—especially over the years from 1995 to 2000—at institutionalizing central control over larger proportions of government revenues, expenditures, and borrowing. In Peru, recentralization was largely subsequent to the resolution of the crisis, occurring mainly in 1992, by which time inflation had subsided considerably.

The preponderance of recentralizing moves in both countries occurred after economic crisis resolution, as path-dependent sequences shaped continued recentralization throughout the 1990s. Yet it should be noted how sequences differed somewhat between the federal case of Brazil and the unitary case of Peru, largely as a function of the countries' prior degrees of decentralization. In Brazil, recentralization was in large part a necessary response to SNG profligacy (since the SNGs were among the actors primarily responsible of the economic crisis), whereas in Peru (where SNGs had little or no role in causing the crisis), the process of recentralization came largely after crisis resolution. The recentralizing sequence under Brazil's federal system was more endogenous and reciprocal, since crisis resolution and recentralization were mutually contingent in ways that did not apply in unitary Peru. The consequence was the more simultaneous interplay between crisis resolution and recentralization in the former case, and the more sequential path in the latter. The particular sequences, and their relationships to the federal–unitary distinction, are further elaborated in the case analyses below.

Taken from a comparative static perspective, it will come as a surprise to observers of Brazilian and/or African politics that Brazil centralized more than the African cases. To be clear from the outset, Brazil remains considerably more decentralized (in the comparative static sense) than any country in Africa. The reasons for Brazil's continued high levels of decentralism are well documented and relate strongly to the historical development of legislative institutions that favor SNGs in national decision making (see, e.g., Ames 2001; Garman, Haggard, and Willis 2001; Mainwaring 1997a, 1997b; Samuels 2003). On the other hand, once power was devolved in each of these cases, Brazil's central government has been successful in clawing back some of the fiscal authority of SNGs. Given Brazil's weak party system, this cannot be explained by partisan powers of the president alone. Despite clear efforts to recentralize, South Africa's African National Congress (ANC) and Senegal's Parti Démocratique Sénégalais (PDS) presidents—with their stronger partisan powers—left revenue provisions and subnational responsibilities largely intact, while the Cardoso government in Brazil reformed that country's fiscal federal system in the wake of economic crisis.

Additional observable implications reinforce the argument about the importance of economic crisis: I show that even small, localized fiscal crises in selected SNGs also generate a centralizing dynamic, but one that is correspondingly weaker than the dynamic created by larger systemic crises characterized by full-blown hyperinflation. Localized fiscal problems of this sort occurred in South Africa, where the central government resolved provincial budget crises, and in so doing intervened directly in provincial fiscal affairs. The key observation is that the extent of recentralization depended on the extent of fiscal crisis: whereas crisis was generalized to the macroeconomic level in the Latin American cases, it was limited to specific provinces in South Africa, and the corresponding recentralization was limited as well. Obviously, limited recentralization in South Africa involved direct inter-executive negotiations between the levels of government. Other reductions in autonomy came through the exercise of executive power in other arenas, most notably within the state and in the legislature.

Institutional Arenas and the Exercise of Executive Power

We can conceptualize the fiscal autonomy of SNGs in three issue areas: autonomy over revenues, autonomy over expenditures, and autonomy over legal and financial contracts. Central governments and SNGs contest fiscal autonomy in these three issue areas, and presidents interact with different actors and exercise their power in distinct institutional contexts that correspond to each of the areas. On revenue issues, presidents (or chief executives) regularly negotiate with elected parliamentary representatives; party systems and the balance of executive–legislative power drive most decisions about the division of fiscal resources. With respect to the administration of expenditures, decisions within the executive branch will matter, such that presidents exercise power relative to bureaucracies, especially ministers and other high-ranking officials within the state; I term this intra-executive relations. In determining subnational contractual autonomy, presidents often engage in direct negotiations with subnational executives such as governors and mayors. Within a framework where decline leads to decentralization and crisis to centralization, these different actors and institutions still shape outcomes. Presidents have greater leverage over bureaucracies than over legislators, on average; this corresponds to greater presidential success in shaping expenditure autonomy (which is controlled through bureaucratic channels) than revenue autonomy (which is regularly debated in the executive–legislative arena).

Changes in the three types of autonomy are usually—but not always—correlated; shifts in one area of subnational autonomy tend to accompany similar shifts in the other areas as well. Broad correlations across these multiple areas underpin existing arguments about decentralization; at least, it is rare that studies can account for enhanced autonomy in one area (such as revenues) but not another (such as expenditures). I place a particular emphasis on the numerous instances when devolution in one area does not correlate with devolution in another, such as when SNGs receive improved revenue guarantees, but remain limited in spending autonomy. In my argument, then, the broad correlations are explained by the "macro" argument that centers on partisan electoral decline and economic crisis; this argument has validity across the three issue areas identified above. Meanwhile, *variations* across the issue areas in the timing and extent of decentralization and recentralization highlight how different institutional arenas may shape political action differently. The three areas together give a relatively holistic view of an entire fiscal system, both in its outcomes and in the complex causes of these outcomes.

Viewing these three distinct areas—revenues, expenditures, and contracts—through the lens of SNG fiscal autonomy clarifies the preferences of subnational actors. For revenues, SNG preferences are relatively clear: SNGs prefer greater (and more autonomous) access to revenues. For expenditures, however, SNG preferences need greater clarification. On the one hand, SNGs may desire the decentralization of expenditures, in order to gain increasing importance in the national political economy. On the other hand, SNGs may desire less decentralization of spending responsibilities because the centralization of expenditures leaves SNGs with greater latitude in spending its revenues. Focusing on subnational expenditure autonomy offers a way through the impasse. For a given level of revenues (that is, holding revenue autonomy constant), SNGs prefer to maximize their own autonomy or discretion over how revenues are spent. Similarly, SNGs prefer to maximize their own autonomy in their forays into capital and labor markets, while passing obligations to the center. The central government, on the other hand, prefers to maximize its own discretion in the distribution of revenues, in the division of spending, and in its action in contracts and markets, while creating parallel obligations for SNG in each of these areas. I consider below how presidents exercise power in each of these three institutional arenas.[10]

Executive–Legislative Relations and Revenue Autonomy

One obvious arena where presidents exercise more or less power is in executive-legislative relations, and much of the decentralization literature shows that revenue autonomy generally depends on the powers of presidents relative to legislatures. Public political debate in the legislative arena largely determines the vertical division of revenue between the center and SNGs, though direct

---

10. Of course, the relationship between these issue areas and these institutional arenas is not wholly fixed. Revenue negotiations may take place directly between presidents and subnational executives, and contractual and expenditure negotiations involve legislators, for example. This division of institutional arenas presents the principal interlocutor for presidents in each issue area, and the division does not suggest that presidents operate exclusively in a given arena for a given issue.

negotiations with subnational politicians also matter here (Eaton 2001). Revenue division can happen either through the passage of laws guaranteeing formulas for the division of revenue and tax authority, or through ad hoc negotiations for patronage resources and pork that legislators deliver to local constituents. Generally, the president's power relative to the legislature can depend on partisan powers or formal powers, as in the case of decree authority or legislative structures that give the president agenda-setting power (cf., e.g., Carey and Shugart 1998, Figueiredo and Limongi 2000; Mainwaring and Shugart 1997).

SNGs seek guaranteed access to high levels of revenue. Access to revenue can come from own-source tax collection or from intergovernmental transfers from other levels of government. Among intergovernmental transfers, or revenues collected by the central government and distributed to SNGs, the most important are automatic, legally mandated transfers. Transfers mandated by constitutions are the most desirable, followed by transfers outlined in ordinary law, and then by transfers over which the central government exercises discretion, since the latter may in principle be revoked by the center at any time. Alongside transfers, SNGs may seek tax authority. If the central government grants SNGs the right to enact taxes that were not previously authorized, this is treated as a move decentralizing revenue. Given the centralized nature of tax collection in the countries examined, shifts in tax authority are less important than intergovernmental revenue transfers, except in Brazil. Still, countries with centralized tax authority score lower on subnational revenue autonomy than countries that do transfer taxation authority.

Presidents facing national decline increased revenue autonomy through legislative channels in all four countries between the years of 1988 and 1996. Brazil's and Peru's presidents both decentralized in 1988, and Senegal's and South Africa's presidents did the same in the mid-1990s. In all four cases, decentralization took place when the governing party had an electoral incentive to empower SNGs. Still, executive–legislative dynamics differed in their details from case to case. In some instances, presidents pushed decentralization through the legislature, while in other cases the legislature pulled resources away from a more reluctant executive on behalf of subnational constituents. Given the momentous occasions that CNAs represent as foundational moments of regime change, these events gave the greatest scope to decentralization processes in Brazil and South Africa.

Though all four countries decentralized revenues, only two central governments were later able to reverse the trend and recentralize certain revenues on a national basis. In Brazil and Peru, presidents who successfully resolved

Table 1.3 Presidential power and changes in subnational fiscal autonomy

Outcome	Increases in subnational autonomy	Decreases in subnational autonomy
Cases	Brazil 1988–1994 Peru 1988–1990 South Africa 1992–1996 Senegal 1992–1996	Brazil 1994–2002 Peru 1992–2000 South Africa 1997–1999 (limited)

economic crises used their reserves of political strength (which were temporary) to assert authority over the legislature and recentralize revenues. Absent such a crisis, even presidents with strong legislative backing (in South Africa and Senegal) were surprisingly weak-limbed in reducing revenue autonomy, and the Decentralization Fund in Senegal and the "equitable share" in South Africa remain intact.

Intra-executive Powers and Expenditure Autonomy

Most of the focus in decentralization literature is on the distribution of revenues, and correspondingly, the literature emphasizes the causal impact of executive–legislative relations and party politics. Expenditure autonomy, however, depends on the establishment and enforcement of spending rules by the central state's bureaucratic apparatus. As Mainwaring (1997a, 101) notes in the Brazilian context, if political institutions are important in shaping presidential successes vis-à-vis the legislature, then "presidents should have been more easily able to implement their preferred policies in areas where Congress and governors are less central actors." Theoretically, we would expect actors in the national executive to have greater leverage over expenditures administered through bureaucracies than over revenues that are subject to political bargaining in the legislative arena, since expenditure rules are more susceptible to executive administration and bureaucratic management. And indeed, central governments generally have given SNGs less autonomy in expenditures than in other arenas where the pro-decentralizing coalition is stronger and more vested.

Executives leading strong cabinet coalitions have opportunities to monitor and control subnational spending. Strong presidential advocates in finance ministries and major social policy areas will use bureaucratic levers to institutionalize power and control subnational action. Presidential loyalists at the heads of key ministries will have different effects on policy from ministers that do not share presidential objectives or that are closely linked to subnational interests. Conversely, presidents with weak partisan support may be required to spread ministerial portfolios broadly to coalition partners, and this will diminish the president's ability to control expenditure patterns and require SNGs to follow national spending mandates. Brazil from 1988 to 1994 was just such a case of a weak president distributing cabinet portfolios broadly in order to assemble a governing coalition, with the result being weaker central government control over subnational spending, or (put another way) increases in expenditure autonomy. On the other hand, the strengthening of presidential prerogatives means presidents can fill important cabinet posts with copartisans who share their preferences and objectives. This occurred in Brazil after 1994, as well as in other cases. In these cases, presidential allies within the governing coalition reduce expenditure autonomy by more tightly monitoring subnational spending.

Presidential partisan weakness thus leads to greater subnational spending autonomy, and crisis resolution (which strengthens the hands of presidents) will reduce this subnational autonomy, but via different mechanisms than is the case with revenues. Patterns differ here from the outcomes with regard to revenue autonomy: in this institutional arena, presidents have given away less and have recentralized more. Decline led to only marginal increases in expenditure autonomy for SNGs in South Africa, Peru, and Senegal, because cabinets remained coherent without a need to distribute spoils, and intra-executive relations thus favored presidents and the centralized exercise of power, even as governments declined electorally. Only in Brazil did a wide distribution of cabinet posts to a broad coalition favor meaningful increases in subnational expenditure autonomy. In terms of reductions, crisis again strengthened the hands of presidents in the Latin American cases and led to more top-down spending mandates set by the center. Additionally, localized crises in South Africa enabled the central government to constrict expenditure autonomy there, but only on a province-by-province basis.

Inter-executive Relations and Contractual Autonomy

Much as expenditure autonomy required an understanding of a new set of actors—the state—in addition to executives and legislatures, so too do new actors emerge in the area of contractual autonomy. Contractual autonomy— or the independence of SNGs in setting their own contracts in labor and capital markets—is partially affected by executive–legislative relations and by intra-executive considerations, and also by its own particular dynamic. The lines of authority between layers of government in intergovernmental systems are often more complex than lines of authority within the state or between branches of the central government. Here, presidents must exercise their authority in direct negotiations with subnational politicians, such as governors and mayors.

Contractual authority is often a function of bargaining between central governments and SNGs over such issues as subnational debt and provisions for the public labor force of provincial or state governments. Evidence from these countries shows that presidential negotiations with subnational officials continued to be shaped by the political-economic environment presidents faced. The decline of the national governing party may be sufficient to lead to greater contractual autonomy under certain conditions, namely if the president and the party's national leadership expect the party to do well subnationally in the future. In this case, subnational contractual autonomy will be strengthened alongside revenue autonomy and expenditure autonomy. Macroeconomic crisis, on the other hand, may give presidents a pretext to assume top-down control of traditionally devolved powers, especially if SNGs played a role in instigating the crisis with profligate spending. In unitary states, SNGs have few constitutional protections, and contractual autonomy may be particularly vulnerable to central government overturn.

The causes of increases and decreases in contractual autonomy again reside in the political economy, but the institutional mechanisms for change are again particular to this issue area. Decline and crisis continue to decrease and increase presidential leverage, respectively, yet the new set of actors is particularly influential: when presidents lose power relative to SNG politicians as a result of decline, contractual autonomy increases; when presidents gain leverage relative to SNG politicians after resolving crises, contractual autonomy decreases. This is not to suggest that SNG politicians matter only in this area, or that legislators or states do not matter for contractual autonomy. Rather, in moving from revenues to expenditures to contracts, this emphasis on new actors highlights what needs to be added to the model to improve our interpretation of each element of subnational autonomy.

Table 1.4 summarizes the three areas of SNG autonomy and the institutional arenas and actors that correspond to each. Immediately apparent is that presidents represent the interests of the center throughout, with the afore-mentioned caveat that presidents will nonetheless sometimes devolve power due to political weakness. When presidents decentralize, they do so not due to innate preferences, but rather because of a loss of authority relative to other actors with subnational prerogatives. Beyond presidents, the principal actors are the national legislature, the state itself, and subnational executives,

Table 1.4 Issue areas and institutional arenas of subnational fiscal autonomy

Issue area	Chief advocates of central power	Presidential interlocutors	Institutional arena of contestation
Revenue autonomy	Presidents	Legislatures	Executive–Legislative
Expenditure autonomy	Presidents	Bureaucracies	Intra-executive
Contractual autonomy	Presidents	Subnational politicians	Inter-executive

with each playing its most significant role in shaping one of the areas of SNG autonomy.

Competing Hypotheses

The focus on presidential powers places this analysis in an institutionalist framework, while the consideration of the political economy gives leverage with regard to dynamic shifts in subnational autonomy over the short term. But could other theories or approaches—either institutionalist, structuralist, or agency-based—explain these outcomes? Not surprisingly, perhaps, explanations from many of the major traditions of political science have sought to explain degrees of centralism and decentralism in the developing world. I argue that structural, cultural, and purely agency-based models offer few opportunities to understand the dynamics of changing SNG autonomy. The most prominent institutional arguments explaining intergovernmental fiscal outcomes, meanwhile, focus on parties and party systems, and most institutional arguments also have relatively little leverage in explaining the timing of outcomes over the short term.

Structural and Cultural Arguments

Structural and cultural arguments jointly share some of the same strengths and weaknesses in their ability to explain decentralization and recentralization. In particular, they are useful in comparative statics but are of less use in predicting or explaining short-term variations. Arguments in the structuralist vein hold that economic and historical legacies have a preponderant effect on contemporary governance outcomes. Truncated processes of state formation in the postcolonial world suggest for some that central governments will be weak and beholden to provincial pressures. For others, it suggests that government will tend to be top-heavy, and local governments will thus be weak. Cultural factors, such as colonization by Catholic (Latin America,

Francophone Africa) or Protestant (Anglophone North America and Anglophone Africa) countries, are also used to explain profound continuities, including greater traditions of centralized or decentralized governance, respectively.

Work in the structuralist vein may be powerful in explaining broad patterns for a given country or region, and economic structure can strongly condition how centralized or decentralized a state becomes, as I will show in the next chapter when I assess the historical development of the cases. Where central government is unable to break the power of traditional local elites, or when subnational elites penetrate national government, SNGs may command considerable power (cf. Abrucio 1998; Hagopian 1996). Similarly, the historical legacies of colonialism may be a deeply structural (or cultural) cause. Strong centralization may be an "imperative of rule" central states inherit from colonizers (cf. Young 1994); or, centralization could simply be a "tradition" colonizers pass on to colonial and postcolonial states (Véliz 1980). Conversely, "decentralized despotism" may be a colonial pattern of rule common to all colonies (French, British, or otherwise) and may be the modal form of the colonial state (Mamdani 1996). Or the sheer costs of projecting power may represent insurmountable state-building challenges for central governments facing difficult political geographies; a difficult territory would represent de facto limitations on the abilities of central governments to rule (Herbst 2000).

I rely heavily upon historical-institutional arguments to explain broad patterns of decentralization, to understand the role of federalism in the process, and to motivate puzzles about recentralization as well. When examined comparatively, socioeconomic structures and political cultures can successfully depict broad patterns in cross-national analysis and can help explain how countries reach the present with higher or lower levels of centralism. Yet these factors alone cannot explain short-term variations within countries as fully as the dynamic institutional model I have proposed. Brazil's historically federal structures, for instance, cannot explain why the country's central government has *reduced* subnational autonomy since 1994. Many structural and cultural arguments also shed little light on the variation among countries in a region or subregion. Frequently (though not always), explanations predict broad regional or national patterns of centralism and decentralism. Why decentralization occurs when it does is often not a central question, unless this is predicted to occur at moments of regime change. While some structural arguments thus go a long way toward explaining persistent tendencies, they are relatively powerless to make more microlevel predictions about the circumstances under which patterns shift.

This criticism will hold as well for those institutional explanations that neglect purposive behavior.

Institutions (and Limitations of Institutional Arguments)

Institutions, including political parties and the state admininstrations have come to the center of comparative political science and have broad applicability to questions of SNG autonomy in developing countries. In Africa, for instance, studies of state institutions in the 1960s found top-down centralization to be instrumental to the aims of single-party states (Lewis 1965; Zolberg 1966). Several works similarly trace the development of centralizing authoritarian states in Latin America to the need to establish order, though these may adopt a more structuralist approach (cf. O'Donnell 1972). Such works are at least partly about attempts to enhance central power.

Highly decentralized countries such as Brazil are regularly assessed in terms of the institutions of federalism; federal institutions explain why power and resources flow to subnational levels (Abrucio 1998; Ames 2001; Mainwaring 1997a; Samuels 2003). Institutions in these studies are a by-product of long-standing political traditions, but they are also of contemporary relevance and have effects on present-day politics. But here again, standing institutions predict broad national patterns rather than changes over time. Indeed, the issue of federalism raises important puzzles in this vein: under what conditions do federations centralize, and likewise under what conditions will unitary states decentralize?

Among institutional literatures, work on executive–legislative relations and political parties in particular is well developed. Willis, Garman, and Haggard (1999; see also Garman, Haggard, and Willis 2001), demonstrate a positive correlation between weak parties and decentralization, with party weakness measured by subnational domination of electoral processes and less party leverage for presidents and national party leaders. This line of argument is strengthened and further specified by other comparative and single-country studies (Ames 2001; Mainwaring 1997a). Where subnational leaders control party nomination mechanisms, national leaders are likely to promote decentralization. Similarly, top-down parties that give nominating authority to national actors will likely produce greater party discipline and a tendency toward centralism.

Comparative static analyses such as these, however, fall short in addressing why such bottom-up dynamics and electoral rules favoring decentralization were developed, and under what conditions these rules were designed.

Strong local elites usually benefit from these arrangements, and it is reasonable to posit that these actors used existing political leverage to create the very institutions that favor their preferred outcomes (cf. Hagopian 1996). Institutions do not arise in a vacuum, and a longitudinal study of decentralization may show that the causal arrows posited by institutionalists are reversed: instead of institutions that favor subnational interests leading to decentralization, decentralized power leads to institutions that favor subnational interests. Analyses such as these offer cross-national correlations between levels of subnational autonomy and institutional frameworks but cannot explain as effectively variations over short time frames in which institutions are stable. The comparative static analysis begs the question of why those institutions were put in place to begin with (cf. Bates 1988). Leading explanations based on institutional rules and party structures are thus useful in studying variations across countries, but have limitations.

Agency, Bargaining, and Choice

In the final analysis, there is little argument that decentralization and recentralization, being shaped through legal frameworks, ultimately occur as a result of choices by politicians. Because choices to reform are the immediate predecessors to decentralization, some arguments about intergovernmental relations reduce the decision to decentralize to the notion of "political will." Assessing the mixed record of decentralization efforts, analysts have made appeals, for instance, to improve "political support" (Cheema and Rondinelli 1983). Unfortunately, this highly voluntarist approach leaves off the table more penetrating questions about political motivations and incentives, and how they may be shaped to compel behavior.

Of greater analytical import is whether agents will decentralize due to ideological conviction. This is particularly true in the era of neoliberal policy reforms, which some suggest played a driving role in decentralization.[11] Eaton (2000) briefly examines this argument cross-nationally and finds no empirical support for the argument that liberalizers decentralize, and the evidence from the four cases here supports the skepticism about the link between

---

11. Several excellent studies of the foundations of economic ideology among elites in developing countries can deepen the argument here. See, for example, Centeno (1994) as well as the extensive literature on Asian developmental bureaucracies.

economic liberalization and decentralization. Similarly, many expect decentralization to be a pet policy of reconstructed post–cold war leftists, since it is often associated with participation, local action, and closer accountability to the populace. Civil society actors may also be potential winners from decentralization, and might be expected to organize collectively to demand it. However, there is also little evidence in the literature to suggest that decentralization is an ideological choice made by left-leaning politicians or civil society (Manor 1999). Even at constitutional conventions, such as those in Brazil and South Africa, where great emphasis was placed on integrating new social actors into politics, the decentralization debates were mainly the domain of parties and politicians (Lodge 1999; Martinez-Lara 1996; Souza 1997).

A more promising line of agency-based argument emphasizes individual incentives to decentralize and centralize under given institutional constraints. Such analyses begin with the premise that political career paths depend on the costs and benefits of holding a particular office (cf. Diaz-Cayeros 2006; Samuels 2003). National politicians (parliamentarians, e.g.) may be eager to decentralize resources if they feel their career paths will likely lead them to a gubernatorial or mayoral seat in the future. Such arguments make reasonable assumptions about political behavior (usually regarding electoral ambitions among politicians), avoid excessive voluntarism, and adopt a specific focus on the relational aspects of governmental power.

Intergovernmental bargaining and purposive action is central to understanding decentralization. For many federalism scholars, SNG actors respond rationally to political incentives presented by fiscal and political arrangements (cf. Rodden 2006; Wibbels 2005). And while work on recentralization is more limited in this regard, the issue is beginning to be addressed more systematically. Alberto Diaz-Cayeros's (2006) examination of Mexico is an example here that begins to bring (re)centralization into a comparative perspective, viewing it as the outcome of intergovernmental bargaining processes as well. Clearly, taking politicians' choices seriously will enable our arguments to address not only cross-national variation, but also crucial questions about the timing and sequencing of change.

Accordingly, I draw heavily on this literature, though I have one significant reservation. Existing rationalist arguments are strongest at explaining why decentralization or recentralization occurred in a single issue area, usually revenues. To understand intergovernmental bargaining outcomes, scholars use mid-range institutional theory, paying particularly close attention to party systems as key variables that mediate intergovernmental relationships, and parties do indeed play a significant role in many of the most important contemporary understandings of decentralization. But these lines of argumentation have greater difficulty explaining more complex outcomes, such as instances where central governments devolve revenues yet retain tight control over spending. If bargaining arrangements favor subnational governments, why would SNGs not gain autonomy in both revenues and in spending? We need an argument that facilitates an understanding that is dynamic over time and across issue areas.

International Actors

Foreign capital and major lending institutions, especially the World Bank and International Monetary Fund, have also tried to play a causal role by rhetorically promoting decentralization. To be sure, the willingness of the World Bank to loan to SNGs in Latin America enhanced subnational autonomy to some extent. Still, decisions about making international capital available to SNGs was rooted more in domestic power than in international imperatives. In the end, foreign capital and the international financial institutions were neither sufficient nor necessary to impose major changes in intergovernmental relations.[12] In fact, work on the power of international institutions openly questions why regimes succeed at resisting international pressures to transform their domestic politics even under stringent conditionality and structural adjustment (Van de Walle 2001).

While the international financial institutions may not be able to single-handedly reconfigure intergovernmental relations, international discourse may still have an influence. Part of the reason for the increasing trend toward fiscal decentralization may be the change in the dominant international paradigms of economic development. The "age of decentralization" (Snyder 2001) arose after the exhaustion of the development economics model of the 1950s and 1960s that emphasized state-led development. The changing nature of the development discourse has thus partially shaped approaches to intergovernmental relations. Again, I control for these effects by looking

12. In fact, however, international pressure on these four countries varies in unpredictable ways, and does not always support decentralization. In all four cases, international pressure for decentralization was either nonexistent (South Africa), weak (Peru and Senegal), or actually worked in favor of centralization to restore fiscal order (Brazil). In all cases, domestic politics was both necessary and sufficient to explain outcomes.

at changes over time (including often surprising recentralizations of power) in the "neoliberal era" from 1980 to the present.

Testing the Argument

The most powerful arguments about the determinants of decentralization and recentralization will combine institutional understandings with historical trajectories to explain the change in fiscal autonomy over time. Only historically informed approaches allow us to understand timing and sequencing in any causal explanation of decentralization and recentralization. Arguments in this historical vein, conversely, are enhanced by analyses that specify the set of conditions under which different levels of government attain their preferred outcomes. The literature on intergovernmental bargaining examines the institutional causes behind which level of government wins the bargaining game, but such an explanation must be made to account for change in bargaining power over time even when certain institutions (such as electoral rules) are held constant. This leads us to examine the underpinnings of central and SNG strength. The changing political fortunes and economic performance of national governing parties provide an explanation here. Political-economic changes, as mediated through different institutional environments, will illuminate the wide range of outcomes.

The structured comparative approach used here contrasts with the monographic studies that have predominated in the study of decentralization, as well as many recent comparative studies.[13] With regard to the former, even those multicountry volumes that attend to important theoretical issues generally arrange evidence into side-by-side single-country studies. As Paul Smoke (2001, 2–3) rightly notes, case studies and individual-country chapters tend to reflect a country-by-country approach, with monographic "snapshots" dominating most publications.[14] Works that do aim to compare across countries are often static, explaining variations in levels of subnational autonomy in terms of prevailing institutional environments. Rather than explaining

13. Examples of monographic studies in the case countries to be examined include Abrucio (1998), Hagopian (1996), and Samuels (2003) on Brazil; Planas (1998) and Zas Fris Burga (1998) on Peru; Diop and Diouf (1997) and Marks (1996b) on Senegal; and Ajam (1998) and Levy and Tapscott (2001) on South Africa.

14. This is true of many of the most prominent and important edited volumes on the subject, such as those by Bird and Vaillancourt (1998), Crook and Manor (1998), Gibson (2004), Levy and Tapscott (2002), Montero and Samuels (2004), and Ter-Minassian (1997).

Table 1.5 Case overview

Region	Federal states / Higher autonomy	Unitary states / Lower autonomy
Latin America	Brazil	Peru
Africa	South Africa	Senegal

"decentralization," they are more accurately described as assessing levels of "centralism" or "decentralism."[15] I provide an alternative to this tendency with a wholly comparative approach using two principal (federal) cases followed by two unitary cases to extend and confirm the initial comparison. This design also complements recent methodologically innovative work in the field, including deductive formal analyses to model individual choice and behavior (cf. Diaz-Cayeros 2006; O'Neill 2005), and monographs that expand on single-country studies using nested, mixed-method designs (cf. Rodden 2006; Samuels 2003; Wibbels 2005). Since much of the literature here is from the Latin American experience, the cross-regional comparison with sub-Saharan Africa further enhances the generalizability of the argument.

Cross-national comparison need not sacrifice understandings of within-country dynamics. Strictly speaking, my cases are country-periods, not countries. I compare not only, say, Brazil to South Africa, but also Brazil pre-1994 to Brazil post-1994. Process-tracing over time allows us to observe causal links and chains in temporal succession, and reduces the risk of mistaking correlation for causation. The countries vary from quite high levels of SNG autonomy to very low levels, both cross-nationally and over time, while also providing a wide cross-section of developing countries on a number of important criteria. Each country provides a periodized case of decentralization, and two of the four (Brazil and Peru) exhibit significant recentralization after decentralization; South Africa is a case of limited recentralization, and Senegal is a case without recentralization.

The four countries fall at vastly different points along a federal–unitary continuum. There is no reason that the logics presented above should be limited to a single geographic region, or only to unitary or federal states. Therefore, I explicitly chose cases that cut across these boundaries, as table 1.5 shows. To examine the effect of party systems, I also selected both tradition-ally dominant party systems (South Africa and Senegal) and traditionally

---

15. Examples here include Willis, Garman, and Haggard (1999) and the majority of the political economy literature on decentralization.

Table 1.6 Sequences of decentralization and recentralization

Country	Decline	Decentralization	Economic Crisis	Crisis Resolution	Recentralization
Brazil	1985–1988	1988	1988–1994	1994–1995	1994–2000
Peru	1987–1988	1988	1988–1990	1991–1992	1992–2001
Senegal	1990–1996	1996	None	None	None
S. Africa	1990–1996	1996	1997–1999 (localized)	1997–1999 (localized)	1999–2001 (localized)

fragmented weak party systems (Peru and Brazil). I consider why decentralization may occur when central governments hold important political cards, particularly when national political parties have strong discipline (Senegal, South Africa); conversely, I consider why states with weak parties would centralize or be highly centralized (Peru, Brazil). Below, I present a brief exposition of the various countries in the study. In each, correlations between party system variables and decentralization and recentralization were sometimes surprising.

Brazil: Robust Federalism

Brazil has consistently been among the most decentralized of all Latin American polities, and SNGs have long had considerable fiscal autonomy; the decentralization that occurred with re-democratization in the 1980s was clearly driven from the bottom up, and subnational power was codified in the 1988 constitution (Samuels and Abrucio 2000). The upper chamber in the legislature, the Senate, was designed to reflect the interests of the *estados,* and the lower chamber, the Chamber of Deputies, also came to reflect parochial interests (Ames 2001; Samuels 2003). Due to electoral rules favoring local-level politicians and to long histories of local networks, deputies are more beholden to patrons in their respective *estados* than to the national party leadership (Willis, Garman, and Haggard 1999). Party switching reached epidemic proportions in 1990s Brazil; the weakness of the party system has contributed to "robust federalism" and "feckless democracy" (Mainwaring 1997a).[16] History and the structure of representation in the legislature have thus militated in favor

---

16. Brazil's system could also be considered a case of "strong federalism" (Samuels and Mainwaring 2004). I prefer "robust federalism" (Mainwaring 1997a) only to avoid any normative implication that Brazil's federal system might be strong in an affirmative sense. "Robust" conveys the extent of Brazilian federalism while acknowledging the weaknesses and imbalances in Brazilian intergovernmental relations. For South Africa, by contrast, "weak federalism" accurately captures the sense that federalism is less developed.

of decentralism in Brazil. For some time, the structure of the executive branch also undermined central power. Faced with weak partisan levers and fragile governing coalitions, the national executive tended to buy votes, offering pork to all and sundry congresspeople in exchange for support.

Only in the mid-1990s did some intimations of change to this political culture arise. Fernando Henrique Cardoso's government (1995–2003) restructured Brazil's fiscal system in the wake of a hyperinflationary crisis, building on the successes of the major economic reforms in the Real Plan. Under Cardoso the center succeeded in limiting certain intergovernmental revenue transfers, reformed the administration of Health and Education, and closed down profligate *estado*-owned banks. While Brazil remains relatively decentralized despite these measures, the Cardoso government dramatically reduced the fiscal autonomy of SNGs. After a first round of recentralizing reforms, a smaller crisis in 1999 generated another recentralizing impetus: in 2000, the Cardoso government capped off its efforts with a major law requiring fiscal responsibility, on pain of imprisonment for subnational politicians who fail to comply.

South Africa: Weak Federalism

South Africa's transition to democracy after the fall of apartheid in the 1990s precipitated a massive set of changes in political representation and greatly increased the autonomy of provincial governments in revenue terms. Suddenly, in 1994 the ANC, which had spent decades in opposition to apartheid rule and was the party of choice for the vast majority of black South Africans, was faced with the daunting task of assuming government at multiple levels. Meanwhile, the apartheid-era National Party (NP) government, controlled by white Afrikaners, sought assurances it would not be excluded from the political game (e.g., Sparks 1994). During the transition, the NP insisted on strong provinces with guaranteed access to revenues. The negotiated settlement at the Constituent Assembly accordingly increased the number of provinces from four to nine, and gave the provinces and municipalities greater political power, including a constitutional guarantee to an "equitable share" of national revenues. As of 1996, the South African government began to decentralize upwards of 55 percent of all government revenues to the provinces.

While South Africa's largely top-down decentralization process was meaningful, the central lessons of the South African case are ways in which central governments can restrict the overall autonomy of SNGs by working through "back door" channels, holding power in one area even as it is devolved in another. Examining centrally imposed restrictions on subnational expenditures and contracting is essential for understanding a country where revenue figures seem to suggest considerable decentralization. The extent of decentralization in historically centralized South Africa never reached the same level as in historically decentralized Brazil, though a cursory glance at revenue distributions may provide a misleading picture of a highly decentralized South African state. Beyond the ways the center holds power, the South African central government has shown some leverage in specific instances actually to reverse subnational autonomy, though the actions were less noteworthy than in Brazil.

Unitary Cases: Peru and Senegal

Not surprisingly, the two unitary states examined here exhibit the lowest levels of subnational autonomy. Peru has rarely had any autonomous regional or provincial government of significance, despite decades of popular support for the principle of decentralization. When SNGs have existed, their autonomy has been highly circumscribed by the center. Following a Constituent Assembly in 1979 and a return to democracy in 1980, Peruvian presidents were charged with the duty of creating viable regional governments. As the presidency of Alan García (1985–90) descended into economic crisis, the president began a largely self-serving process of decentralization in response to his own decline. But when hyperinflation accelerated as a consequence of García's economic mismanagement, the ensuing economic crisis presented a unique set of conditions favoring recentralization under Alberto Fujimori (1990–2000). Fujimori leveraged strong public support in the wake of his successful economic stabilization efforts to dramatically centralize power in Peru and eliminate subnational autonomy. Indeed, revenue recentralization was part of a broad centralization of authority in which Fujimori destroyed political parties, disbanded the legislature, and stacked all branches of government with loyalists.

Senegal, like Peru, is governed by a number of subnational bodies, but these have very low levels of fiscal autonomy. The largest in area are the regions, which have had both elected and appointed bodies since a 1996 Decentralization Law, while local governments also retain some minimal fiscal authority. Yet despite efforts at decentralization by the declining Parti Socialiste in the 1990s, the center retains virtually all political and economic control. Beyond control over (inadequate) decentralized funds, the central government still controls the vast majority of social spending because personnel remain under the purview of the central state, even after the 1996 reforms. Recentralization of previously devolved funds has not occurred in Senegal, however, where it might be most expected. Though Senegal's SNGs have little to lose in their present arrangement, it is striking that the Senegalese president was thwarted in attempts to eliminate the jurisdictional autonomy of SNGs. The ability of SNGs and their allies to resist recentralization, in such inhospitable circumstances, demands explanation. The answer to the puzzle lies in the inherent "stickiness" of reforms such as decentralization that empower new actors: without exceptional justification for removing political authority from a given actor, changes such as centralization are unlikely in a democratic context. The independent variables of interest again predict the outcome: economic crisis has been conspicuously absent in Senegal, relative to other cases, and the center has been unable to reverse revenue decentralization.

Contributions and Organization of the Book

The study of decentralization and federalism is booming. Recent studies in the field are increasingly sophisticated in their comparative research designs and display greater attention to cross-temporal, cross-national, and subnational variations.[17] This study provides a methodological and theoretical complement to the existing literature in several ways. As a point of departure, I have organized the evidence comparatively along thematic lines, and not in country chapters, to trace better why different systems arise and change over time. Cross-national and cross-temporal comparisons also work together here to improve generalizability. Cross-national institutional comparison is essential, but I also use dynamic variables to explain the moments of change when central governments either devolve or reassume authority over fiscal, administrative, and financial power. Variations over time ensure that comparative static "snapshots" are rendered more dynamic. Four key contributions emerge.

The first contribution is the examination of *decentralization and recentralization* in a single analytic framework. Reflecting the fascination with decentralization in international policy, political scientists have gravitated toward the study of decentralization, whereas its converses—centralization

---

17. Many of the aforementioned studies are especially strong in this regard, including Diaz-Cayeros (2006), Eaton (2004a), Falleti (2005), O'Neill (2005), Rodden (2006), Wibbels (2005).

and recentralization—are too often ignored. Focusing only on decentralizing moves and ignoring centralizing moves may lead to biased estimates of central authority; the likely conclusion will be that central governments in the developing world are weak since decentralization studies examine processes where central governments concede or devolve authority to SNGs.[18] Full empirical investigation of central–subnational relations takes into account not only decentralization versus the absence of decentralization, but also why centralizing shifts occur. I measure decentralization alongside (re)centralization and other outcomes imposed by central governments. In other words, I ask a full complement of comparative questions: Why decentralization, and Why not decentralization? *and* Why centralization, and Why not centralization? Failing this, we would miss the ebb and flow of fiscal power, as well as important trends of continued centralism. In cases of persistent centralism, central governments find ways to retain control even as supposedly decentralizing reforms proceed. The center can institutionalize its power over SNGs in many ways, including spending mandates and close monitoring of expenditures, restrictions on borrowing, and statutes criminalizing fiscal irresponsibility. Beyond these processes that institutionalize central control, central governments are actually able to reverse decentralization in some instances. While rarer, recentralization is also a growing policy trend in the wake of 1980s and 1990s decentralization. Most intriguingly, it can even be found in countries such as Brazil where decentralism is robust and seemingly overdetermined. By analyzing both decentralization and recentralization, and by framing a question about why and under what conditions central governments do hold onto fiscal authority, we can get a complete understanding of subnational fiscal autonomy and of national and subnational fiscal power.

A second contribution in this study is the treatment of *subnational autonomy in three key issue areas* in the political economy: revenues, expenditures, and contracts (in capital and labor markets). Studies of decentralization and centralization most frequently examine the divvying up of revenue. Yet major changes often come elsewhere. Important changes in expenditure patterns are often ignored in favor of an emphasis on revenue arrangements

---

18. Thanks to Marta Arretche for making this important point. Of course, it is possible to find ample variation using only decentralization as a dependent variable (Eaton 2004a; O'Neill 2005; Willis, Garman, and Haggard 1999). The point about selection on the dependent variable is more appropriately directed at studies that examine single countries and treat them as static cases, or that look only at similar decentralization processes.

governing taxation authority and IGTs.[19] Fiscal autonomy is not just flows of money but must include analysis of the expenditures of SNGs and of the ability of SNGs to enter into contracts in capital and labor markets. If SNGs are not bound by central legislation governing their spending and contracting, their autonomy is higher, and the country is correspondingly more "decentralized." On the other hand, even high levels of revenue transfers and expenditure responsibilities may be compatible with highly centralized power. In the extreme case, where binding legislation requires SNGs to spend revenues according to fixed criteria, SNGs may be little more than extensions of the central government with little autonomy. This may be considered "deconcentration" rather than "decentralization." The focus on the three areas of subnational autonomy is reflected in the structure of the book, with each area meriting its own analysis.

The third contribution is the *federal–unitary comparison.* To test whether a common logic applies in federal and nonfederal cases, I consider the relationships between levels of government in countries both federal and unitary. I argue that federalism as an institutional arrangement has ambiguous impacts on subnational autonomy. At the most general level, federal states obviously are characterized by much higher degrees of subnational fiscal autonomy than unitary states. Federalism also refers to a set of political institutions—including constitutional and legislative arrangements protecting SNGs—that on average make decentralization likelier and centralization less likely. Nonetheless, federalism per se cannot alone explain how and why decentralization and recentralization happen in either federal or unitary states. While federalism is a useful dichotomous variable in many instances, I argue that instances of decentralization and recentralization should be viewed as taking place along a federal–unitary spectrum. Federal cases vary considerably from one another, as Brazil and South Africa will show. Meanwhile, studies of unitary states in developing countries have been underrepresented in the intergovernmental relations (IGR) literature, but arguably overrepresented in the excitement about decentralization in the 1980s and 1990s, wherein these weaker and smaller states have been pressed to devolve authority to local levels in order to improve economic and social performance. By incorporating both federal and unitary cases into the analysis, it is possible to tease out where federalism matters and where it does not.

19. Part of the reason for this is the implicit assumption among decentralization advocates that "finance follows function" and that revenues and expenditures will thus most often move together in lockstep. While I have noted they often do move together, I frame the question so as to interrogate occasions where they do not move together.

A fourth contribution is the study's *cross-regional comparison*. The cross-regional perspective here highlights Latin America and sub-Saharan Africa, and attempts deliberately to break down regional barriers in order to show that a common set of dynamics can hold across highly variable contexts. The variations in the cases include not only region, but also colonial heritage, levels of economic development and industrialization, histories of democratic governance, and even presidentialism versus parliamentarism (with South Africa an example of the latter). At the same time, comparison is made tractable by the fact that all four cases have recent transitions to democracy and some 1980s and 1990s experience with decentralization.

I organize the book around the three areas of subnational fiscal autonomy and the institutional arenas that most directly correspond to each, rather than directing the focus of the inquiry to individual country cases. This allows for a more complete investigation of the key concepts and theories of inter-governmental fiscal relations in the politics and policy of developing countries. Hereafter, chapter 2 jointly addresses the historical trajectories of the cases, with the aim of illuminating the structures to which these give rise. This informs causal arguments about decentralization in particular: states with unitary or weakly federal histories are likely to witness top-down processes of decentralization that are more fragile in their devolutionary impact, while states (like Brazil) with robust federal histories are likely to see power-ful decentralizing moves driven, from below, by subnational actors. Such cases also suggest the strength of actors arrayed against recentralization, making such change all the more puzzling.

The core empirical work is in chapters 3, 4, and 5. My approach incorporates an understanding of party systems and intergovernmental bargaining with an emphasis on executive power but seeks to explain a wider range of out-comes than SNG access to revenues. This central section of the book focuses on the Brazil–South Africa comparison in detail. Chapter 3 highlights the importance of executive–legislative interaction in shaping SNG revenue autonomy. The findings of this chapter reinforce existing arguments on the roles political parties play in executive–legislative relations, and how these shape intergovernmental relations. In order to understand the full complement of outcomes however, I turn in chapter 4 to the expenditure side of the fiscal equation and account for a crucial arena that is understudied in the literature on IGR: the state. Surprisingly, treatment of states has been thin in studies of intergovernmental relations. Ministers and bureaucrats who share presi-dential preferences are important players in shaping the relationships between different levels of government; the ability of presidents to control subnational expenditure autonomy more than subnational revenue autonomy is largely explicable by intra-executive authority. Direct negotiations between presidents and subnational politicians emerge in chapter 5, where the outcome of interest is the contractual autonomy of SNGs in terms of constitutional independence, access to capital markets, and control over public service contracts. This can be best described as inter-executive negotiation between national and subnational executives. Of course, each of these issue areas is influenced in multiple arenas—executive–legislative, intra-executive, and inter-executive; the division here simply reflects the most salient of the arenas for each issue area.

The last part of the book extends the argument beyond the Brazilian and South African cases. Chapter 6 examines unitary cases in this framework, thus illustrating that a common set of dynamics holds across the federal–unitary spectrum. I focus on Peru and Senegal, thus extending the logic to unitary countries in Latin America and Africa, where unitarism are common. The implications of the findings are addressed in chapter 7, in which I argue that the argument here simultaneously broadens and deepens research into questions of intergovernmental relations. I also argue there that federalism has ambiguous significance for studies of intergovernmental relations. Together, these two chapters in the last section of the book point the way toward areas for further research in the field of federalism, decentralization, and recentralization.

2

———✺✺✺———

HISTORICAL TRAJECTORIES IN SUBNATIONAL AUTONOMY

The development of intergovernmental fiscal relations is a long-term historical process. Present-day patterns of decentralism and centralism can be traced historically to differentiated processes of state formation and state building across countries. Beyond mere correlations between levels of SNG power today and yesterday, scholars have used historical process-tracing to assess the degree to which central and subnational governments (and their politicians) enter into fiscal arrangements, and to elucidate the path-dependent consequences of these arrangements.[1] Understanding contemporary patterns of subnational autonomy in comparative perspective requires an examination of the historical-institutional trajectories in the case countries.

The aim of this chapter is to illuminate patterns of development—in Brazil and South Africa, as well as Peru and Senegal—that gave rise to patterns of centralism or decentralism, and to trace the path-dependent impacts of these patterns for the present. In this chapter only, I analyze the case countries on an individual basis rather than comparatively, in order to capture the historical subtleties of each case. Historical trajectories condition the extent of federalism today, and accordingly shape patterns of decentralization, giving rise to processes initiated either "from above" or "from below." A common set of themes emerges in each country. Early patterns of state formation under colonialism and through the nineteenth and twentieth centuries influenced the federal or unitary structure of the state. As authoritarian regimes gave way to democratization in the four countries in the 1980s and 1990s, decentralization became a salient reform, most notably at Constituent National Assemblies. Democratization processes in turn gave rise to varying

---

1. See Diaz-Cayeros (2006) and Lieberman (2003) on the formation of central tax states.

contemporary political structures and institutions; some of these favored SNGs (especially in Brazil's robust federalism), while others tipped the balance of power to the center. The institutional environments that emerged, including the degree of federalism and executive power relative to other political institutions, are strongly rooted in the past. In short, the structural conditions give rise to the institutional environments that shape the strategic calculus of political actors: the circumstances of democratization in countries with robust federal histories such as Brazil give rise to decentralization "from below" (or bottom-up), while decentralization in unitary states typically occurs "from above" and from electoralist motivations. This not only sets the stage for an understanding of decentralization, but also informs the stakes for subsequent attempts at *recentralization;* the historical underpinnings of contemporary institutions themselves have shaped the bargaining patterns of recent years.

Robust Federalism in Brazil

Brazil is one of the most decentralized countries in the world, as a result of a long legacy of "bottom-up" state formation that dates from the Portuguese Empire through the Brazilian Republic of the nineteenth century and up through the modernizing regimes of the twentieth century. The historical tendency toward decentralized governance has held even through repeated experiences with military rule, which were insufficient to centralize power in a lasting way. Each return to democracy has been associated with strong decentralizing pressures (cf. Eaton 2004b). The Constituent Assembly and the constitution of 1988 epitomized Brazil's pattern, unique among the cases, of decentralization from below in a robust federal system. Strong subnational interests required a weak president to transfer considerable amounts of federal resources to the *estado* and local levels; the 1988 Constituent Assembly also crafted electoral rules that favored subnational interests. Recent experiences with state reform under Fernando Henrique Cardoso have better delimited subnational power, but Brazil remains very decentralized in a cross-national perspective.

The Origins of Brazil's Robust Federalism

From the days of its establishment as a Portuguese colony, the territory of present day Brazil has presented massive challenges for central governments, whether these have been located in Lisbon, on the Brazilian coast in Salvador or Rio de Janeiro, or in contemporary Brasilia. Shifts between autocracy and democracy in Brazil did not alter the problems the central government had in projecting power over the country. Periods of military rule in Brazil have meant the centralization of social services and state functions, first in the 1930s, and later under the bureaucratic-authoritarian military regime that began in 1964 (Souza 1997, 29–32). During democratic periods, on the other hand, subnational elites have restored their own powers (Hagopian 1996). The concentration and dispersal of power occurs with changes of regime type: democracy has not simply dispersed power among national actors such as unions and parties, but instead has divided it on a geographic basis, while military rule attempted to concentrate power at the center as well. Yet even under military rule, the center in Brazil was regularly beholden to local oligarchic elites, including the famous *coroneis,* the local bosses that under-pinned the country's political system.

In 1930, Getúlio Vargas, from the southern state of Rio Grande do Sul, came to power at the head of a military junta, with the backing of civilians in several less-powerful states. The Vargas administration (1930–45) broke with the tradition of presidents from the economically powerful states of Minas Gerais and São Paulo; Vargas had a contradictory relationship with *estado* elites; he wrote off *estado* debts (especially in São Paulo) and enforced supports for coffee production during the Great Depression, but also replaced civilian governors (with the exception of Minas Gerais) with central appointees (Burns 1980, 402–3; Souza 1997, 27). After São Paulo went into open revolt in 1932, Vargas militarized state power in the late 1930s with the proclamation of the Estado Novo ("The New State"), reflecting the belief that Brazil's centrifugal forces could only be overcome by dramatic top-down action, most notably in the state-led political incorporation of newly powerful urban industrialists and laborers (Burns 1980, 375, 414; Collier and Collier 1991). Vargas was unable, however, to break definitively with the power of regional interests even after the Great Depression upset Brazil's agricultural trade.

Several civilian presidents presided over the continuation of industriali-zation over the next decade, including a second Vargas administration (1951–54), which ended with Vargas's suicide as he faced a military ultimatum to resign or be deposed. Under Juscelino Kubitschek (1956–60), the federal government carved out a new federal district on a cleared plain in the muggy Center-West of the country, far from the coastal power centers of Rio de Janeiro and São Paulo, and within it built the new capital of Brasilia. The new city was meant to isolate the bureaucracy from societal pressures and to project central power into the interior of the country, but even Brasilia did not enhance the center's leverage. After the brief seven-month presidential stint of the eccentric Jânio Quadros (1960) ended in a surprising resignation, the leftist João Goulart assumed the presidency. Goulart lasted four years, but increasing acrimony on the part of the military due to his uncertain economic policies eventually led to the 1964 coup that placed the military in power as a "bureaucratic-authoritarian" regime from 1964 to the 1980s.

This military regime, unlike other "caretaker" regimes that saw their tasks as stabilizing the country for future civilian rule, planned to govern indefinitely in an attempt to overcome the structural blockages in the development process (O'Donnell 1972). The military's impulse was to centralize power and to repress dissidence.[2] The regime turned Brazil into a nominally unitary state, but the military's political power continued to be underpinned by the collaboration of powerful civilian actors at the *estado* and local levels (Hagopian 1996; Souza 1997, 33).[3] While the military presided over the deepening of industrialization and a substantial portion of the "Brazilian Miracle" of the postwar era, the longer-term failures of import substitution, the 1980s debt crisis, and the growing pressures for political liberalization ultimately signaled the exhaustion of military rule.

The military controlled the process of political liberalization in the initial stages but found itself required to make moves toward fuller democracy (Haggard and Kaufman 1995). Change accelerated after Brazil's debt crisis destroyed the argument that authoritarian rule was necessary for strong economic performance. Subnational leaders, including influential senators from São Paulo and other large states, led the political pressure on the regime and pressed for more autonomy at the subnational level. Decentralization was thus driven by state elites who recognized their bargaining power relative to the military regime. By the mid-1980s, millions took to the streets to demand elections, and trade unions (particularly São Paulo unions led by political hopeful Luiz Inácio Lula da Silva) called for massive strikes and protests. These culminated in rallies in the early to mid-1980s calling for "Direct Elections Now" (*Diretas já!*), supported not only by trade unions but also business community and the growing official opposition. Faced with the endgame, the military made a number of tactical moves, including

2. A particularly important legal statute was Institutional Act number 5 (Ato Institucional No. 5), passed in 1968, which among other items banned assembly and union elections.

3. Among those who collaborated with the military regime were many state-level politicians who later held crucial roles in democratic Brazil, such as Antônio Carlos Magalhães (future minister, governor, and senator from Bahia) and José Sarney (future president and senator from Maranhão).

a push to create several new states in the North with low populations to stack the senate in favor of promilitary traditional conservatism. As the military regime lost its grip on power, some of its signature actions were decentralizing in nature: it first reinstituted subnational elections in 1982, followed by national elections in 1985.

Democratization and Decentralization from Below

Brazil's decentralized processes of state formation strongly conditioned the democratic transition as the election cycle moved beyond the election of mayors and governors to the restoration of national democracy. The elections resulted in a massive victory for the official opposition candidate, Tancredo Neves, who defeated the military-backed candidate convincingly. Neves, however, died before assuming office, leaving vice president José Sarney, a traditional politician from an oligarchic background in the northern state of Maranhão, to assume the presidency.

The new civilian president convened a Constituent National Assembly (Assembléia Constituinte) for 1987–88. The form of the assembly helped subnational interests: it brought together governors and local elites in a situation where they could act collectively to enforce their preferred outcomes (cf. Martinez Lara 1996). By 1987, Sarney realized that his rule would be dependent on the cooperation of the increasingly emboldened elites from the *estados* (Souza 1997, 43). In a miscalculated attempt to increase his authority, Sarney bargained away considerable authority to subnational elites in order to secure an extra year in office (Souza 1997, 73). The 1988 constitution thus restored power to the *estados* and *municípios,* which received generous revenue transfers and tax authority with only limited corresponding responsibilities, as well as electoral rules that guaranteed strong subnational leverage in the Congress.

In many ways, the return to democracy in Brazil was not a wholesale reconfiguration of Brazilian politics (Abrucio 1998; Hagopian 1996; Samuels and Abrucio 2000). The power of state elites had been persistent, though not constant, under military rule. In fact, some degree of fiscal decentralization actually preceded the full restoration of democracy (Samuels and Abrucio 2000). While authoritarianism and democracy mean different patterns of resistance and political maneuvering, the power of state-level elites, the "Barons of the Federation," holds across regime type, with the weak center depending on local power brokers in the form of the governors and mayors (cf. Abrucio 1998). The restoration of *estado*-level elites returned Brazilian politics to its historical patterns (Hagopian 1996). The "new politics of the governors" returned to dominate not only state-level politics, but national politics (Samuels and Abrucio 2000).

Institutions of Robust Federalism in Contemporary Brazil

Brazil's federation comprises three levels: the federal government, states (*estados*), and municipalities (*municípios*). At the highest level, the central government includes a bicameral National Congress, the Supreme Court and the federal judicial branch, and the presidency and ministries. In post-1988 Brazil, the federal government assumed numerous expenditure responsibilities in areas such as health and education, in addition to such areas as national defense and macroeconomic management. The responsibilities of the federal government in these areas is best interpreted as symptomatic of the center's weakness: in the wake of democratization, the center was unable to force subnational governments to assume responsibilities in correspondence with the revenues devolved.

As suggested above, Brazil's transition to democracy created a bottom-up system that favored subnational interests. Weak political parties became a dominant feature of the political landscape. Party weakness, and the structural strength of Brazil's subnational elites, was written into the institutions of representation: the Congress was organized around territorial interests, and electoral rules gave national party leaders no control over nomination procedures or party lists (Garman, Haggard, and Willis 2001; Mainwaring 1997a, 1997b; Willis, Garman, and Haggard 1999). In this environment, legislators seek parochial support from home districts, and party switching is common. Because of the lack of party discipline and the fragmentation of the party system, commanding a parliamentary majority is difficult, and pork barrel projects become a principal means of gaining support (Ames 2001). Career paths also reflect the appeal of being a subnational executive, as prominent politicians often use national office to gain access to mayoral or gubernatorial positions (Samuels 2003).

Like the Sarney (1985–90) years, the Fernando Collor (1990–92) and Itamar Franco (1993–94) governments epitomized the difficulties of governance in democratic Brazil. Collor sought to revise the fiscal federal relationship with an omnibus amendment to the constitution (*emendão*), but this effort largely failed. When Collor was impeached for corruption, Franco acceded to the office. He fared little better, instead presiding over the persistent decline of Brazil's macroeconomy. A substantial cause of these macroeconomic troubles was uncontrollable *estado* spending and the revenue shortfalls that faced the central government as a result of fiscal decentralization. Faced with hyperinflation, Franco appointed São Paulo senator Fernando Henrique Cardoso to head the Ministry of Finance. Cardoso's orthodox stabilization plan, which ultimately became the Real Plan, succeeded where earlier heterodox efforts had failed, and this gave Cardoso a springboard to the presidency.

The Cardoso government (1995–2003) could not correct all the deficiencies of Brazil's federal system, but succeeded in strengthening the hand of the central government. Even analysts who criticize the weakness of Brazil's center recognize the shifts in the mid- to late 1990s, though they characterize these gains as costly and temporary (cf. Abrucio 1998; Ames 2001; Samuels 2003). Institutions and political career paths continued to be unfavorable to the federal government, yet the center reduced and reapportioned revenue transfers to the *estados* and *municípios,* and pushed expenditure requirements to the subnational levels.[4] In some sense, the most important changes in federal- state relations came not in 1988, but in 1994. With regard to the sorting out of fiscal rules, the Real Plan in some ways meant more than the constitution itself. The fiscal stabilization of the Real Plan was the first step in recentralization.

Weak Federalism in South Africa

While originally founded as a union of four distinctive and culturally varied provinces, the history of modern South Africa centers on the rise and fall of apartheid, the formal separation of the races that codified and reinforced racial inequalities. The country's impressive economic development and comparatively strong state were enabled by a climate propitious to colonial investment, the discovery of precious metals in the nineteenth century, and a unified white minority that repressed the black majority (cf. Lieberman 2003). The political union of two British and two Boer Dutch colonies took place in 1910. From 1948 to 1994, the National Party's (NP's) apartheid rule mandated strict racial segregation. The NP increasingly militarized the state, in an effort to eliminate the African National Congress (ANC) and other anti-apartheid groups both within the country and in exile. In doing so, the

---

4. Other analysts have noted the ways in which the Brazilian president overcame party weakness by using the internal structures of the Congress to command a majority (Figueiredo and Limongi 2000). This was certainly part of Cardoso's success, but the inability of previous presidents to command such a majority means a full explanation must show why Cardoso succeeded where previous governments failed.

apartheid state centralized power and curtailed the autonomy of the four provinces. Given the abysmal history of race relations, the transition from apartheid to democracy from 1990 to 1996 was stunningly successful; despite some violence in the early 1990s, the NP and ANC remained committed to a full transfer of power and coordinated the transition process in a series of increasingly formal discussions, which reached its conclusion in the 1994–96 Constituent Assembly. There the NP bargained for federalism and the ANC for a unitary state. Ultimately, the ANC got most of what it sought—including central control over many of the institutions of government—but the NP also secured a set of institutions that greatly strengthened subnational governments.

The Origins of Weak Federalism: Apartheid from 1948 to 1994

South Africa never came under direct military rule, but the country's history hinges upon white dominance of politics and a militarization of the state, particularly in the form it took after the NP's emergence as the dominant party in 1948. In that year, the Afrikaner majority among the white population coalesced enough to elect the NP to power. Upon assuming power, the NP promptly set to the business of establishing the apartheid system of draconian racial segregation that would be the country's dominant symbol for over four decades. While segregation had prevailed under the Unionist governments before 1948, the apartheid system instituted under the Nationalists further formalized and reinforced white dominance: blacks were required to reside in barren homelands and townships on the peripheries of large cities. Blacks could not formally own property but could live as squatters; this township arrangement was necessary to provide an ample labor supply for white-owned businesses in the cities. Among numerous other humiliations, apartheid outlawed interracial marriage and required blacks to carry passes to enter white districts.

Under apartheid, South Africa was a unitary state, run from the top down, in which provincial governments had largely administrative roles. Line-item budgets for the provinces passed down directly from the center. Meanwhile, many of the major provisions enacted by the NP operated directly through local government and had a lasting impact on the perception of local government by the African majority.[5] First among these was the Urban Black Councils Act 79 of 1961. This empowered the White Local Authorities (WLA) to delegate authorities to Black Councils. Such a move was viewed

---

5. These provisions can be found in Reddy 1996, 53.

as a first step in removing white authorities' responsibility for the development of black populations. This was followed ten years later by the Black Affairs Administration Act 45 of 1971, which delegated to the Black Councils the responsibility for the management the of townships, thereby definitively freeing the WLA from the task.[6] Finally, Black Local Authorities (BLA), ostensibly designed to parallel the WLA, were established in Act 102 of 1982. Of course, the BLA were of little consequence, and had even less legitimacy than their predecessor councils (Reddy 1996, 58). While depriving the BLA of any real economic or political power, the NP transferred responsibilities to these local collaborator institutions to defuse political tensions and deflect criticism from its rule, a form of "decentralized despotism" (cf. Mamdani 1996).

The NP engaged in a constant battle with the black-led ANC, which was outlawed in 1960 and whose principal leaders were exiled, imprisoned, or killed by the 1970s. A succession of National Party premiers maintained a hard line toward the ANC and maintained the apartheid system.[7] The NP repressed black resistance most infamously at a police massacre in Sharpeville in 1960 and in the death of activist Steve Biko in 1977. Amid social conflict, B. J. Vorster (1966–78) and P. W. Botha (1978–89) tried to decompress racial tensions by granting nominal "independence" to several black homelands in the late 1970s and early 1980s. The tactic failed: the ANC continued its guerrilla campaign unabated, and international pressure on the NP increased, even after South Africa opted out of the Commonwealth of Nations in 1961, eventually resulting in trade sanctions and divestment from Europe and the United States. More significant, however, was local protest. The 1980s became the "decade of defiance," replete with street riots and boycotts, and a "culture of boycott" that spread throughout the townships and homelands (Swilling 1996, 19–21). Growing numbers of black residents refused to pay for rents or public services. The legitimacy of the BLA was left in tatters, and most became insolvent. The dysfunction of apartheid pushed the NP toward preliminary talks with imprisoned ANC leader Nelson Mandela.

Democratization and Decentralization from Above

Given the history of mistrust and the increasingly violent conflicts between the NP and the majority black population, the transition from apartheid to

---

6. In the 1970s new Black Community Councils were created (Act 125 of 1977) in an attempt to shore up the legitimacy of the subordinate black local governments.

7. Prime ministers included D. F. Malan (1948–54), J. G. Strijdom (1954–58), H. F. Verwoerd (1958–66), B. J. Vorster (1966–78), and P. W. Botha (1978–89).

democracy came as a surprise. F. W. de Klerk's election as National Party Prime Minister in 1990 proved to be the trigger event. De Klerk, seen at the time of P. W. Botha's resignation as possibly the most conservative of NP candidates, shocked South Africa and the world when he announced at the opening of Parliament in 1990 that he would release ANC icon Nelson Mandela from prison, along with several other political prisoners, and would begin the process of systematically dismantling many of the most egregious acts that underpinned apartheid.

Violence erupted in numerous incidents throughout South Africa—including between black South Africans in the ANC and those in the Zulu nationalist Inkatha Freedom Party (IFP)—but the transition to democracy received a major boost when a referendum among whites on a transition to "multiracial" democracy passed in March 1992, with two-thirds of the white electorate supporting reform. The 1993 assassination of popular Communist Party activist Chris Hani by white extremists (including a Conservative Party parliamentarian) also, paradoxically, strengthened the democratization process as major actors united to condemn the action. NP reformists and the ANC moved the country toward free and fair elections in 1994, in which Nelson Mandela was elected president handily.

Though the majority of white South Africans favored democratic reforms, the transition still proved treacherous. During the two years from 1994 to 1996, South Africa operated under a set of transitional institutions and maintained some power-sharing arrangements that protected the NP. Moving from this to a new constitution proved thorny. Before a Constitutional Assembly could be convened, the NP and the ANC engaged in extensive "talks about talks," in which both sides laid out the basic conditions for moving forward. Aware that it was doomed to lose a free and fair national election, the NP insisted on principles of federalism and power sharing (cf., e.g., Sparks 1994; Spitz with Chaskalson 2000). The ANC preferred a unitary state. Early in the transition, the NP held the upper hand in bargaining; as the transition progressed, and the costs of a reversion to apartheid grew, the emboldened ANC commanded more authority.

Throughout negotiations at the Constituent Assembly, each party supported certain elements of a new governmental system. The "negotiated settlement" in the constitution of 1996 gave the ANC reasonable expectations that it would dominate South African politics indefinitely, with "one person, one vote" and the elimination of formal racial divisions in terms of political rights. Some degree of redistribution from the privileged white localities to the black and colored communities came to be accepted by all parties. The major concessions from the ANC to the NP, meanwhile, were twofold. First was the maintenance of a relatively independent state bureaucracy, based on the preexisting civil service, which would merge previous white and black authorities into a single system. The outgoing NP sought guarantees that the ANC would not turn the state apparatus into the party's patronage machine and insisted that the ANC include even old apartheid collaborators in the new state: civil servants from the black homelands were to be incorporated into the bureaucracy. The other major concession to the NP was the strengthening of provincial government, decentralization, and a form of federalism. The 1996 "final" constitution gave provinces greater access to resources than they had had at any time in South African history.

Institutions of Weak Federalism in South Africa

Unlike Brazil, South Africa is a parliamentary system (though the head of government is called the president). Executive–legislative relations both under apartheid and after apartheid have been quite tight as a result of the fusion of the branches. While the end of apartheid did not change parliamentarism, it did result in much stronger SNGs. Under apartheid, subnational autonomy was subordinated to the overarching national state task of securing white privilege (cf. Lieberman 2003); provinces existed largely as deconcentrated entities of the state with little autonomy and minimal political identity. As of 1996, the legislature came to consist of a National Assembly elected by proportional representation and an upper chamber, the National Council of Provinces (NCOP), comprising representatives elected indirectly by the nine provincial legislatures. Both bodies are dominated by the ANC. In the National Assembly, the ANC alone has (or has nearly) commanded a two-thirds supermajority since 1996. With occasional support from small splinter groups, this gives the governing party the ability to amend the constitution with relative ease. Given historically weak regional identities in South Africa and the ANC leadership's weight in nominating parliamentary candidates, even proponents and members of the NCOP recognize that it is only beginning to lobby effectively for subnational autonomy.[8]

Each province, meanwhile, has its own executive (premier) and its own legislature, which have discretion over provincial budgets. However, nearly all premiers are members of the ANC, with exceptions having occurred only in the Western Cape and KwaZulu-Natal provinces; the ANC governing

8. Interviews: Murphy Morobe, Hildegaard Fast, Mohammed Enver Surty.

structure is based on strong top-down discipline, forged during years of exile and resistance and codified in party rules that give the president control over the political fortunes of parliamentarians and premiers. This presidential power severely constricts the autonomy of the subnational executives in all areas of governance; ANC premiers depend on the president for many fiscal decisions.

The central state plays an important technical role in the partition of fiscal resources but has little discretion over what percentage of revenues are distributed to subnational governments, as these distributions are made on the basis of an "equitable share" formula. Calculations for the equitable share are made in the National Treasury (formerly the Ministry of Finance), but are fixed by preestablished criteria. Revenues are then divided up annually in a national Division of Revenue Act, submitted by the Treasury and passed by Parliament. While provinces have little tax capacity, they have received considerable transfers from the center since 1994, and these transfers have remained robust throughout the years of ANC rule. These generous distributions substitute for locally collected revenues, which make up only a small percentage of provincial budgets (RSA/NT 2001, 2003). Local government receives its own equitable share, but relies much more heavily on its own sources of revenue, mainly property taxes and user fees.[9] Coordination between the different levels of government is ensured by a complex set of institutional bodies, most notably the Ministers and Members of the Executive Council (MinMECs), which bring together national ministers and their provincial counterparts on a regular basis. Together, these institutions ensure the provinces of access to revenue and a meaningful role in the implementation of policy, though the center continues to effectively dominate decision making.

Unitarism and Centralism in Latin America: Peru

Until 2006 Peru was one of the most centralized countries in Latin America and in the world. In the 1990s Peru's local governments were responsible for about 4 percent of total government spending (Mejía Navarrete 1990, 154). The centralist tendency in Peru has persisted despite nearly half a century of debate on the importance of the devolution of political authority from

9. Cf. Ministry of Provincial Affairs and Constitutional Development 1998. White Papers are declarations of law to be implemented by the parliamentary majority; they trace out the broad parameters of law, with detailed enabling legislation following later.

the central state to subnational levels of government. Decentralization has been a political issue for decades, but actual devolution has been scanty. Regional and local governments have been weak, and presidents have controlled and reversed processes of decentralization as they arose. This long-term centralist trend was propagated through an elite-controlled democratization process at the end of the 1970s. At that time, the military called a Constituent Assembly, but the assembly did not reflect a broad cross-section of social actors and did little to decentralize power. A weak democratic president from 1980 to 1985 also did not push for reform, though his successor, Alan García, finally did in 1988. Attempts to reform Peru's government structure were short lived: they were reversed by Alberto Fujimori in the early 1990s. Fujimori's dictatorial reign ended only in 2000, leaving another president, Alejandro Toledo, to weigh the merits of decentralization.

The Origins of Centralism in Peru

Whereas Brazil's autocratic governments could not break the trend of very decentralized governance, Peru's democratic governments did not succeed in breaking the centralization of power. Alternating regime types reinforced centralism. During the early years of the Peruvian Republic, prominent politicians urged the central government to decentralize power, but each time rhetoric outpaced reality. In 1919 a coup d'état and installation of military rule heralded a new centralist era. President Augusto Leguía (1919–30) restored central control over departmental budgets, annulled the mandates of mayors (*alcaldes*) and local councils, and passed a new budget law (Ley Orgánica de Presupuesto) that ensured central government domination of national resources (Planas 1998). In what would foreshadow the lack of decentralizing follow-through at the end of the twentieth century, Leguía's civilian successors ignored the provisions of the 1933 constitution, which stipulated that new local councils (Consejos Departamentales) be established. Also unheeded was the Economic and Administrative Decentralization Law (Ley Orgánica de Descentralización Económica e Administrativa) created in September 1933 (Planas 1998, 14).

In 1948 Manuel Odría (1948–56) took office after another military coup and pushed an export-led growth model. The Odría years favored Lima in the distribution of government-financed public works, thereby reinforcing the capital's preponderance in the economy. Economic centralization hardened the tendency toward political centralization (Gonzales de Olarte 1997; Gonzales de Olarte, Pinzás García, and Trivelli Avila 1994). After Odría consented to free elections for 1956, Peru witnessed over a decade of relatively ineffectual civilian regimes. Civilian rule then broke down again in 1968 when a new military junta took command under Juan Velasco Alvarado, who surprisingly emphasized popular sector organization, enacting land reform measures and organizing peasant and labor groups. While the pro-poor focus was new to the Peruvian military, the structure of politics was little changed: Peru remained centralized under Velasco, just as it had been under civilian and military rule for decades (Contreras 2002, 27).

Democratization and Decentralization in Peru

Following the Constituent Assembly of 1979 and the return to democracy in 1980, Peruvian presidents were charged with the duty of creating viable regional governments. During redemocratization, Peruvian politicians developed a consensus, in principle, on the need for regions. After floundering under Acción Popular (AP) President Fernando Belaúnde Terry (1980–85), these processes were finally initiated by President Alan García (1985–90) of the Alianza Popular Revolucionária Americana (APRA) party, which claimed its first presidential victory after six decades of frustration and repression. During the first two years of his mandate, García too equivocated on the decentralization process, as is common for presidents in unitary states with no particular incentive to devolve power. In fact, in these early years (before his administration's later disastrous decline), García attempted to promote an alternative to the proposed regions that had been the subject of the decentralization debate since 1979. In lieu of regions, García mooted the idea of constructing "microregions," entities similar to prefectures that could be controlled from the center.

In 1987, however, García's presidency took a considerable turn for the worse, and the government's dramatic weakening and decline generated a truly decentralizing impulse. The impetus came from woeful economic mismanagement. Faced with a deteriorating economic situation, García suddenly and shockingly nationalized the Peruvian banking system in July of 1987. The extent and rapidity of the measure stunned international investors and Peruvian depositors, and the result was economic disaster and plunging popularity for García's government. In the decentralization arena, this provided García and APRA with instant motivation to create stronger regions, in an attempt to build on its subnational power base, given the improbability of an APRA reelection to the presidency in 1990 (O'Neill 2005). García thus moved quickly and decisively to ensure that regions would become elected bodies in 1988, as a clear and direct consequence of his national decline.

Elected in 1990 on the back of a populist campaign that discredited traditional parties (notably APRA), Alberto Fujimori shocked the country using orthodox measures to resolve the economic crisis precipitated by García; the new president was rewarded with high levels of public approbation, reinforced by his largely successful campaign to disarm and defeat the Sendero Luminoso (Shining Path), a Maoist insurgency that had terrorized the Peruvian highlands and increasingly the capital city of Lima during the 1970s and 1980s. Fujimori interpreted his burgeoning popularity as a mandate to reform Peru's entire system of governance, and his centralization of power was part of a larger effort to eliminate political opposition; in this case, crisis resolution facilitated subsequent recentralization.[10]

The regions still had an unclear political mandate and little fiscal power by the time Fujimori categorically disbanded them as part of his authoritarian *autogolpe* in 1992. At that time, Fujimori replaced the elected regional governments with appointed "transitional councils for regional administration," the Consejos Transitorios de Administración Regional (CTAR). While provisional in theory, the CTAR in effect served as part of a plan toward consolidating power in an authoritarian regime. Subsequent abuses of power by Fujimori and the armed services turned into an authoritarian regime from 1992 to 2001.

The Ministry of the Presidency, created by García, was given far greater authority and scope under Fujimori. The presidency, along with the Council of Ministers (Consejo de Ministros), became a sort of "super-ministry" designed to coordinate the political programs sponsored by the regime, and served as the principal channels of information flows between the cabinet and the president. Fujimori dominated relationships within the state, conferred responsibilities to members of the armed services and intelligence community, and constructed vertical relationships with society, deliberately avoiding the development of a political party base (Kay 1996). These choices had serious consequences for subnational government, as the executive assumed many of the social service tasks otherwise attributable to SNGs (Schady 1999).

10. As noted in chapter 1 and in chapters 3, 6, and 7 hereafter, the sequence of recentralization differs slightly between the Brazilian and Peruvian cases. Brazil underwent a more simultaneous process of crisis resolution and recentralization, while Peru's was more sequential, with recentralizing efforts following the resolution of the economic crisis. This difference in modality is attributable to Brazil's robust federal system, in which reforming the fiscal federal system was a necessary component of an economic stabilization package, as contrasted with Peru where the economic crisis had little to do with SNGs.

After the protests and sham elections of 2000, Fujimori's regime quickly crumbled amid scandals that exposed the power of the intelligence services and the extent of regime corruption. Fujimori's principal adviser and the head of the intelligence services, Vlademiro Montesinos, was caught on video-tape buying the vote of a congressman. Montesinos promptly went into hiding, and Fujimori himself began a televised soap-operatic hunt to track down his erstwhile associate. Fujimori was eventually forced into exile in Japan and threatened with imprisonment and high treason should he return to Peru. With the collapse of Fujimori's government, Peru's Congress transferred interim authority to the long-respected politician Valentín Paniagua, who paved the way for free and fair elections.

Institutions of Centralism in Peru

Peru's second democratic transition in twenty years took place in 2001. In special presidential elections that year, Alejandro Toledo narrowly defeated a resurgent Alan García (though the latter would regain the presidency in 2006). Toledo had a brief honeymoon in which he appointed several key advisers, including international banker Pedro-Pablo Kuczynski, but the new president quickly faced popular frustration. Toledo decided to eliminate the Ministry of the Presidency as part of a gamble that disassembling the centralist institutions created by Fujimori would provide a substantial boost to his popularity. This did not pay off in the short term, as his support plummeted.

Peru's vacillations between authoritarian and weak democratic regimes—including the challenges of the 1990s—have contributed to the weakness of legislatures and political parties. Throughout the 1990s, the country was governed by a unicameral parliament, with legislators picked in a single national district by proportional representation. Tanaka (2002, 10) notes that Fujimori did so despite advantages that would have accrued to his movement from majoritarian rule; Fujimori implemented proportional representation not to advantage his allies, but for personalist reasons to avoid the emergence of any regional or local elites. In Peru's single nationwide district, legislators had few incentives to deliver particularist services to constituents and little allegiance to specific districts. Under normal circumstances, a single national district with closed party lists and proportional representation would be expected to strengthen the hand of national party leaders, who would control nominations to political office, but in Peru the effects were different. From 1979 onward, the party system in Peru declined precipitously as personalist vehicles emerged in the 1990 election. Parties constructed around individuals, such as Fujimori's Cambio 90, had no regional base and as a result did not press for decentralization. The single national district thus exacerbated the centralizing dynamic of the party system by undermining APRA and giving Fujimori a direct, populist relationship with the citizenry that precluded allegiance to local constituencies.

After 2001 the Congress reverted to district-based constituencies for its 120 members, but remained unicameral. Also in 2001 Toledo called for regional elections to break decisively with the Fujimori centralization. By 2002 Toledo regretted this move, as APRA reasserted its claim to be the leading opposition party with a convincing set of victories in the regions. Toledo correspondingly began to backtrack on his original claims to decentralize the country's resources to the regions, fearing that in this new environment APRA would stand to gain most from decentralization. With the reelection of the once-disgraced Alan García to the presidency in 2006, APRA regained central control, signaling the possibility of a new phase in central–regional relations.

Unitarism and Centralism in Africa: Senegal

In Senegal, patterns of state construction and development led to a central government that dominated local governments. Centralism was a result of French efforts to administer West Africa directly, the pattern of the country's economic development, and the legacy of one-party rule after independence. In the 1800s French colonizers founded semiautonomous urban communes at four locations along the Senegalese coast. The development of the export-oriented groundnut trade under French rule and thereafter gave the central state a product that could provide a steady stream of revenue while providing leverage over established local elites (Boone 1992, 27–30). After independence in 1960, Senegal's single party regime moved slowly toward fuller democracy and also slowly dropped the insistence on central planning that was associated with the socialist parties of the moment. In Senegal's gradual transition to democracy, no Constituent Assembly was called. Rather, Parti Socialiste (PS) presidents gradually watched their party's electoral dominance wane and enacted limited state reform at each step of the process. Strong presidential control of the governing party enabled the presidents to adopt relatively top-down measures, though even these national prerogatives were necessitated by growing disaffection among party elites.

The Origins of Centralism in Senegal

By African standards, Senegal has exhibited exceptional stability and very high levels of democracy in its postindependence period. Though the PS dominated politics during the entire period from 1960 to 2000, elections were increasingly free and fair over that time. In fact, of the four countries in this study, Senegal has since 1960 had the most consistent history of democracy and the least repression. This does not mean that governance was entirely benign or constructive, as clientelism prevailed. The PS elite controlled politics for decades and developed a complex patronage network that systematically excluded the opposition from power and access to resources. As Bratton and Van de Walle (1997, 82) note with respect to Senegal and other selected African countries, "African multiparty systems can be thought of as hybrid regimes in which the formal rules of electoral democracy vie with informal personal ties of 'big men' to define and shape the actual practice of politics."

In the forty-year history of the dominant party-state, political conflicts between central and local governments took place within the party structures of the PS (Diop and Diouf 1990). Many of the shifts in governance reflected shifts in the balance of power between national leaders and local operatives, as the PS quickly recognized the need to extend benefits downward to well-located elites (Adamolekun 1971; Boone 1990a). The extension of patronage and the management of clientelism did not come without conflict. In the 1960s in particular, Léopold Sédar Senghor increasingly concentrated party power. Senghor won an early power struggle with Prime Minister Mamadou Dia; this enabled the president to arrogate greater powers to his own office and person (Hesseling 1985, 231–37). A new constitution in 1963 and a constitutional revision in 1967 strengthened Senghor's hand (Hesseling 1985, 237, 258–60). The concentration of power in the hands of the president could not continue indefinitely in a broad movement such as the PS, however, and Senghor came under increasing pressure in the late 1960s and early 1970s. One reform in particular allowed Senghor to appease party militants while continuing to institutionalize the PS's hold on power: the creation of rural communities (*communautés rurales*) in 1972. With a single act, Senghor extended government across the entire national territory, including that portion of Senegalese territory hitherto governed only by customary leaders.

While the 1972 creation of the rural communities was a top-down move, the 1960s and 1970s also saw urban pressure for increased autonomy. Throughout these decades, demands for local autonomy were most acute in the capital,

Dakar. The city had the only truly viable city budget; whereas other cities floundered when required to perform such basic tasks as urban sanitation and lighting, Dakar found the requisite resources more easily. The primacy of Dakar is not merely a function of its economic preeminence, but also of its political centrality. The threat posed by Dakar's autonomy to central party leadership was evidenced in 1964, when Senghor suspended the city's municipal statute, bringing it directly under national control and thereby avoiding the insurgence within the PS of rival factions with a strong local power base (Marks 1996b).

In 1980, Senghor surprised the country (and much of the world) by announcing he would leave the presidency, an event virtually unheard of in Africa. Prime Minister Abdou Diouf, a young PS technocrat, assumed the office and began to push through several reforms, including some further concentration of presidential power. At the same time, Diouf set to the task of strengthening Senegal's democratic credentials, which had received a boost from Senghor's decision to leave office without duress. During the 1980s, Diouf and the PS continued to dominate politics through control of all branches of government, but the president recognized the increasing difficulty of maintaining a satisfied party under increasingly democratic norms.

Democratization and Decentralization in Senegal

Senegal's democratization process was very different from the processes in the other countries cited here. The process was gradual, and did not culminate in a Constituent National Assembly. In fact Senegal was one of the few countries in francophone Africa to avoid having a regime-threatening National Conference, and this is largely attributable to its experience with multiparty democracy (Bratton and Van de Walle 1997, 69). On the whole, Senegal made a much less dramatically punctuated move toward democracy in the 1980s and 1990s, but not a less complete move.

One of Diouf's governmental reforms in the 1990s was a decentralization process. In the context of the increasing political opening, the PS passed laws reforming the government structure in 1996 by creating elected regions and by delegating major public service responsibilities to SNGs, along with some increases in revenue transfers. The country's ten regions (later changed to eleven), which before the change were politically irrelevant, corresponded to a Parti Socialiste need to shore up a subnational political base. The creation of the regions with elected councils and presidents gave the PS "control over this stratum of government . . . insofar as regional voters will come overwhelmingly from rural areas—creating hundreds of elected positions for PS rank-and-file" (Marks 1996b, 141).

The 1996 reforms were acclaimed in Africa as a major advance in decentralization, but on the whole the reforms decentralized responsibilities without transferring the revenues necessary to realize these functions. In fact, most government activity, including the payment of civil service salaries, remained in the hands of state-appointed administrators. The laws were in effect a set of unfunded mandates.

Senegal's dominant-party system finally gave way to an *alternance* of power on April 1, 2000, when long-time opposition leader Abdoulaye Wade was sworn in as president at the head of a coalition known as Sopi (for "Change"), led by his PDS (Parti Démocratique Sénégalais). To that date, Senegal had had only two presidents since independence in 1960, both from the PS. Wade led the drafting of a new constitution, which was passed on January 7, 2001. For all the excitement about the change, the Wade administration has taken much the same approach to intergovernmental relations as the PS governments did: it is a potential tool for political use, but an uncertain one. The ambiguity surrounding local and regional government is a function of Wade's uncertainty about how well he can control subnational allies.[11]

Institutions of Centralism in Senegal

For a relatively small unitary state, Senegal is governed by a surprising number of subnational bodies. The largest in area are the country's eleven regions, and the smallest are the local governments (*collectivités locales*), which take two forms: the municipality (*commune*) in urban areas and the rural community (*communauté rurale*) in the countryside. Sandwiched in between elected regional and local governments are two layers of unelected state administration intended to coordinate the state's governance in a deconcentrated fashion: the *département,* governed by a prefect, and the *arrondissement,* governed by a subprefect. Municipal officials (in the urban communes) have been elected since before Independence (with occasional interruptions) and local officials in rural governments have been elected since 1972. Since 1996 the regions have had both elected and appointed bodies. They are governed by a regional council, which elects its own president; the region also has a

---

11. Interviews: Seynabou Ba, Christian Fournier.

governor who serves as a representative of the state and who works alongside the elected council.

Senegal's legislature remains weak and has feeble links to SNGs. Under the country's relatively strong presidential system from about 1963 to 2000, the legislature was relatively unimportant. Strong discipline within the PS and the formal powers of the president enshrined in the constitution marginalized the Parliament in policy making. During the forty years leading up to 2000, the PS leadership controlled the lists for election to the lower chamber, the Assemblée Nationale, which ensured allegiance to the national party instead of local constituencies, and meant that the Parliament was not an effective channel for subnational governments to exert pressure on the center. The Senegalese senate, ostensibly created to represent the regions or subnational governments, was largely an echo chamber to endorse the interests of the national PS leadership, as the president nominated a large percentage of the members. After his victory in 2000, Abdoulaye Wade abolished the senate, citing it as an institution of the old order, and took Senegal to a unicameral system until 2007, when the senate was reestablished. Elections to the assembly in 2001 were modified to include a new combination of proportional representation and district voting for the 120 seats. After dismissing Parliament, holding a referendum, and approving a new constitution, Wade's coalition commanded nearly a three-fourths majority in the legislature (with 89 seats). The defeat of the PS meant that control of the legislature had shifted from a single relatively strong party to a more fractious coalition. Following its loss at the national level, the PS also watched its local power wane, though it remains strong in some rural areas where older clientelist patterns are retained. Changes in electoral law have not altered the disconnect between local power and parliamentary representation.

PS presidents had strong formal powers and partisan powers (cf. Mainwaring and Scully 1995). Senghor and Diouf were rarely required to use formal powers throughout their presidencies because they could rely on the levers of the PS, which commanded a majority in the legislature. On the other hand, the strong endowments offered to the president in the constitution were reinforced over time, as the prime minister (head of the Parliament) became more a subordinate to the president than a head of government. On several occasions, both Senghor and Diouf abolished the position of prime minister, moving Senegal to a strongly presidential system (Hesseling 1985).

Senegal's bureaucracy retains considerable control over national revenues. The Ministry of Economy and Finance and the Local Government Bureau (Direction des Collectivités Locales) are responsible for the division of transfers to municipalities, with little input from expenditure ministries. The only place where the expenditure and revenue ministries coordinate appropriations and distributions is the annual National Conference for Local Collectivities (Conférence National des Collectivités Locales, or CNCL), a political forum involving the various ministries at which presidential direc- tives for the budget year are tabled. At this conference, national ministers meet to discuss national priorities, and a set of political decisions are made, based on the government's policy priorities. Technical elements of revenue distribution are left to the discretion of the Local Government Bureau, which places considerable bureaucratic limitations on Senegal's decen- tralization process. The realities of Senegal's state thus vacates much of the purported decentralization.

Understanding History's Causal Impact

Trajectories of economic development, patterns of industrialization, exper- iences with democracy, and the strengths of subnational elites varied considerably as these four countries approached the 1990s (see table 2.1). Brazil had a strong historical tendency toward decentralized government, while the other three countries had much weaker subnational governments. State formation in Brazil's robust federal system meant that even episodes of military rule did not change the basic facts of national politics. Ultimately, the decentralization that accompanied 1980s democratization was not the result of an electoralist calculus, but rather the path-dependent consequence of decades of subnational power. In South Africa, by contrast, the creation of quasi-federalism in the 1990s was a much more narrowly electoralist initiative propagated from the top down. The top-down logic was also apparent in the historically unitary states, showing that decentralization is likely to occur for different reasons in states with different trajectories of state formation.

Viewed from historical distance, processes of state formation and state building resulted in lower degrees of subnational fiscal autonomy in unitary states relative to the federal states. In Brazil's robust federalism, the *estados* successfully retained tax authority for themselves (Diaz-Cayeros 2006). In South Africa, by contrast, the constituents of the apartheid-era NP struck a virtual bargain with the central authorities, resulting in a powerful central tax state (Lieberman 2003). The fact that many of the proponents of the centralized tax state were in the private sector rather than the public, and that subnational politicians had minimal authority, only reinforces the

Table 2.1 Historical trajectories in four countries: From state formation to democratization

	Brazil	South Africa	Peru	Senegal
Degree of centralization in state formation	Decentralized	Centralized, with early provincial autonomy	Centralized	Centralized
Episodes of military rule	Yes	No, but militarized state	Yes	No
Local elite strength at democratization	High	Moderate	Low	Low
Contemporary structure	Robust Federalism	Weak Federalism	Unitary	Unitary
Decentralization bottom-up or top-down	Bottom-up	Top-down, with some bottom-up pressures	Top-down	Top-down

argument that bargaining over tax systems can result in high degrees of centralization. Finally, in the unitary states, the preeminent position of the central government from a very early stage made possible the imposition of a unitary solution to the questions of revenue collection. Examining the logic of decentralization is best done with a broad selection of federal and unitary cases. These cases show that federalism is not a necessary cause of decentralized government, yet they suggest federalism does condition decentralization. Federalism and decentralization correlate but are properly viewed side by side as outcomes of historical processes, rather than as one causing the other.

State formation and building have bequeathed to contemporary Brazil its robust federal system, to Peru and Senegal the bases for centralized, unitary systems, and to South Africa its quasi-federal system that intermediates between these two poles. These varied trajectories shape decentralization in ways that analysts too infrequently recognize. Decentralization from below (bottom-up decentralization) is a function of historically powerful actors located at subnational levels; it is more structural in nature than simple electoralist approaches to decentralization can account for. Meanwhile, top-down decentralization is likelier to occur as an electoral strategy, or as an outcome of more contingent and conjuncturally specific bargaining, in societies where power is historically centralized. In the examinations across issue areas in subsequent chapters, this difference proves vital in comprehending how and why Brazil witnessed a more thorough and complete decentralization across multiple issue areas. As for recentralization, the expectation would be that reducing SNG autonomy would be easiest in historically centralized societies, but the cases do not covary in this way (as Brazil saw some of the most thoroughgoing recentralization and Senegal the least). History thus motivates an additional puzzle and demonstrates the peculiar power of the independent variable—economic crisis—that is capable of explaining recentralization.

The "telescopic" view of taxation and intergovernmental fiscal relations offered in this chapter must hereafter be complemented by a "microscopic" view. Building on history, we can examine when the center has held power and when it has conceded power during the last twenty-five years. In the next chapters, I place two federal countries—Brazil and South Africa—under the microscope. To this end, histories treated here have served three purposes. First, to explain the modalities of decentralization across states with different historical trajectories, since there is no one single model that can account for decentralization across all polities; state formation has path-dependent effects that condition whether decentralization will happen from below or from above (Eaton 2004a, 2004b). Second, to motivate the subsequent questions and puzzles that arise for each country. Why does historically decentralized Brazil see a democratic central government make a "comeback" by reducing subnational power in the 1990s? Why does historically centralized South Africa, on the other hand, decentralize so much revenue to the provinces in those very same years? Perhaps most intriguing are the questions that the historical analysis presented here cannot answer. Why do shifts toward and away from decentralism take place when they do? Given the popularity of decentralization as a political and institutional reform, what explains the timing and sequencing of short-term variations in subnational autonomy? Third and finally, the current chapter has presented the antecedent conditions against which contemporary politics plays out in each country.

In subsequent chapters, I assess the recent shifts in decentralization in each country on its own terms. That is, I consider how much a country has changed relative to its own historical tendency. The cross-national comparison of overall levels of subnational autonomy across countries is not the principal variation explained, but rather the timing and direction of changes in each country. This is essential, because even substantial reductions in autonomy in Brazil will not make it as centralized as Senegal or Peru; similarly, even significant decentralizing reforms in the latter countries will not make them as decentralized as a robust federation. Decentralization and centralization must not be viewed as static, even if the rank order of countries is stable. The next several chapters address each of three areas of subnational autonomy over the last twenty-five years in Brazil and South Africa; I extend the logic to the unitary states thereafter, in chapter 6.

3

—⟨o/o/o⟩—

SUBNATIONAL REVENUE AUTONOMY

In recent years, studies of federalism and decentralization have focused on the transfers of revenue and tax authority from national to subnational governments. In this chapter, I examine fiscal decentralization and recentralization, assessing the revenue autonomy of SNGs under Brazil's robust federalism and under South Africa's much weaker federalism. The operating assumption in this and subsequent chapters is that SNGs prefer and seek increased fiscal autonomy. In the case of revenue autonomy, preferences are for more autonomous access to revenue in the form of tax authority and guaranteed revenue transfers. Central governments, meanwhile, seek to limit revenue and tax transfers, retaining revenues for themselves, and aiming to make transfers discretionary rather than mandatory. In short, SNGs prefer fiscal decentralization, while central governments prefer fiscal centralization.

In Brazil and South Africa the weakening of the chief executive's partisan powers is a central cause of fiscal decentralization, and fiscal crisis drives processes of revenue recentralization. These moments of change are mediated through particular institutions that shape revenue autonomy. Executive–legislative relations—specifically the shifting balance of power between presidents and legislators within governing parties—is at the heart of contestation over subnational revenues. Political parties play key roles in shaping battles between presidents (who represent the interests of the central government) and legislators (who often represent more centrifugal interests by virtue of representing local constituencies). When presidents lose authority relative to legislators, SNGs gain revenue autonomy; when presidents increase their ability to compel legislation, SNGs lose revenue autonomy. While future chapters reach new conclusions regarding subnational autonomy in other issue areas, this chapter in part reinforces arguments in the literature that link parties and decentralization, while also developing a political economy argument about recentralization.

The arguments about decentralization forwarded here synthesize two growing literatures that view decentralization as (1) a top-down strategy initiated by central government actors, or (2) a bottom-up process masterminded by powerful subnational elites. Eaton (2004a) develops these twin logics, terming them "decentralization from above" and "decentralization from below." The former includes electoralist approaches resulting from political calculations by national governing parties, while the latter expands the logic to include decentralization processes where subnational actors drive the process, whether from within the national governing party, within a governing coalition, or from opposition. Whether decentralization is top-down or bottom-up varies as a function of the extent of federalism and the power of subnational actors, as seen in chapter 2. Decentralization in Brazil and South Africa, which started from quite different levels of centralization, illustrates these two patterns. Brazil is a quite decentralized federal country where fiscal decentralization occurred from below, while postapartheid South Africa is only weakly federal, and revenue decentralization occurred from above.

In "top-down" cases where central governments have partisan reasons to decentralize, electoral politics can drive processes of decentralization to regional governments.[1] This may be especially salient when governing parties foresee (with some certainty) electoral defeat at the national level; under circumstances where national governing parties also envision an electoral future at the subnational level, decentralization emerges as a politically appealing solution. Kathleen O'Neill's (2003, 2005) work on Andean countries shows that decentralization was a strategy of governing parties at the national level seeking to build up regional power bases when faced with national defeat. Eaton (2004b, 19) further notes cases such as Chile and Uruguay where decentralization generated political advantage for national governing parties even where these were not weakened. In other instances, quests for legitimacy by authoritarian governments—as in the later years of Mexico's Partido Revolucionário Institucional (PRI)—may explain top-down processes of decentralization (Rodriguez 1997). Such logics prevail in the South African case.

"Bottom-up" processes, or "decentralizations from below," may be explained by another set of political motivations: central government requisites to ensure governability. Central governments in these instances may prefer not to decentralize, but must distribute power and resources to subnational actors

---

1. On electoralist approaches to decentralization, see Montero and Samuels 2004, 20–25.

in order to govern and legislate. Particularly where party systems are weak and power regionalized, and/or where electoral rules provide subnational officials with leverage on national issues, central governments will often succumb to bottom-up pressures (e.g., Abrucio 1998; Garman, Haggard, and Willis 2001). Subnational politicians whose preferences conflict with those of the center may include a president's copartisans or fellow coalition members, as well as opposition party members. Brazil is a crucial case in this regard, given its historically "robust federalism" and weak party system (Mainwaring 1997a, 1997b). Subnational officials demanding decentralization systematically force Brazilian presidents to govern via the distribution of considerable resources.

These motivations explain increases in revenue autonomy, but decreases in SNG autonomy are more problematic for central governments to achieve. Decentralization, like reforms in other policy areas, proves sticky as it invests increasing numbers of political actors with greater power and resources. Once empowered, subnational politicians concede authority reluctantly as each level of government seeks to maintain its own autonomy. Reversing decentralization requires more than central government preferences for recentralization. Central governments wishing to recentralize require extraordinary justification to do so, especially in federal states where SNGs have institutional bases of power, in the form of representation in the national legislature and constitutional protections. The justification for recentralization occurs with economic crisis. Crisis, as is documented extensively in the broader literature, creates unique governing opportunities for central governments in a variety of political outcomes; with respect to issues of SNG autonomy, it creates the possibility of recentralization. In Brazil, national economic crisis preceded and facilitated reductions in SNG revenue autonomy across the board, while in South Africa more localized economic crises enabled only a correspondingly more localized centralization. This despite the fact that partisan powers favor far greater recentralization in South Africa than in Brazil.

To address subnational revenue autonomy, I first discuss the concept of revenue autonomy and propose a means of measuring it, arguing that this variable enables an interpretation of fiscal decentralization that facilitates a comparison with other areas of subnational fiscal autonomy. In the same section, I lay out briefly the argument about presidential power in relation to the legislature and why this matters for revenue autonomy. In doing so, I argue that the electoral decline and partisan weakness of presidents leads to fiscal decentralization, and that economic crisis resolution enables fiscal recentralization. Following this, I turn to governing structures in Brazil and South Africa to examine how these affect subnational revenues. A section on democratization and Constituent National Assemblies (CNA) explains fiscal devolution in the two countries in detail. The penultimate section treats the extent of revenue recentralization in each case as a function of the extent of macroeconomic crisis, and I conclude with a comparative analysis of the findings.

Explaining Revenue Autonomy: The Executive–Legislative Arena

Subnational governments draw revenues from two major sources: taxation and intergovernmental transfers (IGTs) from central governments.[2] This distinction between own-source revenues and IGTs applies to both state/ provincial governments and to local governments. In countries such as the United States, local governments may receive some grants from higher levels of government, but generally draw the largest proportion of their revenues from an own-source: property taxes. Local governments also draw heavily on user fees, for services such as utilities, waste collection, and recreation.[3] State and provincial governments often rely more heavily on IGT from the central government, though they may also have the independent right to place surcharges on national income taxes or occasionally on value-added taxes.

Measuring revenue autonomy, as opposed to simply subnational revenues, clarifies the preferences of SNGs. Varied assumptions can be made about the preferences of SNGs, with one of the central points of disagreement being the desirability of various means of procuring revenues. Whether SNGs most prefer the devolution of tax bases or IGTs is a key source of debate.[4] As Diaz-Cayeros (2006) rightly argues, SNGs prefer more options for raising

---

2. In keeping with the focus on (domestic) economies, I do not consider foreign aid here.

3. The emphasis in this chapter is on provincial government, though I occasionally make reference to local government. On the three-way relationship between central, regional, and municipal government, see, e.g., Dickovick 2007; Samuels 2004.

4. Diaz-Cayeros (2006) argues that SNGs prefer decentralized tax collection to transfers, as collecting own taxes reduces dependence on potentially fickle central governments. Taxation authority also enables SNGs to set rates and to use the prospect of tax breaks for political gain. On the other hand, SNGs may find raising taxes from constituents too politically costly and may prefer to operate on transfers from the center; the desirability of transfers is particularly high if transfers are predictably large and create implicit soft budget constraints for SNGs (cf. Rodden 2006; Wibbels 2005). Transfers allow SNGs to externalize the political costs of taxation, while internalizing the political gains from spending. SNGs prefer greater revenues, but may not always prefer tax responsibilities.

revenue rather than less, and less formal dependence on national governments. To be sure, the assumption that SNGs prefer more revenue to less is safe as well, but the emphasis on revenue autonomy helps us bracket the debate about *from where* SNGs wish to draw their resources. By focusing on revenue autonomy, we can talk about both cash transfers and the transfer of tax authority as movements in the same direction, both of which favor SNGs.[5]

While different forms of revenue decentralization may have different consequences, subnational officials seek greater autonomy both in the form of enhanced tax authority and increased transfers. In terms of IGTs, automatic, legally mandated transfers are of greater value to SNGs than discretionary transfers. Transfers mandated by constitutions offer SNGs the highest degree of revenue autonomy, followed by transfers outlined in ordinary law, and then by transfers that are voluntary or over which the central government exercises discretion. For tax authority, if the central government grants SNGs the right to enact taxes not previously authorized, this too is considered a decentralization of revenue.

Ideal type measures of subnational revenue autonomy are shown in table 3.1. The strongest guarantees of subnational revenue autonomy are written into constitutions. Decreases in the solidity of legal guarantees diminish autonomy. Low levels of autonomy occur when SNGs are subordinated to the whims of central governments. For transfers, this would mean transfers are discretionary; for own-revenues, this would mean SNGs are not empowered to raise taxes.

Of course, in order to calculate subnational revenue autonomy, one must also consider not only the type, but also the *amount* of revenues they receive. High degrees of legal autonomy are less important if very little money is transferred or if SNGs do not have the necessary capacity or economic base to collect tax revenues. Meaningful amounts of transfers are the *sine qua non* of these processes. A reduction in the financial value of transfers to SNGs can reasonably be treated as a reduction in subnational revenue autonomy. As a result, a discussion of revenue autonomy must include both legal autonomy and fiscal salience.

---

5. Additionally, framing revenue preferences in terms of autonomy enables analytical symmetry in the consideration of entire fiscal systems. In subsequent chapters, I forward a unifying framework that enables us to incorporate the numerous aspects of these systems, including autonomy over less-quantifiable areas, such as expenditure management and contracting. Measuring revenue autonomy rather than revenue totals means explicitly examining a political relationship. The concept of revenue autonomy dovetails with the broader examination of SNG autonomy seen in subsequent chapters, enabling clearer comparison across the issue areas of intergovernmental fiscal relations.

Table 3.1 Subnational revenue autonomy: Ideal type measures

Score	Characteristics
High	Large amount; constitutionally mandated transfers Constitutional guarantees for major tax bases Ad hoc transfers consistently large
Moderate	Large amount; legally mandated transfers Legal guarantees for major tax bases (income tax, VAT, e.g.) Ad hoc transfers inconsistent or occasional
Low	Small amounts of legally mandated transfers Legal guarantees for minor tax authority (fees, e.g.) Ad hoc transfers minimal
Very low	Exclusively voluntary transfers, or no transfers Subordination to center on taxation matters Ad hoc transfers minimal

Since subnational revenue autonomy is conditioned on a set of legal guarantees, caution must be used when considering measures for cross-national or intertemporal comparison. Marginal changes in taxation law in larger, more industrialized countries such as Brazil may dwarf huge budgetary overhauls in smaller unitary countries, for instance. That said, considering the various components of revenue autonomy enables a more accurate qualitative assessment of the phenomenon. I opt for this approach, examining countries qualitatively to assess the magnitude and direction of changes in revenue autonomy, considered relative to the size of each country. The change over time in a given country is a more significant study than a determination of the relative position of the countries in a static cross-national rank order.

The consensus in the literature on decentralization is that national bureaucrats and presidents generally favor centralized revenue and resist attempts to decentralize resources (Levi 1988). The question that arises, therefore, is under what conditions the preferences of the president and national bureaucracy will prevail. What are the mechanisms through which the central government can control revenue? This chapter builds on the existing literature on revenue patterns.[6] As mentioned previously, Brazil and South Africa will not be considered static cases. Rather, I look at variation over time in each country throughout the past twenty years.[7] Treating subnational autonomy

6. In particular, I draw on Ahmad 2003; Ames 2001; Bird and Vaillancourt 1998; Eaton 2001, 2004a; O'Neill 2001, 2003; Rodriguez 1997; and Samuels 2003.
7. Important changes that increased the revenue autonomy of SNGs also occurred in other instances that are beyond the scope of the study. These include moments when politically autonomous local governments were created where only appointed officials had

as a set of relationships that is constantly in flux, certain historical moments are likelier to produce change than others. Two particular types of moments often lead to changes in autonomy: first, times of decline for a government (to include government dissolution at Constituent National Assemblies); second, economic crises.

Increases in subnational access to revenue in these countries occurred at moments when national executives had weak partisan prospects. Declining governments sought to shore up their political futures by decentralizing, though the process was top-down in South Africa and bottom-up in Brazil. This occurred at Constituent National Assemblies that represented the pinnacle of democratizing movements (with Brazil's occurring in 1987–88 and South Africa's in 1994–96), and in anticipation of national and subnational elections. Public and constitutional law governing revenue distributions is the outcome of constitutional bargaining processes, which are crafted and voted upon by sovereign or semi-sovereign constituent assemblies, typically at a time of regime change. Decentralization thus occurs alongside democratization, with Constituent Assemblies the bodies responsible for the charters that define both democracy and decentralization.

Of course, revenue can be recentralized as well, and economic crisis plays a key role in shaping recentralizing changes (cf. Dillinger and Webb 2001). At moments of crisis, the stakes for different levels of government are raised, contributing to greater institutional upheaval (Haggard and Kaufman 1995), as well as bolder policy initiatives (Weyland 2002). Actions that may be tolerated in times of crisis appear to be antidemocratic power grabs by presidents during "normal" times. The resolution of crisis reconfigures the balance of power between different actors in the political system, offering temporary windows of opportunity to executives. Crisis operates causally by increasing presidential leverage in ways that both substitute and complement partisan powers. Centralizing initiatives in Brazil's weak party system, for instance, followed on the heels of economic crisis, and these were translated into increased presidential authority in negotiations with the legislature, when compared with previous time periods (cf. Power 2002). Recentralization occurred in both countries in the wake of economic crises, and the extent of recentralization depended on the extent of crisis. National macroeconomic crisis in Brazil in the early 1990s engendered the central government's comprehensive reassertion of fiscal authority against all odds. Meanwhile, limited crisis in South Africa in the late 1990s led to more-limited centralization.

---

existed before, such as in Brazil in 1982 (the subnational elections that signaled the beginning of redemocratization).

Both decentralization and recentralization are mediated through party systems. Accordingly, political party structures and strength are probably among the most tested variables in the decentralization literature (cf., e.g., Ames 2001; Lodge 1994; Marks 1996b; O'Neill 2005; Samuels 2003; Willis, Garman, and Haggard 2001). In particular, analyses of institutional arrangements have led many to conclude that decentralization increases as a function of decentralized party structures, party incoherence or fragmentation, and the expected future electoral strength of governing parties at subnational levels. It is clear, then, that parties and legislatures play important roles in revenue distributions, where outcomes depend on the partisan powers of chief executives. The mechanisms through which laws change are found in executive–legislative relations, where parties have their undeniable mediating impact.

Legislative Structures, Executive Structures, and Partisan Powers

Political structures in Brazil and South Africa—beginning with weak presidentialism in the former and a centralized parliamentary system in the latter—suggest that decentralization should be extensive and perpetual in Brazil and that centralization should prevail in South Africa. While Brazil has clearly been the more "robust federal" case, legislative and executive structures motivate the puzzle about why decentralizing change occurred in South Africa and why recentralization occurred in Brazil.

In Brazil, the cross-pollination of military-era elites with democrats in the wake of re-democratization led to a plethora of small- and medium-sized parties, each of which performed well in one or two regions of the country at most. President Fernando Collor (1990–92), who was ultimately impeached and forced from the presidency, belonged to a tiny regional party with almost no following beyond his person. Fernando Henrique Cardoso won his 1994 and 1998 presidential elections in generally convincing fashion, but in Brazil's disintegrated party system, presidential coattails proved to be chronically weak (Samuels 2003). Cardoso had to piece together a broad four- or five-party coalition that housed social democrats, ideological neoliberals, and old-style patronage bosses. This inchoate party system was reinforced by open-list electoral rules that nullified party discipline and favored individual campaigns (Samuels 2003; Willis, Garman, and Haggard 1999). Moreover, Brazil's *congressistas* were long able to switch parties with impunity, and chose to do so with great frequency. Executive–legislative relations favor legislators and their subnational allies because *deputados* and *senadores* have strong electoral links to governors and mayors and not to national party leadership. Weak party discipline complicates efforts to ensure subnational fiscal responsibility. For Brazil, then, the causes of revenue decentralization are well established: exceptionally low party discipline and fragile partisan support for presidents.

Despite the institutional challenges arrayed against the center, the centralizing efforts of Fernando Henrique Cardoso differed dramatically from feeble concessions to SNGs under previous administrations. Whereas presidents elsewhere can use their party's chain of command as their principal tool in passing legislation, Cardoso had to struggle for fiscal order despite the weak party system.[8] The Cardoso years give rise to differing interpretations of central government power, as a result of the costly nature of the reforms, but it is clear Cardoso progressively regained control of the political economy for the center, relative to previous presidents; this demands explanation, given Brazil's long legacy of decentralized power and undisciplined party coalitions. The Brazilian government's surprising degree of coherence in the 1990s (despite its fractious coalitional nature), is due in part to the centralization of decision-making power within the Congress (Figueiredo and Limongi 2000; see also Power 2002). Members of Cardoso's coalition frequently supported the president. However, Cardoso's comparative success over previous presidents can be attributed less to partisan powers (per se) and more to Brazil's economic crisis, as well as to a lingering propensity to distribute pork within and among members of the coalition (Ames 2001). In order to cobble together support for presidential reforms in a context of frequent floor crossing, the central government had to satisfy legislators in the National Assembly and the Senate alike with massive payouts, in the form of individually sponsored amendments (Ames 2001; Samuels 2003). State governors and mayors likewise received massive transfers to their constituencies, and this deepened their powerful patronage networks based on extensive hiring and contracting. Cardoso, like other Brazilian presidents, clearly could not promote reform by pulling party levers in the ways used in countries with stronger party systems, yet early reforms begun during temporary windows of opportunity had long-term reform consequences.

Some observers of Latin American politics emphasize the importance of the formal decree powers of presidents, and Cardoso used such powers extensively during his eight years in office (Carey and Shugart 1998). But

---

8. For a fuller comparative treatment of presidential partisan powers in Latin America, see Mainwaring and Shugart 1997.

formal powers did not carry the day in Cardoso's rationalizing reforms either. While the *medida provisória,* a temporary decree authority, allowed Cardoso to impose a number of policies (and, in fact, the successful Real Plan for economic stabilization and reform had its birth as a *medida provisória*), it did not figure heavily in the ability to commandeer the federal political economy. In fact, substantial changes in Brazil operated through negotiation; the major advances, including the Real Plan and later the indispensable Fiscal Responsibility Law of 2000, were considered consolidated only when they became either full legislation or obtained de facto currency, even if they originated as temporary decrees. That Cardoso gave away a great deal to secure support for his laws favoring fiscal responsibility suggests the limited value of decrees, and that lasting institutional changes require a wrangling with the underlying powers of subnational politicians.

Unlike Brazil, South Africa is a parliamentary system. The head of state and head of government—called the president—is elected by the National Assembly and is the head of the largest party in this lower house of Parliament. Since the end of apartheid, the ANC has consolidated its dominant position in the party system, and the ANC president has consolidated executive power over the legislature. Party discipline within the ANC comes from two principal sources: electoral rules and a tradition of top-down loyalty that was crucial to the organization's survival as a militant opposition movement during the apartheid era.

As regards federal institutions, the upper legislative chamber (the National Council of Provinces, or NCOP) represents the provinces. Its ninety members are chosen by the nine provincial legislatures, with each province having ten delegates. To date, the NCOP has not assembled any meaningful provincial front in opposition to the wishes of the central government and the ANC's national party leadership. A first reason for this is the relative newness of the chamber. More important is the redundancy of the chamber in a dominant party system. Given the ANC's dominance of the lower chamber (National Assembly) and of the majority of provincial governments, and strong party discipline within the ANC, the NCOP largely reflects national priorities rather than provincial interests.[9] Moreover, several have noted the NCOP's weak links to other governmental bodies (cf. RSA/NT 2001).[10] The NCOP is

9. In this context, the ANC leadership works primarily through the National Assembly, tabling the Division of Revenue Act and ensuring that it passes through both chambers of Parliament without significant discussion.

10. Interview: Hildegaard Fast.

thus often perceived as a second chamber that rubber-stamps ANC policy and offers little to the provincial cause.[11] For the near term, it seems unlikely that the NCOP will have a significant role in lobbying for increased transfers to the provinces. This gives an image of a South African system in which power is much more centralized than in Brazil: the ANC president wields considerably greater partisan powers over members of both chambers of the Parliament, reinforced by proportional representation electoral rules and formal powers.

Democratization, Constituent Assemblies, and Revenue Decentralization

If presidents are the principal advocates of strong central authority, then presidential weakness will likely favor decentralization. Constituent National Assemblies are political moments when presidential power is at its most fleeting. When assemblies are convened with the task of writing a constitution, fundamental questions of sovereignty and state leadership are at issue. Accordingly, a theory of decentralization as a function of presidential weakness would expect such assemblies to be crucial moments when substantial decentralization would occur, and both Brazil and South Africa show that constitutional assemblies are indeed decentralizing. In part, this echoes arguments that decentralization follows democratization, and that decentralization would have an elective affinity with democratization. More concretely, however, democratization cannot be said to cause decentralization unless it can account for the timing of decentralization. Constituent Assemblies deserve greater consideration in this regard.

Brazil: Revenue Decentralization in the 1988 Constitution

The major increase in revenue autonomy for SNGs in recent years was the establishment of the constitution of 1988, which greatly empowered SNGs. In Brazil at that time, revenue decentralization was more an effect and manifestation of subnational power than a cause of it. Politics in Brazil had long centered on local "colonels" and their relationships with governors and mayors; even recurrent episodes of authoritarian rule did not succeed in

---

11. Some defenders of the NCOP argue that the institutions may increasingly find its feet as provincial political identities develop (interview: Mohammed Enver Surty).

centralizing power (Abrucio 1998; Hagopian 1996; Samuels 2003). In 1988 subnational actors were on the ascendant, and the constitutional provisions merely codified (and cemented into place) this political fact. With democratization in the 1980s and the constitution of 1988, both chambers in the national legislature—the Senate and Chamber of Deputies—came to reflect parochial interests (Ames 2001; Samuels 2003; Stepan 2000). Electoral rules, most notably Brazil's open-list electoral system, led to weak party discipline and ensured that politicians cultivate subnational power bases; combined with long histories of subnational networks, this ensured deputies were as beholden to patrons in their respective *estados* as to national party leadership (Willis, Garman, and Haggard 1999).

Fiscal decentralization "from below" peaked during the Constituent Assembly under President José Sarney (1985–90). Subnational elites seized the agenda and ensured massive revenue transfers. Sarney was no match for the strong representatives of *estado* interests at the assembly (Samuels and Abrucio 2000).[12] Major taxes were assigned to the states, among the most important being a value-added tax on the circulation of goods and services (Imposto sobre a Circulação de Mercadorias e Serviços, or ICMS) and a tax on industrial production (Imposto sobre Produtos Industrializados, IPI). Intergovernmental transfers were also substantial, as revenue sources assigned to the central government had a guaranteed proportion reserved for the *estados* and *municípios*. At the heart of these arrangements were the State Participation Fund (Fundo de Participação dos Estados, or FPE) and Municipal Participation Fund (Fundo de Participação dos Municípios, or FPM), which guaranteed a large percentage of national revenues to both levels of SNGs. With the FPM, municipalities also became directly involved in the fiscal federal system, along with the *estados;* like the increases in transfers to the states, municipal power in the new federation is largely attributable to the strong position of subnational officials at the time of the constitution (Martinez-Lara 1996; Souza 1997). Alongside these established revenue sources for SNGs came other resources which were less regularized, but scarcely less significant in pecuniary terms: transfers arising from pork barrel legislation in the Brazilian Congress. Together, devolution of tax authority and regular and pork barrel transfers represented a revenue bonanza for SNGs. This fiscal devolution was a consequence of presidential partisan weakness—as evidenced by the splintering of the president's Partido do Movimento Democrático Brasileiro (PMDB) coalition—and pressure for revenue decentralization remained strong from 1988 through the mid-1990s.

12. Interview: Luiz Carlos Bresser Pereira.

Importantly, the strong decentralization of revenues in 1988 was not matched by a corresponding transfer of expenditure responsibilities.[13] The fiscal outcome of the Constituent Assembly was the opposite of an unfunded mandate to the states: it was cash devolved, with few strings attached. The combination of hefty revenue decentralization and limited central control over spending meant that states and municipalities in Brazil had arguably one of the most favorable fiscal dispensations in the world. In short, Brazilian revenues were excessively decentralized from 1988 until after 1994, as a result of the weakness of an executive whose rule depended on the support of subnational politicians. In Brazil's weak party system, the need to form coalitions dictated a wide distribution of particularistic benefits. José Sarney and successors Fernando Collor (1990–92) and Itamar Franco (1992–94) sacrificed the central government's fiscal reserves to make Brazil governable. Transfers to SNGs were the prerequisite to earning the support of the powerful mayors and governors who controlled congressional deputies and senators. Revenues were passed to the *estados* to shore up coalitions rather than for a coherent decentralization program.

A final point should be made about soft loans from state banks, which were later eliminated by Cardoso on the heels of the Real Plan. Bailouts provided to *estado* banks represented a form of extra-constitutional revenue windfall for SNGs, as will be discussed in chapter 5. In the absence of party mechanisms to pull subnational strings, the central government was unable to impose effective budget constraints on states, which led to spending even beyond the transfers from federal government. States not only had the legal right to issue debt, but also had "morally hazardous" incentives to do so, as the central government had no mechanisms to credibly commit not to bail out indebted SNGs (Dillinger and Webb, 2001). Some states—particularly in the industrialized Southeast—were deemed "too big to fail." Once the bailout precedent was established in the 1990s, other states ensured their own bailouts through their strong (overrepresented) positions in the Senate. In this situation, the center proved unable to allow the state banks to fail. This represented a massive transfer of funds from the federal to the state governments clearly not foreseen in the constitution; this question is best treated

13. Some have noted that the failure to equate revenue transfers with expenditure responsibilities in the constitution is not necessarily a shortcoming of the Brazilian transition. For one thing, the Brazilian constitution of 1988 is widely viewed as overly detailed, even without specific entries specifying expenditure responsibilities. One can maintain that the decentralization of expenditures was a matter best left for ordinary legislation, while the decentralization of revenues needed to be constitutional. I am thankful to Luiz Carlos Bresser Pereira for this point.

further in the discussion of contractual autonomy but has clear links to questions of revenue autonomy.

South Africa: Decentralization in the 1996 Constitution

Top-down logics apply clearly in South Africa's fiscal decentralization to the provinces in the 1990s, though subnational actors also played a partial role. The apartheid-era National Party (NP) proactively "decentralized from above," calculating that its electoral prospects were strongest at the provincial level after democratization, as it could be expected to do well in the major province of the Western Cape (cf. Sparks 1994). Among black South Africans, the Zulu-nationalist Inkatha Freedom Party (IFP) sought powers for another of the new South Africa's largest and most important provinces, KwaZulu/Natal. The majority African National Congress, which expected to dominate in national elections, favored a strong center with weak provinces. Given their presumptive success in the provinces and expected defeat at the national level, the NP and IFP championed federalism and conditioned their support for democratization on power-sharing arrangements and guarantees for the provinces. The result was the distribution of a guaranteed "equitable share" of national revenues to both provincial and local levels.[14] With the NP insisting on federalism "from above" and the IFP demanding federalism "from below," South Africa's regional decentralization mixed top-down elec-toralist incentives with bottom-up pressures. Of the two, the top-down logic was the more fundamental, given the NP's strong bargaining hand and its domination of apartheid-era institutions; while the IFP collaborated with these, it was without any significant national political power.

The new South Africa greatly increased the fiscal salience of the provinces with major grants and revenue transfers.[15] It was at the Constituent National Assembly that the dispensation was altered dramatically. The most important institutional development with respect to revenue was the creation of the formula-bound equitable share that allocates revenues across the three "spheres"

14. While NP–ANC negotiations were at the heart of the transition, the IFP's dissent could also conceivably have stopped South Africa's democratization process. Violence between the ANC and IFP erupted frequently, and the ANC accused the NP of provoking such violence and/or failing to prevent IFP attacks. Heightened tensions often placed the transition itself in grave peril. The IFP's importance in the process was evidenced by repeated ANC attempts to incorporate the IFP into the final approval of the constitution.

15. As will be discussed in the coming chapters, many scholars suggest that South Africa's provinces remain weak, and that the country still has essentially an "hourglass" shape with a strong center, strong cities, and a "missing middle" (cf. Ahmad 2003).

of government: central, provincial, and local. One of the steps in the establishment of the equitable share is to take under advisement the recommendations of the Financial and Fiscal Commission (FFC), an independent body established by the constitution to serve as a safeguard (reporting to Parliament) against particularistic concerns. Beyond the establishment of the FFC, the South African constitution of 1996 established a set of institutions to ensure that national revenues are divided equitably among the various spheres of government. The result is an annual Division of Revenue Act outlining generous revenue guarantees for provinces and municipalities, such that SNG were responsible for about 50 percent of total government spending for the period from 1996 to after 2003.[16]

Given that substantial changes occurred in the mid-1990s, the question becomes: Why did the ANC, a party long associated with a desire for centralized control, allow such high levels of revenue decentralization, and why has it not reversed this once taking national power? The transition to democracy required a bargaining process that locked in major gains for SNGs. The National Party, on its way out of power at the time of the Constituent Assembly in the mid-1990s, still held many cards and used these to press for subnational power in postapartheid South Africa. As the NP's authority has waned, the ANC has also increasingly come to dominate subnational politics. Yet, as will be discussed subsequently, the interests of ANC leaders in recentralization have been unfulfilled. While the reasons for this lie in the difficulty of recentralization itself, there is one point relevant to the NP–ANC dynamic to make here. The ANC's current strength at all levels of government removes one primary impetus for recentralization, insofar as the calculus of power does not demand changing the status quo. On the other hand, given the dominant-party system in South Africa, the ANC is increasingly aware that its political supremacy is at greater risk from internal splits than from external competitors, portending changes in the party's internal balance of power between the center and subnational politicians over time. That is, the need to accommodate SNG politicians within the party is growing, increasing the costs of recentralization.

Beyond the mandated division of revenue, SNGs have one other principal mechanism for securing revenues: "conditional grants" for infrastructure and investment. Yet as the name suggests, the central government has discretionary

16. In recent years, the accounting for social security pension administration shifted from provinces to the center, altering the calculations for revenue transfers without any significant change in policy and reducing the SNG percentage to less than 50 percent. This is discussed in the subsequent chapters.

authority over these conditional grants. While equitable share funds are nominally at the discretion of the provinces, conditional grants are made for explicit, earmarked projects. These account for less than 15 percent of all transfers in any given year, but they do give the central government a set of intergovernmental transfers that it controls. Coincidentally, conditional grants are most prominent in the sector where policy has led to the most conflict between center and SNGs: health. Social policy provisions will be treated in greater detail in the next chapter, but the substantial role of conditional grants must also be stressed as a revenue issue, mostly because conditional grants predominate where funds are to be spent on capital investment. The equitable share provides revenue mainly for recurrent expenditures, and provinces have almost no independent revenue streams to finance investments in schools, hospitals, and the like. This means that, as a question of revenues, provincial governments are in effect required to submit requests to the central government for funds to expand physical plant and capacity. This serves as a substantial limitation on the opportunities for provincial governments to engage in politically expedient, capital intensive projects without the support of the center.

Crisis Resolution and Revenue Recentralization

The resolution of economic crisis played a significant role in efforts at revenue recentralization in Brazil. While the understanding of Brazil's fiscal recentralization is contentious, it is clear that Fernando Henrique Cardoso's presidency advanced further in fiscal federal reforms than did previous administrations. Where economic crisis is absent, so too are attempts at revenue recentralization unsuccessful. The South African case should be optimal for presidential centralization: a dominant party and a parliamentary system with strong top-down presidential control over the legislature. Yet South Africa's reductions in SNG revenue autonomy were far more restricted than Brazil's in the 1990s, and were limited to precisely those provinces where (localized) fiscal crises emerged.

Brazil: The Cardoso Years, the Real Plan, and Recentralization, 1994–2006

From the end of the 1980s through the Fernando Collor presidency, hyperinflation raged in Brazil, eventually reaching several thousand percent. After Collor resigned in the wake of numerous corruption scandals, Itamar Franco assumed the presidency in 1993 and appointed Fernando Henrique Cardoso as Minister of Finance. Cardoso used this powerful position to enact an orthodox economic stabilization policy aimed at ending the hyperinflationary spiral. Unlike numerous previous attempts at economic stabilization and reform, the program succeeded, and laid the groundwork for what would later become the Real Plan (Plano Real). From this point forward, Brazil's story has changed considerably, with the central government reducing the revenue autonomy of SNGs, against most predictions.

The challenge for Cardoso was the fiscal instability caused in large part by subnational overspending, facilitated by the ability of *estados* (with their strong representation in Congress) to "roll over" debt obligations to the central government. Subnational politicians had thrived in Brazil's inflationary crisis, as it allowed them a veil under which to contract unsustainable debt and hire extensively. Lifting the inflationary shroud was a prerequisite to other lasting reforms (Dillinger and Webb 1999, 2001). The implementation of the Real Plan, in which a new currency was initially tied to the U.S. dollar at parity, halted hyperinflation in short order, reducing it from approximately 1,500 percent to about 30 percent (Dillinger and Webb 1999, 2). The stunning success of the plan led to Cardoso's selection as the candidate of both the center-left and the right for the 1994 presidential election, and resulted in high levels of public approval for years thereafter.[17] The macroeconomic stabilization was instrumental in Cardoso's election to the presidency in 1994 and in his subsequent reformation of the intergovernmental system.

The resolution of hyperinflation enabled the center to force a more accurate nominal accounting of subnational spending, due to a number of direct effects in intergovernmental finance (many of which will be treated in greater detail in chapter 5, which looks directly at capital markets and the relationship between states and state banks). Most notably, the plan exposed *estado* finances, making the costs of expenditures more transparent by eliminating the ability of the *estados* to "inflate away" liabilities; the increased interest rates associated with the Real Plan also raised the cost of future borrowing (Montero 2004, 153).

Despite Cardoso's success on the macroeconomic front, little political reform was possible without the support of top subnational officials, most notably governors. Congressional support for fiscal reform must be understood as an outcome with its own causes: changing subnational support for

17. Importantly, even as late as 1998, Cardoso was reelected in the first round of voting, without the need for a runoff vote against Luiz Inácio Lula da Silva.

Cardoso's policies. The popularity of the Real Plan—contrasted with the sudden transparency of the financial situations of the *estados*—encouraged even reticent governors to back fiscal responsibility.[18] In assessing how the Cardoso administration succeeded in winning governors over to the side of fiscal responsibility where others had failed, a top presidential adviser noted the particular importance of governors in the key states of São Paulo, Rio de Janeiro, Minas Gerais, and Pernambuco, as well as key support from the governors of Rio Grande do Sul and Bahia; this made binding legislative action possible.[19]

Through its effects on the calculations of governors and their "ambassadors" in Congress, the stabilization plan strengthened Cardoso's hand within an otherwise weak party system. By exposing the link between intergovernmental fiscal patterns and macroeconomic instability, Cardoso used the Real Plan as the basis of his attempts to reform the central government's relationship with the *estados*. Combined with the unifying fear of a leftist challenge from Luiz Inácio Lula da Silva, Cardoso's success encouraged a variety of politicians and parties to join a coalition led by the Partido da Social Democracia Brasileira (Brazilian Social Democratic Party, or PSDB). The government that emerged was quite stable by Brazilian standards, centered on Cardoso's PSDB, Sarney's (and later Franco's) PMDB, and the Northeast-dominated Partido da Frente Liberal (Liberal Front, or PFL). Even as Cardoso grabbed the third rail of Brazilian politics by restricting the revenue autonomy of the *estados*, he retained the highest coalition discipline of any president from the 1980s up through at least 1998 (Amorim Neto 2002, 64). Some refer to the Cardoso coalition as "pathologically pro-government" (Power 1998, 131), while those most skeptical of central government power in Brazil argue that Cardoso held particularly favorable cards relative to other Brazilian presidents (Abrucio 1998, 226–31; Ames 2001, 3).

Reformers argue that the resolution of Brazil's macroeconomic crisis represented a unique moment in which Brazil's governors and legislators accepted fiscal compromises, because at these moments public pressures for fiscal responsibility outweighed the patronage benefits that could accrue from overspending.[20] This window of opportunity may have been temporary, but the Cardoso reforms took on a path-dependent quality of their

18. Interview: Marcos Mendes.
19. Interview: Eduardo Graeff.
20. Interview: Erika Amorim Araújo.

Table 3.2 Popularity of the Real Plan and public support for Cardoso

Date (1994)	Favorable view of Real Plan (%)	Intention to vote Cardoso (%)	N
May 25	28	17	3,911
July 5	62	21	3,915
August 9	75	36	20,603
September 9	76	44	10,560
September 15	77	45	21,074
September 28	75	47	21,292

SOURCE: Meneguello 1998, 139.

own that gradually reinforced the center's leverage.[21] State and local politicians' initial willingness to back Cardoso's reforms came coupled with demands for compensation in the short term, in the form of pork barrel projects. As a result, a first Social Emergency Fund (Fundo Social de Emergência, or FSE) was secured through a messy amalgam of one-off transfers. First initiated under the Franco government in 1993, this temporary legislation was designed to correct for short-term fiscal crises by allowing the federal government to halt (among other items) transfers to state and local governments. Stabilizing measures in the Real Plan were thus enforced with reductions in transfers through the FSE, and this began a long chain of improvements in the fiscal federal arrangement that included the Lei Camata (Camata Law), a law that limited subnational spending on personnel.

The Brazilian case is thus one where the logic of recentralization and the logic of crisis resolution were necessarily intertwined in the early 1990s, since excessive SNG autonomy in revenue was one of the key elements of the inflationary spiral. Imposing greater central control over SNG spending was an endeavor that simultaneously undercut a major cause of the economic crisis and initiated a sequence that furthered the recentralizing effort over the next half-decade and more. In 1996 the FSE morphed into the Fiscal Stabilization Fund (Fundo de Estabilização Fiscal, or FEF), an institution originally planned for a two-year existence, but with a more permanent design that would enable it to be renewed periodically. The FEF differed little from the FSE, but its passage incrementally reinforced the institutions responsible for limiting revenue decentralization. Despite the increasing resistance of politicians to the FSE and FEF, Cardoso successfully pushed through renewals and updates of the laws. The FSE and FEF gave the central government an

21. I am especially thankful to Al Montero for highlighting the importance of this path-dependent quality and the temporariness of Cardoso's opportunities.

Table 3.3 Presidential election results in Brazil, first round

Year	Top vote getter %	Second place %	Others %
1989	F. Collor de Mello 30.5	Lula da Silva 17.2	52.3
1994	F. H. Cardoso 54.3*	Lula da Silva 27.0	18.7
1998	F. H. Cardoso 53.1*	Lula da Silva 31.7	15.2
2002	Lula da Silva 46.4	José Serra 23.2	30.4
2006	Lula da Silva 48.6	Geraldo Alckmin 41.6	9.8

* Elected in first round; no runoff required
Source: Dados Eleitorais do Brasil (1982–2004). Available at
http://jaironicolau.iuperj.br/database/deb/port/index.htm (accessed June 29, 2008).

increasing share of total government revenues, and established the principle of delinking certain taxes from SNGs.[22]

Even more important than either the FSE or FEF was the comprehensive Fiscal Responsibility Law (Lei de Responsabilidade Fiscal, or LRF) of 2000, which followed an additional macroeconomic crisis (of much smaller scale) in 1999, and which will be discussed in greater detail in chapter 5. The LRF codified the principle of withholding federal transfers to the states or municipalities if these SNGs failed to make scheduled debt payments to the federal government. The clause was invoked on numerous occasions by the Cardoso government, and has been used by the Lula government in a fight with a host of states seeking to return to the heyday of massive revenue flows with soft budget constraints. Cardoso mustered support for the law using the precedents of the FSE and FEF (and used these as models for certain LRF provisions), and counted on the increasing fiscal responsibility being exhibited by reformist governors in São Paulo and other states. While the new LRF reiterated the provisions of the former FSE and FEF in certain areas, the new law also imposed stringent budget requirements on SNGs, backed by criminal penalties for those governors and mayors responsible for infractions. An additional important difference was that the LRF became a "complementary law" (*lei complementar*) to the national Constitution. With the LRF, Cardoso moved beyond the reactive tendency to govern by decree and passed binding legislation whose legal stature makes it difficult to water down through ordinary legislation (Miranda 2001, 18).

President Luiz Inácio Lula da Silva (2003–2011) has explicitly followed Cardoso's trail on the economy and especially on relations with the states.

22. Samuels (2003) emphasizes the one-off costs of the reform and the fact that states saw no decrease in their absolute level of revenues. I treat the *relative* power of central governments and SNGs as the crucial outcome, and view the central government's growing proportion of revenue throughout the Cardoso period as more puzzling and noteworthy than the fact that states retained revenue levels in nominal terms.

Table 3.4 Provisions reducing subnational revenue autonomy in Brazil

Event	Year	Change in revenue autonomy
Social Emergency Fund (FSE)	1993	Intergovernmental fiscal element of the Real Plan removes certain amounts from the pool of federal transfers to the states.
Fiscal Stabilization Fund (FEF)	1996	Reiterates provisions of FSE and retains 20% of constitutionally mandated transfers to subnational governments for central government.
Debt service provision	1998	Transfers to subnational governments made conditional on SNG completion of debt service requirements.
Fiscal Responsibility Law (LRF)	2000	Stipulates subnational governments will receive transfers only after debt service obligations met. Requires budget surplus for SNGs in certain conditions. Criminal punishment for subnational politicians who exceed spending limits.
Budget requirements	2003	Lula government proposes increases in budget surplus requirements at all levels of government.

Lula has even gone so far as to demand greater budget surpluses from all levels of government, thereby outflanking conservative opposition while alienating the more traditionally leftist wing of his Worker's Party, the PT (Partido dos Trabalhadores). Early in his first administration, Lula showed that his administration would continue to adopt a hard line toward SNG spending in particular, by asserting that the Ministry of Finance would increase required SNG budget surpluses to 4.25 percent from a prior level of 3.75 percent.

Brazil's central government now sits on a stronger legal framework than it had in the early 1990s. With the LRF behind it now, the Brazilian executive has seen its formal power enhanced. From various points on the political spectrum come arguments that the LRF is an unfair piece of legislation. For some on the left, the LRF is a draconian, anti-Keynesian measure designed to stunt sometimes necessary deficit spending; the LRF essentially removes any budgetary flexibility in a crisis-prone economy (Miranda 2001). For some center-right officials favoring fiscal reform, the LRF failed to distinguish between good governance and irresponsibility at the *estado* level, and a preferable solution would simply be legislation proscribing bailouts.[23] The fact that any central government measure vis-à-vis the states could be considered remotely draconian is ample evidence that power shifted, at least temporarily, toward the center. The enhanced legal framework backing the

23. Interview: Yoshiaki Nakano.

national executive on fiscal matters is based largely on Cardoso's handling of the aforementioned fiscal crisis.

This assessment of change over time offers a dynamic perspective of Brazilian politics that differs from more static views. Recent scholarship on Brazil seems to provide complementary evidence that the country is not merely stuck in a bad institutional equilibrium, but rather that certain aspects of Brazilian politics have followed a trajectory away from institutional mayhem and in the direction of improved governability. Power (2008, 84), for instance, characterizes the Cardoso era as one in which the Real Plan began a sequence of events that altered the balance of power in coalition building and partisan politics. Cardoso's governance generated a form of "coalitional presidentialism," the net result of which was a "rebooting" of the polity after the disastrous years from 1988 to 1994. In this changing Brazil, centrism increasingly prevailed in party politics, and elected officials exhibited some moderate shifts toward accepting party discipline. Similarly, Power and Zucco (2009) find that the party system has become increasingly clarified by the presence of the PSDB as the principal party of the center-right and the PT as the principal party of the center-left.

Perhaps most importantly, this change in Brazil suggests the reforms have gone beyond the passage of legal prohibitions on bailouts (as with the LRF), and have taken root and institutionalized. Hagopian, Gervasoni, and Moraes (2009) find that Brazil has increasingly (and surprisingly) come to be characterized by more disciplined legislators who focus increasingly on programmatic and policy issues, and less on patronage. This is a function of politicians observing greater returns to programmatic appeals, while "state reforms that shrank the scope and resource base for state patronage diminished the efficiency of personal, patronage-based electoral strategies" (Hagopian, Gervasoni, and Moraes 2009, 362). The state reforms that originate this sequence are Cardoso's macroeconomic changes. This party system change is especially consequential because it suggests a self-reinforcing equilibrium in which politicians act in ways that promote the deepening of reform, rather than attempting to subvert it. The Cardoso reforms that culminated in the Fiscal Responsibility Law are much likelier to persist when backed by increasingly programmatic and policy-oriented behavior in the Congress.

South Africa: The Mbeki Years, Limited Crisis, and Limited Centralization

Recentralizing power was a clear executive goal in Thabo Mbeki's (1999–2008) South Africa. The proof that Mbeki sought centralization is laid out most clearly in subsequent chapters treating other institutional areas, where South Africa's ANC government centralized the most. Yet the South African case also shows the limits on revenue recentralization where the crisis resolution logic found in Brazil does not exist.

Without strict controls, subnational malfeasance in countries with high revenue decentralization can lead to overspending and central government bailouts. And indeed, the South African government witnessed a rash of provincial overspending in the late 1990s. At the time, the situation evoked Brazil's disastrous experience triggered by *estado* overspending. The South African government, however, was empowered (by section 100 of the constitution) to take extraordinary measures to intervene in provinces under such circumstances. When the provinces of Eastern Cape and KwaZulu-Natal overspent their budgets in 1997–98, the result was an advance from the center of 1.5 billion rand, to which austerity conditions could be attached, including detailed spending plans and monthly progress reports; the Department of Finance invoked this section 100 provision again for a third province in early 1999 when the Free State announced an expected annual deficit of about 170 million rand (Wehner 2000a, 258–59). Several provinces threatened to go bankrupt in 1998 and thereafter: Mpumalanga province (formerly known as the Eastern Transvaal) overspent by 618 million rand in 1997–98 and 110 million in 1998–99 (Wehner 2000a, 258). Mpumalanga was bailed out by the central government when short-term expenditures looked to be beyond the province's capacity to repay. The terms of the provincial bailouts were increasingly draconian, including details such as the elimination of cell phone privileges for provincial officials. And beyond the fiscal whipping it took, Mpumalanga's leadership suffered the humiliations of both public rebukes and back-room censure from within the party.[24] Its reputation for hard budget constraints credibly established, the center moved to improve the quality and nature of provincial spending. Of course, this involved greater monitoring and evaluation, largely driven by the National Treasury.

Out of the rash of fiscal irresponsibility came greater central government control over subnational finances. Unlike Brazil, South Africa's dominant party system allowed the rapid implementation of measures to reduce provincial spending. This was facilitated both by ANC control of the relevant provinces and the close relationships within the bureaucracy.[25] The turnaround was swift, with a 2001 internal Treasury "audit" of the intergovernmental

24. Interview: Tania Ajam.
25. Interviews: Theo Bekker, Tania Ajam.

fiscal system noting "a major turn around in provincial fiscal performance"; the audit thereupon viewed provincial overspending as a transitory problem at a particular conjuncture in the years following the constitutional establishment of stronger provinces with greater autonomy (RSA/NT 2001, 109). Indeed, after the brief bouts of provincial overspending around 1998, South Africa's provinces had the opposite problem, as revenue transfers from the center were more than a match for provincial spending capacities. Incredibly, after the brief bout of budget deficits in the late 1990s, several provinces *underspent* their transfers from the center, citing the impossibility of managing the funds.[26]

The localized crises in several provinces were nipped in the bud before they could affect the macroeconomy, and these moments constituted the only major opportunities for reducing subnational revenue autonomy. Two important points emerge. First, and most importantly, the localized fiscal crises did not result in reductions in the equitable share provision for the provinces. In fact, provinces continued to receive ample revenues, to the point that transfers more than met all expenditures, resulting in the aforementioned underspending. Localized fiscal crises led to reductions only in the localities where the crises occurred, and they did not justify a more comprehensive revisiting of SNG revenue autonomy the way macroeconomic crisis did in Brazil. The second point links this finding with analyses of other arenas: the principal limitations on SNG autonomy come not from insecurity in access to revenue, but rather in government control over SNG expenditures. Mpumalanga's cell phone provision, for instance, represents a limitation on how revenues can be spent; this will be taken up in the next chapters.

Despite the apparent revenue autonomy provided by access to the equitable share, the provinces are also limited in another sense that highlights the importance of analyzing revenue and expenditure autonomies distinctly, yet conjointly. In 2000–2001, over 95 percent of provincial budgets came from central government transfers (NSA/RT 2001, 15). This indicates an almost total lack of own-source revenue, even in relatively wealthy provinces. Dependence on the center for revenues means that provincial leaders do

26. The Treasury came to believe that problems in contemporary South Africa are not a result of fiscal imbalance, but of poor delivery and implementation, and a low budgetary absorptive capacity in the provinces. The central government viewed improving provincial spending capacity (to spend the full equitable share attributed to them) as the principal challenge of the transfer system, not preventing overspending. The low absorptive capacity of provinces can be traced to provincial bureaucratic weakness, combined with effective state monitoring that prevents the diversion of funds to political ends. The state's ability to limit provincial spending led to this counterintuitive result.

not build up independent tax bases and remain dependent on the center's political support. Combined with the central government's power after 1997 to dismiss provincial premiers, this lopsidedness with regard to the origin of revenues may be construed by some as a restriction on provincial revenue autonomy. Of course, the relative importance of own-source revenues and intergovernmental transfers is a source of some debate. IGTs are likelier to result in less subnational autonomy than decentralized tax authority, yet IGTs may also enhance revenue autonomy by generating softer subnational budget constraints, as vertical fiscal imbalance creates a disconnect between public perceptions of who is responsible for taxes and who is responsible for spending.

The examination of South Africa's situation presents a way through this analytical impasse: constitutionally protected transfers constitute a very high level of *revenue autonomy* for provinces there, regardless of a lack of taxation power, but the predominance of transfers in the SNG budgets means that *expenditure autonomy* (examined in the next chapter) is the "make or break" criterion for whether SNGs are truly autonomous. High levels of revenue transfers coexist with low levels of overall fiscal autonomy in cases where the center tightly controls spending, but mean extremely high levels of overall fiscal autonomy where SNGs control their own spending. As seen in the next chapter, the former reflects the South African case, the latter the Brazilian before 1994.

Comparative Lessons

Executive–legislative relations and political parties are crucial to the revenue autonomy of SNGs. This finding concurs with much of the literature on decentralization, though I have extended the argument in several ways. In both South Africa and Brazil, the decentralization of revenue was pushed by parties and politicians whose political futures were brightest at the subnational level, as predicted by the rationalist models forwarded by O'Neill (2003, 2005) and Samuels (2003). More specifically, increases in revenue autonomy occurred when politicians with subnational interests held important cards at a Constitutional Assembly and when governing parties deemed their future electoral prospects to be best at the subnational level. Chief executives, who generally prefer limiting subnational revenue autonomy, are more susceptible to decentralizing pressure under these conditions.

On the flip side of revenue decentralization, substantial reductions in subnational autonomy (via the centralization of certain revenues) occurred in Brazil under Cardoso, even though Brazil's central government suffers from a notoriously weak party system (cf. Mainwaring and Scully 1995). Partisan power alone cannot adequately explain centralization. Rather, the Cardoso administration created an extraordinary political opportunity by resolving Brazil's hyperinflationary crisis. In the wake of fiscal crisis, Cardoso faced exceptionally fragmented partisan opposition by Brazilian standards. Presidential success in recentralizing in weak party systems suggests that the capacity for cohesive collective action by opposition parties is as important as the partisan powers of presidents; where opposition actors are divisible and incapable of "ganging up" in an all-on-one fashion against the center, presidents may have exceptional opportunities to (re)centralize revenue authority (cf. Montero 2004).

Cardoso's recentralization occurred without strong partisan powers and independent of formal decree powers. Brazil's pro-reform consensus arose not through party pressures, but through the executive's successful foray into macroeconomic stabilization; the Real Plan provided the springboard for a national–subnational fiscal compromise that was costly to the center in the short term, but favored the center over the long run. Even Cardoso's 1990s reforms reducing revenue autonomy did not reverse the fundamental features of Brazilian federalism. The resolution of crisis allowed Cardoso to work through an otherwise fractious coalition to promote new laws governing revenues.

In debates about presidential weakness and strength in contemporary Brazil, the most prominent explanations for Cardoso's legislative successes rely heavily on the centralization of the decision-making process in the Congress, which Figueiredo and Limongi (2000) found could provide cohesion and discipline even in Brazil's inchoate party system. The perspective here is consistent with these findings, at least with respect to the Cardoso years, but addresses a question about intertemporal variations across administrations that Figueiredo and Limongi do not address: why did the Cardoso administration succeed relative to previous presidents in reforming the political economy of fiscal federalism? In a similar vein, Amorim Neto, Cox, and McCubbins (2003, 552) highlight the importance of this question with their finding that Cardoso was the only Brazilian president who constituted an effective majority and "agenda cartel" in the years after redemocratization. The emphasis on the path-dependent consequences of crisis and recentralization serves to explain the underpinnings of Cardoso's relative ability to centralize decision making and coordinate support for the presidential agenda.

In South Africa's less historically robust federalism, revenue decentralization was more top-down than bottom-up, yet efforts at recentralization were surprisingly less successful. Revenue decentralization to the provinces occurred in the first half of the 1990s, as the country transited from apartheid to democracy via a Constituent National Assembly. Democratization and the CNA coincided with fiscal decentralization to the provinces, while also resulting in an increase of their number from four to nine. Yet this alone does not necessarily reflect a major transfer of fiscal power. With respect to intergovernmental relations, South Africa's state carefully details the final destination of the vast majority of provincial revenue. South Africa serves as an example to demonstrate why revenue figures are insufficient to comment on the distribution of power in decentralized federations. This will be shown in subsequent discussions of subnational expenditure autonomy and contractual autonomy.

While state authority over spending limits South African SNGs, the case also shows that subnational revenue autonomy, once increased, is sticky in the absence of crisis. South Africa under Thabo Mbeki (ideologically a would-be centralizer working in an institutional and political environment that is much more favorable to recentralization than Brazil) is a much more limited case of recentralization. The center was not able to reappropriate SNG funds from the key "equitable share" provisions for the distribution of revenue. Absent the governing opportunities created by Cardoso via the resolution of macroeconomic crisis, Mbeki has been unable to trim subnational revenue autonomy. The limited recentralization reflected the limited nature of crisis in South Africa: the president could only reduce provincial revenues on a case-by-case (that is, localized and temporary) basis.

Beyond an explanation of key variables, this cross-national comparison has the advantage of presenting a theory with predictive power about the timing of change, with constituent assemblies and the resolution of economic crises being vital antecedents. Decentralization followed on the heels of the electoral decline of sitting governments. Founding moments, usually in the form of Constituent National Assemblies, tend to be profoundly decentralizing in revenue largely because they represent the twilight of declining regimes. The exhausted National Party in South Africa held enough cards in the early 1990s to ensure some decentralization, while the myriad actors at Brazil's Constituent Assembly overwhelmingly came from the subnational level and together ensured extensive decentralization. Constituent Assemblies may be seen as "special cases" of presidential partisan weakness wherein the government may also represent a declining regime.[27] Presidential weakness also occurs in times of "normal politics," of course, and when governments are on their way out but have strong subnational bases, they prefer to decentralize, though this would seem to require acute political incentives for the national government; such "nonfoundational" moments will be found in the unitary cases in chapter 6. The other observed triggers for changes are fiscal crises. In Brazil macroeconomic crisis spurred the revision of revenue-sharing patterns in ways that favored central governments. The presidential reaction to economic crisis in the form of a stabilization plan formed the basis for a recentralization of revenue, even though Brazil remains highly decentralized in a cross-national perspective. In South Africa, meanwhile, crisis was more attenuated and centralization was correspondingly more limited. This "no crisis, no centralization" pattern is confirmed by the unitary Senegalese case in chapter 6; political costs preclude recentralizing unless crisis exists.

Finally, with respect to the scope conditions of this analysis, federalism per se mattered only in a limited sense, though both countries are nominally federal. Two points merit consideration. Brazil is clearly the more federal of the two cases, yet was also the case where the more noteworthy recentralizing changes occurred. While federalism affects the overall level of revenue autonomy, it cannot explain the dynamic changes over time. The second conclusion regarding federalism links to subsequent chapters and illustrates the need to move beyond the examination of revenue: higher levels of revenue autonomy alone cannot ensure robust federalism. In fact, when assessed purely on the basis of revenues, South Africa's provinces have as much or more access to guaranteed revenue than Brazil's *estados*. Yet it would be wrong to characterize South Africa as the more federal of the two countries. The difference between Brazil's robust federalism and South Africa's weak version is not rooted in the distribution of revenues, nor are there substantial political-institutional differences in the forms of federalism (since both countries provide constitutional guarantees for SNGs, have independent elections for SNG legislatures, and have upper chambers in the national Parliament that are intended to protect the interests of SNGs). Rather, the principal difference between the two cases is in the center's power to control spending. This question will be treated in the next chapter.

27. Properly speaking, Brazil's CNAs did not end a "declining regime," since a civilian president had become the head of state in 1985; nonetheless, the CNA can be seen as the completion of the transition from authoritarianism to decentralized democracy.

4

—⟮⟯⟮⟯⟮⟯—

SUBNATIONAL EXPENDITURE AUTONOMY

States have been at center stage in the political science of recent decades, yet they are treated in a relatively cursory fashion in much work on the causes of decentralization. This is startling, since close examination of state structures would seem particularly crucial for intergovernmental relations. Most studies, however, portray these relations as a set of conflicts (which result in bargains) between presidents and subnational elected officials or locally interested legislators. And indeed, intergovernmental revenues are often contested in legislatures, shaped by executive–legislative relations that are in turn mediated by power within political parties. Yet state bureaucracies also play key roles in intergovernmental relations. National executives have a "back door" way of reducing subnational autonomy: through state policies governing expenditures, ministers and bureaucracies can require SNGs to assume policy mandates. While the devolution of revenues and revenue sources to subnational governments has captured the imagination of political scientists and policymakers, it is only a partial story. Autonomous access to revenue does not equal fiscal autonomy. The division of expenditure responsibilities and the extent to which central governments can compel subnational spending behavior also matters. In this issue area, we must once again "bring the state back in" as the central arena in which contestation occurs.

For any given level of revenue decentralization, states may exert greater or lesser control over SNG spending, and SNGs may receive more or less specific obligations that correspond to the revenues they receive or raise. Some stylized examples illustrate the significance of considering both revenue and expenditure autonomy simultaneously, yet independently. Consider two countries. In both cases, SNGs receive guaranteed transfers and/or independent tax authority, and therefore have considerable revenue autonomy. In one of these cases SNGs are free from central government influence over spending, with revenues coming in the form of block grants and unrestricted transfers; there are no federal mandates on spending. In a second case, SNGs are compelled by the center to spend their money on detailed line items; in these circumstances SNGs are hardly autonomous, but rather are tantamount to deconcentrated entities of the central government; this may be true even if subnational politicians are duly elected.[1]

The former story may be seen in Brazil, circa 1988: high levels of revenue decentralization, and the use of these revenues for patronage by SNGs. Contemporary South Africa, by contrast, is closer to the other extreme, wherein central governments successfully monitor and shape spending not through any restriction on revenue autonomy, but through tightly constraining autonomy on the spending side. South Africa's federalism is weak precisely because of these restraints on expenditure autonomy; this story finds an echo in the examination of unitary cases in chapter 6.

At the macrolevel, the same variables affect expenditure autonomy as affect revenue autonomy: governmental decline and economic crisis shape presidential power, and these interactions condition expenditure rules. But to explain how expenditure autonomy is shaped distinctly from revenue autonomy, we must look to new institutional arenas. In the mechanisms of change, expenditure autonomy is not contested only in legislatures. Rather, it is shaped profoundly within the executive branch. The arena shifts, in other words, from an executive–legislative to an intra-executive arena. The principal interlocutors situated within the executive are elected officials and the state bureaucracy. When their partisan powers weaken, presidents lose power to control the executive branch ministries and bureaucracies that govern expenditures, and when presidential power increases, they gain power to control those same ministries from the top down.

Central governments on the whole do not empower SNGs as much on the expenditure side as on the revenue side, largely due to the fact that expenditure determinations play out in the intra-executive arena rather than the executive–legislative arena. Presidents, ministers, and bureaucrats are all

---

1. An important question that is not resolved in full here is whether "earmarked" revenues should be viewed as the prerogative of central governments, or are requested by officials representing subnational interests, as well as how "tight" earmarking can be. Given the comparative scope, I do not address this in detail, rather leaving the analysis at the level of whether SNG are receiving "block grants" or funds that are designated for certain functions. I am thankful to Al Montero for raising this question.

central government officials and often share a preference for central government bureaucratic controls to limit subnational expenditure autonomy (while SNGs continue to seek increased autonomy, in this case over their spending).[2] Preferences of central government actors may diverge when declining presidents have incentives to increase subnational autonomy, such that the central bureaucracy may represent the strongest actor favoring central authority. There thus remains a powerful constituency, even in federal states, that resists spending devolution. The loss of presidential power relative to bureaucracies differs from the loss of presidential power vis-à-vis legislative opposition. While pressures for decentralization are thus lessened in this arena, crisis resolution continues to have a centralizing impact; in these instances central actors work together to strengthen the center.

In this chapter I first develop the concept of expenditure autonomy and argue that *intra-executive relations,* or politics within the state bureaucracy, shape expenditure autonomy. A subsequent section deals with the fungibility of subnational revenues and the locus of decision making about spending. Two empirical sections then highlight the principal actors in the intra-executive arena: ministries. Ministries of finance are treated in one of these sections as key advocates of central control over the political economy. Social policy ministries, specifically health and education, are then highlighted as examples of how central governments can control subnational spending. The final section offers a brief conclusion on the important—but often overlooked—role states play in intergovernmental fiscal relations.

Explaining Expenditure Autonomy: The Intra-executive Arena

This chapter contemplates the intergovernmental division of social policy outputs.[3] Expenditure autonomy is high when SNGs can spend their revenues as they see fit, including in the form of political goods and patronage. Lower levels of expenditure autonomy exist when SNGs are required to

2. I do not assume that ministerial and bureaucratic preferences always mirror presidential preferences. Indeed, presidents often do seek administrative reforms of the state that will meet bureaucratic opposition (cf. Geddes 1994). The way in which the national executive coheres (or fails to) will influence subnational fiscal autonomy. I am not looking at the ways central bureaucrats stick up for their own sinecures and patronage interests, but the ways in which the policies they create and enact constrain SNG politics.

3. Whereas the examination of revenue autonomy enabled an analysis of fiscal decentralization and recentralization, this treatment of expenditure autonomy enables us to capture outcomes commonly referred to under the rubrics of *administrative* decentralization and recentralization.

spend on nationally established priorities, which often (but not always) take the form of broadly distributed public goods. The question is the extent of SNG accountability to the center for the provision of public goods, and systems for financing the provision of social services. Clearly, this implies a large variety of content. To make this tractable, I focus in particular on two major social policy expenditure areas—education and health—in which SNGs play major roles.[4] Expenditure autonomy is highest where SNGs can transfer resources from sector to sector at will, and lowest when specific rules state on which line items revenues must be spent. Key questions include which levels of government build and manage schools and hospitals, and which pay the teachers and doctors who staff them.

Expenditure autonomy is not the same as expenditure totals (or which levels of government spend money). Tracing aggregate spending does not capture the crucial findings. The decentralization of expenditures *may* empower SNGs, since it enhances political relevance and prestige, yet the decentralization of expenditure responsibilities is often sought by central governments and not by SNGs. Central and subnational levels of government may both have ambiguous preferences with respect to expenditure decentralization. The center may prefer to *decentralize expenditures*, to promote efficiency or simply to offload responsibilities in the form of unfunded mandates. Pushing responsibilities to lower levels of government may relieve pressure on the national budget and reduce the discretion SNGs have to divert funds into their own patronage networks. Meanwhile, subnational insistence on greater access to revenues is tempered by concerns about spending mandates. SNGs may have clear preferences for more revenues, but preferences over the distribution of expenditure responsibilities is much more ambiguous.

The more interesting measure with respect to expenditure decentralization is not overall proportions of spending, which closely approximates overall revenue decentralization, but the *use* of decentralized funds. When Brazilianists, for instance, say revenues were more decentralized than expenditures in 1988, they often mean that SNGs did not receive spending mandates for the revenues they received. Expenditure totals were very decentralized in

4. This choice of relatively decentralized issue areas is deliberate, as health and education constitute "crucial sectors" for the study of decentralizing dynamics. Moreover, health and education are among the most significant functions of government in developing countries, and their benefits are generally among the most widely distributed public goods. However, I also examine the roles of finance ministries' more general efforts to constrain all SNG spending. I am thankful to an anonymous reviewer for comments on the need to consider the potential bias in this sectoral choice.

Table 4.1 Subnational expenditure autonomy: Ideal type measures

Score	Characteristics
High	Little central government guidance on spending Extensive freedom to transfer funding across sectors Block grants, little or no earmarking
Moderate	Central government monitoring Spending autonomy for large sources of revenue Earmarking for some/minor sources of tax revenue
Low	Spending autonomy for small sources of revenue Earmarking used for most/large sources of revenue Binding norms and standards set by center
Very Low	Budgets only applicable in given sector or detailed line item Spending determined by national formula Deconcentration, budget execution without decision making Unspent budgets revert to central government Binding mandates (funded or unfunded)

Brazil; SNGs spent their generous revenue receipts and then some, going into chronic deficits as a result. The relevant point is that expenditure *obligations* were not decentralized. SNGs therefore spent considerable revenues on political goods rather than public goods. Administrative decentralization was insufficient to require SNGs to take on expenditures in a way consistent with central government preferences. Mere spending totals are insufficient to measure *how* SNGs spend resources. Measuring aggregate expenditures and aggregate revenues by level of government will prove largely redundant, but measuring subnational revenue autonomy and subnational expenditure autonomy captures two fundamentally different (and substantively important) features of intergovernmental relations. Aggregating expenditure totals does not show the vast difference between SNGs spending, say, 60 percent of the national budget with no strings attached and SNGs administering the same 60 percent of the national budget, but on specific line items of a president's choosing. A governor using central government funds to extend a patronage network has expenditure autonomy; a governor that merely executes and administers a centrally controlled budget does not.

Subnational autonomy depends—as table 4.1 shows—on the latitude SNGs have in the use of revenues. Higher autonomy arises when larger sources of revenue are free for spending per the wishes of SNGs, and lower autonomy occurs when only minor sources of revenue can be diverted from one sector or budget item to another. In between, national governments impose partial limits on the shifting or diversion of resources. Generally, central governments seek to ensure that SNGs comply with national standards and norms, apply resources according to top-down directives, and not divert resources to other ends.

To be sure, a simple measure of the proportion of expenditures at the subnational level might be a tempting measure of subnational expenditure autonomy for its quantifiability, but using such a measure would sacrifice measurement validity for two reasons. The first reason for using a statutory approach to measure the expenditure autonomy of SNGs are the set of theoretical and conceptual considerations just mentioned: the real autonomy of SNGs is found not only in the amount of resources to which they have access (which was treated in the discussion of revenue autonomy in chapter 3), but also their freedom over the spending of those resources. Subnational expenditures measured as a simple proportion of government expenditures will be highly correlated with subnational revenues as a proportion of government revenues, yet the statutory autonomy of SNGs may vary meaningfully even at comparable revenue levels. Conversely, as Falleti (2005) finds, the true autonomy of SNGs may not vary even as revenue transfers occur. The apparent puzzles of "centralization under decentralization" require a perspective that analytically separates statutory autonomy over expenditures from the intergovernmental distribution of funds expended.

The second reason to focus on statutory fiscal autonomy is empirical: statutory autonomy for SNGs varies meaningfully even across federations and even in public services (health and education) that are quite decentralized relative to other areas. This variation can be seen both cross-nationally and inter-temporally. Looking at cross-national variations, Boadway and Shah (2009) examine a sample of federations in the policy areas of health and education, and they find that most federal systems operate under a regime of concurrent responsibilities, where central and subnational governments share responsibilities for public goods provision. Responsibilities in health and/or education are shared in distinct fashions in at least eight of the twelve countries summarized: Belgium, China, Germany, India, Indonesia, the Philippines, and Mexico, as well as Brazil. It is less common to find federations where SNGs retain exclusive constitutional authority over a policy area. Germany and Belgium leave exclusive responsibility for education (but not health) to SNGs, as do Canada and the United States. The latter two countries are nearly unique in that they have also devolved health care provision to subnational levels. Exclusive central government provision, meanwhile, is found in highly unitary states.

Statutory rules for health and education provision will be varied and complex across federal polities that have concurrent arrangements. Concurrent responsibility is neither uniform across countries nor a stable equilibrium, making variations in statutory fiscal autonomy a rich area for investigation. For instance, the United States, a robust federal country where much of the health and education sectors are decentralized, illustrates the complex and contested nature of the center's statutory control over SNGs. On the health side, the central government has a prominent supervisory role in health insurance provision for low-income citizens via Medicaid, which states administer and manage subject to federal government oversight and monitoring.[5] Since the central government regulates and conditions how states must spend their funds in order to receive federal transfers, SNG autonomy is in question. Increasingly stringent controls over state Medicaid spending would reduce SNG autonomy, while the loosening of these controls would increase SNG latitude in expenditures. An illustration of statutory changes that alter SNG expenditure autonomy came in the education sector with the No Child Left Behind Act of 2001, which placed new requirements on states to adopt learning standards. While states have latitude in the establishment of specific standards, the debate over local autonomy versus central control of expenditures continues to be engaged in national education debates. For this reason, the United States is portrayed as exhibiting small reductions in expenditure autonomy in figure 4.1.

Figure 4.1 illustrates a spectrum of possibilities with respect to subnational expenditure autonomy, based on the indicators outlined above and using education as a sectoral example.[6] To begin with the comparative statics, the left-hand side of the spectrum shows countries where the central government predominates in the funding, administration, management, and monitoring of public service provision by SNGs. This will be typical in centralized unitary states, such as Italy (to 1993), historically centralized France (before modest decentralizing reforms since the 1980s), or many unitary countries (including Senegal and Peru). Countries with the highest levels of expenditure autonomy, by contrast, would allow SNGs to run education with very little central government oversight. Canada is an example of relative stasis here, since the country has no central government education ministry and relies almost exclusively on local and provincial management. In the middle of the spectrum are cases where responsibilities are concurrent and contested between

5. Medicare, as a federally run program, may be seen as different from Medicaid with respect to SNG autonomy. Of the two programs, Medicaid is the one where issues of central government control over subnational expenditure autonomy come into play.

6. The location of countries on the spectrum relies on the author's categorization, building especially upon Ter-Minassian 1997 and Boadway and Shah 2009.

Figure 4.1 A spectrum of expenditure autonomy: Centralization and decentralization of education in comparative perspective

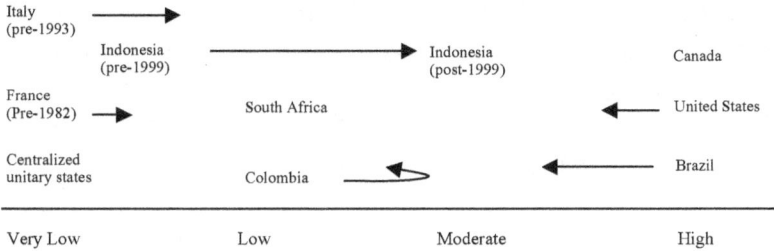

levels of government. Some countries with some federal features—including South Africa—exhibit a degree of provincial autonomy in administration, but a continued central government presence in shaping how funds are spent. In education, this may involve extensive national standards, requirements for certain expenditures, and extensive use of conditional grants or transfers conditional upon compliance or performance.

Several cases also illustrate mobility along the spectrum in the form of decentralization and centralization. In the "age of decentralization," to use Snyder's (2001) term, many changes worldwide increased the spending autonomy of SNGs. For instance, with its big bang decentralization of 1999 to 2001, Indonesia transferred considerable authority to subnational levels, including responsibility for teacher salaries. However, autonomy remains below the level of SNGs in, say, Canada because the central government retains minimum standards that schools must enforce; the center requires provinces to monitor localities for compliance. Statutory authority can also oscillate over time in a given country. For instance, Colombia devolved health and education responsibilities in 1993 with the Law on Assignment of Responsibilities and Resources, accompanied by increases in automatic transfers or *participaciones* (Daughters and Harper 2007, 226–27). Given the automaticity of the grants and the relatively limited strictures on spending, this entailed an increase in expenditure autonomy as well as revenue autonomy. However, the central government also curtailed SNG spending autonomy in 2000 by establishing indicators to ensure SNG compliance with central directives, and then in 2003 passed a Fiscal Responsibility Law governing SNG actions.

Statutory fiscal autonomy over expenditures varies according to the degree to which central governments control SNG outlays. The principal mechanism for central governments to control outlays is to set national standards or benchmarks for SNG outputs or spending, requiring that expenditures be directed to certain functions and responsibilities. This is most effective when backed up with sanctions for those SNGs that fail to comply. Perhaps the most notable weapons in the central government arsenal are conditional grants and conditional transfers, from which the center can remove funding from when SNGs do not follow central rules. South Africa is one significant example examined here, but the principle extends even to developed federations such as the United States, where the issue of national education standards highlights debates over states' rights and federal control over fiscal federalism.

If central governments have clear preferences to reduce the expenditure autonomy of SNGs, when do they succeed? The partisan strength of the executive matters once again, but here the distribution of ministerial port-folios is the important intervening variable. Decisions about rules governing expenditures are largely intra-executive deliberations, though they may be open to public political debate. Different distributions of cabinet posts lead to more or less presidential control over expenditure policy. The partisan coherence of presidents and their ministers influences the degree to which expenditures are seen as a technical issue (as opposed to an issue of the political distribution of favors), and the partisan composition of ministerial portfolios should be a predictor of subnational expenditure autonomy. Where presidents must build a cabinet coalition (i.e., where various parties have some control of the commanding heights of the state), fractious relation-ships are likely to predominate. Weak coalitions and wide distributions of ministerial appointments lead to higher levels of SNG expenditure autonomy, as coalition partners use their portfolios to extend patronage to subnational allies, rather than to support the president. When a single, coherent political party or group controls the state, resistance to central control over expendi-tures will weaken. Copartisan ministers give presidents important levers in shaping the expenditures of SNGs, as happened in South Africa, and in Brazil after 1994. In short, a wide distribution of cabinet posts enhances SNG autonomy, and tighter coalitions reduce autonomy.

The preeminence of the intra-executive arena in this analysis does not preclude a continued role for the national legislature. Presidents still need legislative support to pass expenditure statutes, as well as various forms of enabling legislation. Expenditure decisions operate in part through congres-sional action, so executive–legislative relations matter at an initial stage for the passage of laws, and parties continue to mediate the process. Beyond this, however, comes implementation through state channels, and the monitoring and management of expenditures within the executive branch. The intra-executive arena is not a substitute for executive–legislative relations but a complement to it. This additional arena shapes subnational autonomy in conjunction with executive–legislative relations, and the focus on executive branch dynamics should not obscure this. Rather, considering this arena adds explanatory power for varying outcomes across diverse issue areas, and helps explain a conundrum of intergovernmental relations: why spending obligations are not always devolved in parallel with revenues.

Variation across issue areas—with SNGs having low levels of expenditure autonomy compared to revenue autonomy—is a first major finding of this chapter. For revenues, both democratizing assemblies and electoralist calculations favored SNGs. Central government control over expenditures, on the other hand, is much stickier. Increases in expenditure autonomy have been fewer and more limited in scope.[7] The most compelling case here is Brazil, because increases and decreases over time have been most dramatic. In South Africa subnational officials inherited responsibilities from previously deconcentrated appendages of the central government. The increases in expenditure autonomy in South Africa involved giving SNGs authority to administer spending under the monitoring of ministries. With these inheritances came much tighter expenditure mandates than in Brazil. In South Africa bureaucracies prevailed in monitoring SNG spending closely and little change occurred. Taken together, these reductions in expenditure autonomy in Brazil and the continued power of the South African state to control SNG spending suggest a trend of increasing central government control over expenditures that should temper enthusiasm over decentralization. The avenue to (re)centralization is broader than existing studies of decentralization admit.

The second major finding—which is related to the above—deals with variations across the cases. Despite the broad finding of greater centralization in this issue area, not all central governments dominate subnational budgets and spending. Ministerial-level politics are key to explaining this. The ideological and partisan proximity of ministers to the president increases the likelihood that expenditure autonomy will be low. By contrast, a more fractious executive comprising a broad coalition and characterized by internal opposi-

---

7. There are also interactions between revenue and expenditure autonomy. In the previous chapter, I distinguished between own-source revenues and intergovernmental transfers (IGTs). Laws governing IGTs shape revenue autonomy. Yet a dependence on IGTs *can also compromise expenditure autonomy* by making SNGs vulnerable to central mandates. Own-source revenues are much more difficult for central governments to compel than transfers.

tion will lead to higher subnational autonomy. Presidential partisan weakness leads to such fractious executive branches as ministerial portfolios are distributed to coalition members. Economic crisis resolution tightens intra-executive coherence by enhancing the roles of technocrats closely aligned with presidents and by inducing coalition members to follow presidential prerogatives for electoral reasons. In South Africa's provinces, expenditure autonomy remained low even when revenues were transferred. On the other hand, SNGs lost expenditure autonomy in the wake of economic crisis, just as they lost revenue autonomy. The pattern of massive decentralization and substantial recentralization occurred in Brazil under Cardoso.

Budget Fungibility and the Locus of Spending Power

The central issues of expenditure autonomy revolve around which level of government is able to decide on how public monies are spent. Highly fungible budgets for SNGs (as in Brazil before Cardoso) mean that the locus of spending power is subnational. Low fungibility (as in South Africa) means that the locus of decision making over expenditures is in the central state. I began with the assumption that SNGs seek greater expenditure autonomy (i.e., greater spending power) in order to internalize the political benefits of spending. Not all SNG expenditures can be considered political goods or patronage, of course, but if subnational officials can claim credit for expenditures, they will seek to do so. In more centralized systems, where subnational expenditure autonomy is lower, central governments can target social programs according to national political priorities.

Brazil: High Fungibility and Decentralized Spending Power (1988–94)

From 1988 to 1994 Brazil's central government had little control over the spending of the monies it sent to the *estados*. Governors and mayors commonly financed large-scale projects that resulted in some investment in infrastructure, but that also diverted considerable amounts to private purposes.[8] Investments in broad-based social services such as primary education and primary health were scanty by comparison. Confusing the expenditure situation was the

---

8. For instance, Souza (1997) documents that agricultural projects in rural areas benefited politically well-placed entrepreneurs, while in urban areas public funds were often used in the construction industry.

existence of "concurrent competencies." No particular level of government had a clear mandate for the provision of health care, schooling, housing, or welfare. Instead, all three levels of government overlapped in all these areas; wealthier communities thus ended up well-supplied with public goods and other (poorer) locales were neglected. Decentralized patronage is well documented by Brazilianists, as Ames (2001) and Samuels (2003) show the extent to which subnational actors were able to command and direct resources from the center. In the state of Minas Gerais, Hagopian's (1996) work suggests that traditional oligarchs ensured that they would have considerable spending power into the 1990s. The epitome of the well-connected subnational politician came from the neighboring state of Bahia, where Antonio Carlos Magalhães (known as ACM) served as a major power broker in Brazil's new republic (Souza 1997).

Brazil's social service administration suffered up to the mid-1990s from mismanagement in the state bureaucracy. Health and education expenditures were poorly managed (Weyland 1996). Public services lacked accountability systems between layers of government, and policy outputs were remarkably regressive, with tertiary services such as hospitals and universities taking precedence over primary services. Nonetheless, even those who would later wrestle with the issue forwarded arguments in favor of the high expenditure autonomy of the Brazilian states and municipalities. Noting the detail in Brazil's constitution, one former minister said it was folly to suggest expenditure mandates were incomplete.[9] Remarking that it was fashionable to say that the Brazilian constitution transferred revenues, but not expenditures, Luiz Carlos Bresser Pereira argued that it was not reasonable to specify responsibilities in greater detail than existed in the charter. Dividing revenues was indispensable, whereas the division of expenditures had to come later through ordinary law.[10] However, while increases in revenue decentralization and spending autonomy may have been a priority in 1988, it is clear that Brazil's public finances later suffered from an unclear specification of expenditure responsibilities. High levels of spending autonomy led to battles over fiscal irresponsibility that plagued Brazil through the 1990s. Only with enhanced ministerial control, state reform, and technocratic competence did subnational spending improve.

9. Brazil's constitution (of October 5, 1988) included 245 articles plus 70 complementary acts. It fills a small book of 193 pages.
10. Interview: Luiz Carlos Bresser Pereira.

South Africa: Low Fungibility and Centralized Spending Power

As noted in chapter 3, South Africa's provinces were granted real revenue autonomy with the end of apartheid, such that South Africa's revenue decentralization compares to that of Brazil. Provinces have responsibility for a large percentage of the national budget and are responsible for the management of health, education, and much social welfare, in collaboration with the national ministries. Ample revenues and numerous expenditure responsibilities enhanced the provinces' importance. Yet the fiscal autonomy of provincial governments in South Africa is quite limited on the expenditure side. The ANC ministries have made several moves to ensure provincial compliance with central government objectives by enacting standards for public service inputs and performance.

The annual Division of Revenue Act—which defines the considerable revenue autonomy of the provinces—is the first step in South Africa's intergovernmental relations process. It has been complemented in recent years by the preparation of a budget review and a so-called Medium-Term Expenditure Framework (MTEF), which is essentially a set of five-year projections for public spending. Both of these documents have been developed with a view toward close monitoring of fiscal inputs. Beyond the vertical relations within sectors and sectoral ministries, the South African state includes a Department of Provincial and Local Government (DPLG), a structure that allows the ANC leadership in Pretoria to appoint a coordinating body charged with the relationships with SNGs. The DPLG has a role in vetting major legislation (including the Provincial and Municipal Financial Management Acts), and annual budget processes, particularly the Division of Revenue Act.[11] In addition to these mechanisms, the National Treasury releases an annual Intergovernmental Fiscal Review that highlights the areas of collaboration (and monitoring) between the center and SNGs. All this contrasts with the Brazilian case, where locally interested deputies and senators help to channel spending in an ad hoc fashion on a ministry-by-ministry basis.

Central control over South African provincial revenue is indirect, being applied via ministerial mandates and standards rather than outright prohibitions on fungibility. The Division of Revenue is first based on criteria that correspond to expected spending inputs. For example, the funds provinces receive increase as a function of school-aged children, since this implies more education inputs. Once the equitable share block grants to the provinces are

11. Interview: Derek Powell.

made, there are few specific statutory requirements to spend the transfers on given services, and no explicit prohibition on provinces transferring funds from one sector or line item to another. In fact, provincial departments for different social services may consider themselves to be competing for resources with other departments in the same province.[12] Yet the fungibility of provincial funds is prevented via national performance standards and the multiyear budgeting guided by the National Treasury, as well as strict party discipline within the ANC. Provinces cannot transfer resources across budget items de facto, even if it is not prohibited de jure.

The power of the central government in South Africa is evidenced in works by many of the country's practitioner-scholars (Abedian, Ajam, and Walker 1997; Ahmad 1998, 2003; Ajam 1998, 2001; Momoniat 1998). Major features of the system demonstrate provincial political weakness (cf. Ahmad 2003). For several years capital expenditure budgets from the central government actually surpassed the capacity of provincial governments to absorb them, and unspent monies reverted to the center. By the same token, despite low spending capacity and an inability to manage significant transfers, numerous provinces were placed on strict austerity regimens. Moreover, the center has intervened in provincial affairs on several occasions, with many interventions coming through the National Treasury, to be discussed next.

Ministries of Finance and Mechanisms of Central Control

Limiting subnational spending autonomy is the prerogative of states, and particularly of certain ministries. Line ministries will be treated shortly, but probably none are as significant as ministries of finance, though other special reformist ministries (such as the case of a ministry charged with bureaucratic reform in Brazil) may also play a major role. Presidential imperatives to reduce the autonomy of SNGs regularly come through this channel, and finance ministries are key for several reasons. First, they link directly to questions of macroeconomic stability and intergovernmental fiscal relations, and thus have prominent places in the distribution of fiscal resources in federal systems. Second, they are likely to share the preferences of chief

---

12. Interviews: Helen Zille, Russell Wildeman. This conflict is usually muted because the vast majority of provincial spending is essentially predetermined. The remainder is often funded out of "conditional grants" earmarked for specific projects. The conditional grant mechanism serves to reduce the tension between departments at the provincial level by mitigating the competition for unrestricted equitable share resources.

executives, as this ministry (due to its importance) is one of the likeliest to be retained by presidential confidants even in a coalition government; this is evidenced in Brazil's weak party system. Third, the importance of finance ministries is heightened even more at moments of fiscal crisis. Where macro-economic crisis occurs, these ministries are the prime venue for imple-menting new fiscal rules governing subnational spending. In both Brazil and South Africa, finance ministries proved especially adept at executing presidential prerogatives.

Brazil's Finance Technocracy

Starting in 1994, Cardoso (who himself came to the presidency from the Ministry of Finance) assembled a cabinet-level team that began increasing monitoring of subnational expenditures. As shown in the previous chapter, his formulation of the Real Plan ended hyperinflation and cemented his reputation as a fiscal conservative. As president, Cardoso in turn placed a high premium on stability in financial administration. His appointment as finance minister, Pedro Malan, remained at the post for all eight years of Cardoso's administrations, a long stint at the helm of a volatile economy. Brazil's "expenditure" ministries were also configured in the Cardoso-Malan mold: ministers with strong social credentials alongside a reputation for techno-political competence. The result was a ministerial team that succeeded, over the course of eight years, in transforming Brasilia's traditional bureaucracy into a force for decentralizing expenditures in ways that more tightly circum-scribed state and municipal autonomy. State-level officials who participated actively in the intergovernmental bargaining process of the late 1990s high-light the importance of Brazil's bureaucracy in fiscal processes, arguing that the entrenched bureaucracy compromised the autonomy of SNGs.[13] More sanguine observers asserted that Cardoso's ministers in Brasilia maintained a commitment to decentralization but successfully rationalized the fiscal system by focusing on the decentralization of expenditures.[14]

Related to efforts at economic stabilization within the Finance Ministry, some of the important improvements resulted from Cardoso's appointment of Luiz Carlos Bresser Pereira to another post, that of Minister of Adminis-tration and State Reform (MARE), in his first term. It was Bresser's persistence and strategic decision making that got both the governors and the Brasilia

13. Interview: Yoshiaki Nakano.
14. Interview: Luiz Carlos Bresser Pereira.

bureaucracy on board with administrative reforms that limited the use of patronage (Melo 2003, 9–12, 24). Tactically, Cardoso and Bresser Pereira established extra-ministerial structures that insulated MARE proposals from bureaucratic resistance at an early stage, until a broader pro-reform coalition could be assembled on the back of increasing pressure for subnational accountability. In conjunction with the Finance Ministry technocracy, MARE was a crisis-inspired move to better monitor SNG spending.

Constraints on subnational expenditures under Cardoso also took the form of financial rules put in place to enforce specific requirements on expenditure levels. Most of these were fully implemented with the Fiscal Responsibility Law (LRF) of 2000 (noted in chapter 3 and detailed again in chapter 5).[15] The principal provision of the law relating to spending autonomy sought to reduce subnational spending on patronage posts by limiting expenditures on personnel to less than 60 percent of revenues. The result was a 10-percentage-point reduction in the proportion of spending on personnel, from 61 percent to 51 percent in just the three years between 1997 and 2000 (Afonso 2002). Also with respect to expenditures, the LRF required Brazil's three levels of government to reduce their total debt burden to specific limits; this implied spending reductions in many *estados*. Finally, the proponents of the LRF foresaw the establishment of primary surplus targets of over 3 percent for the various levels of government; again, this required a reduction of expenditure relative to revenue and heightened the role of the Finance Ministry in oversight.

South Africa's "Team Finance"

South Africa's management systems in the national executive closely monitor SNG spending, mostly through the National Treasury (formerly Ministry of Finance). Provinces are mandated to meet specific service standards and fixed output targets, and the Treasury has constantly increased its monitoring of SNG expenditures. Many of these mechanisms emerged in response to localized provincial deficit and debt crises in the late 1990s. These crises were more contained than in the Brazilian cases: provincial overspending never compromised the national macroeconomy in the way seen in Brazil. Rather, the South African central government dealt with the crises on an

15. For text of the law in English or Portuguese, as well as a host of primers and other documents on the LRF, see the Brazilian Development Bank Web site at http://www.bndes.gov.br /SiteBNDES/bndes/bndes_en/ (accessed July 29, 2010).

individualized basis, and this implemented localized forms of expenditure control—with provinces placed on individual adjustment plans—that corresponded to the local (versus national) nature of the crisis.

Once provincial spending came under control in the late 1990s, the techno-political team at the National Treasury moved to implement multi-year public finance plans and turned its focus to creating MTEFs—which plan expenditures over a three- to five-year time frame—and annual budget reviews for all levels of government.[16] Urgency in developing frameworks such as the MTEFs came not from overspending, but rather the opposite. Officials responsible for the Budget Review noted that the main efforts of the Treasury by 2002 were to *increase* the spending of provincial governments, since the central government was comfortable with its ability to monitor increased expenditures.[17] Provinces have lacked the technical capacity to expend their budgets appropriately, though they have generally strengthened their capacity over time, according to Treasury officials (*Business Day,* May 2002).[18]

At fiscal year's end, South Africa's provinces do not retain the resources that they were unable to spend, because unspent monies revert to the National Treasury. The center thereby maintains tight control over provincial spending; if the provinces had any meaningful degree of expenditure autonomy, they could surely divert funds to other purposes, be it in other public service sectors or to patronage. South Africa's top-down control means that line items are not fungible; unspent money designated for textbooks, for instance, reverts to the central government coffers rather than ending up in pork projects. National Treasury officials note the importance of central government pressure on the provinces; as the Director of Intergovernmental Relations at the Treasury noted, "[e]very day you get to kill a dinosaur."[19]

One of the principal features of South Africa's relatively harmonious fiscal system is the strong set of relationships between the National Treasury and the provincial treasuries. This collegial relationship between the different ministers of finance (national and provincial) has ensured some commonality across the national–provincial bureaucratic divide and has strengthened

16. Interviews: Tania Ajam; Ismail Momoniat. Members of the team at the Ministry of Finance (later National Treasury) included Maria Ramos and former World Bank experts such as Junaid Ahmad and Anwar Shah, among others with professional economics backgrounds in the World Bank and abroad.

17. Interview: Tania Ajam.

18. Interviews: Ismail Momoniat, Iraj Abedian, Tania Ajam.

19. Interview: Ismail Momoniat.

Table 4.2 Provisions managing subnational expenditures in South Africa

Measure	Year	Change in expenditure autonomy
Structural Adjustments Plans	1996– 1998	"Structural adjustment" plans stipulate multiple specific spending reductions for provinces on a case-by-case basis.
Medium Term Expenditure Framework (MTEF)	1997– present	Develops multiyear budgeting plan designed to hold provinces to spending targets.
Budget Review	1997– present	Builds on MTEF to develop three-year budgeting cycle, beginning with 1998 budget. Projects intergovernmental division of revenue.
Public Finance Management Act (PFMA)	1999	Tighter monitoring of provincial budgets.

the principle of cooperation on the division of revenue. Far from conflicting over revenues, officials representing these institutions at both levels boast that they are part of "Team Finance" and emphasize their common techno-cratic outlook.[20] Thabo Mbeki's minister of finance, Trevor Manuel, was applauded by upper-level officials at the National Treasury for changing the atmosphere in the ministry, calling it a "place for open debate."[21] In addition, the conflicts between National Treasury and the ministries responsible for public expenditures remained muted.[22] The cohesive nature of interactions within the National Treasury, and between the national and provincial treasuries, contributes to a fiscal system in which the financial ministry at all levels of government responds as a unit to those line ministries with incentives to spend. Relations are correspondingly less cordial between the provincial treasuries and the provincial expenditure portfolios.[23] The finance depart-ments remain frustrated over the low capacity for spending and delivering services exhibited by departments such as Education and Health, especially in poorer provinces such as the Eastern Cape, where the capacity to plan, budget, and execute budgets is suspect.[24]

Despite relative intergovernmental harmony between finance officials at the central and provincial levels, there is little doubt where power lies, as table 4.2 shows. An internal government "IGR Audit" conducted in 1999 shows

20. Interviews: Ismail Momoniat, Tania Ajam.
21. Interview: Ismail Momoniat.
22. Interview: Murphy Morobe.
23. Interview: Murphy Morobe.
24. Interview: Ismail Momoniat.

other bureaucratic institutions also favor the center. Among the principal institutions addressed in the audit are the MinMECs, councils that bring together national ministers with their provincial counterparts (Members of the Executive Committee, or MECs). Of particular importance here is the Budget Council, which brings the National Treasury and provincial finance ministers together: the so-called "Team Finance." These sectoral meetings were designed to accommodate a principle of interdependence between the national and provincial spheres, but the audit found MinMECs on the whole to be largely dominated by representatives of the center:

> There was general concern as to the limits imposed on debate, dialogue and participation in the policy process by the national minister. . . . The question of the predominance of the national perspective at MINMECs was a common concern among the majority of officials interviewed in the provinces and SALGA [South African Local Government Association]. Respondents pointed out that co-operative governance required respect for the integrity of each sphere of government and that this was not always adhered to when national ministers dominated the proceedings. . . . National ministers used it as a clearing house as well as a forum to secure the necessary support for their policies. (RSA/DPLG 1999, 43)

The MinMECs are the state institution through which provincial demands are channeled, with provinces asserting that it is where the center brings "errant provinces into line" (RSA/DPLG 1999, 43). The ability of national ministers to dominate proceedings is largely traceable to strong discipline within the ANC, which facilitates provincial adherence to national demands. Provincial legislators are less likely to check the actions of provincial department officials than provincial treasury departments, though the NCOP is seeking to develop provinces' capacities to engage in their own budget oversight.[25]

Controlling Social Policies: Education and Health

Beyond ministries of finance, other ministries and bureaucracies within the central state also shape the expenditures of SNGs. I focus here in particular on the expenditures in the areas of health and education. These areas constitute

25. Interviews: Tania Ajam, Ismail Momoniat, Mohammed Enver Surty.

two of the largest expenditure areas in most fiscal federal arrangements. In the Brazilian case, increasingly competent technocratic management reduced SNG spending autonomy from extreme to more moderate levels. In South Africa, top-down control of spending is ensured through the aforementioned controls, such as standards on performance and inputs.

Brazil: Improved Social Policy Management

Cardoso's team overhauled funding patterns in two of the most important portfolios in the revenue-expenditure equation: Education and Health. Both ministries were led by Cardoso colleagues with similar technocratic stature to Pedro Malan of Finance. Paulo Renato Souza (Education, 1995–2002) and José Serra (Health, 1998–2002) implemented innovative measures that decentralized expenditures in efforts to change the pattern of unrestricted transfers.[26] In both cases, programs linked increases in transfers to increased provision of services (Arretche 2000).

The willingness of the subnational–congressional nexus to tolerate improved central control over expenditures is puzzling, and again must be explained with reference to the resolution of Brazil's economic crisis. Erika Amorim Araújo argues that subnational actors (and their agents in Congress) engaged in two stages of rational calculation with respect to supporting the Cardoso reforms. In a first stage, the exposure of state finances forced SNG officials to back reforms to the fiscal system, as the popularity of the Real Plan and the challenges of *estado* finances necessitated discipline; the new conditions of fiscal responsibility and the ending of bailouts also had the subsequent effect of forcing subnational actors to find new areas for credit-claiming, most notably in improvements in the subnational provision of social services that deepened the fiscal federal reform.[27] This logic is further supported in recent work that suggests Brazil's legislators have become more programmatic and policy oriented, and less focused on dwindling patronage resources (Hagopian, Gervasoni, and Moraes 2009).

Education funding reform, initiated in 1996, can be almost exclusively attributed to the Cardoso administration, which instituted the Fundamental Education Fund (Fundo de Manutenção e Desenvolvimento do Ensino

26. Serra was Minister of Planning in the first Cardoso government (1995–98), where he was involved in efforts to bring subnational finances under control through tax revisions.
27. Interview: Erika Amorim Araújo.

Fundamental e de Valorização do Magistério, or FUNDEF).[28] The FUNDEF stipulated that *estados* should reach minimum spending levels in primary education and provided incentives for SNGs to voluntarily assume educational responsibilities. The FUNDEF was not simply a concession to the states and municipalities, despite its "decentralizing" nature; Cardoso's government desired the transfer of primary education, believing reforms of this type necessary to equilibrate the prior decentralization of revenue from 1988.

Predating the FUNDEF were constitutional provisions governing education funding that required 25 percent of expenditures at each level of government to be dedicated to education. The FUNDEF reinforced this provision by further mandating that 15 percent of expenditures in each state government (i.e., three-fifths of the 25 percent designated for education) be directed to primary education; this ensured that no states would invest the majority of resources in tertiary education at the expense of primary schools. Beyond these rules, the FUNDEF began transferring revenues to SNGs as a function of the number of pupils enrolled, with each municipal district being publicly assigned a funding coefficient based on its numbers of schoolchildren as evaluated in an annual School Census. The FUNDEF's primary mechanism thus gives municipalities incentives to increase the supply of school spots on offer in order to receive additional transfers.[29]

The FUNDEF has a net redistributive effect, as wealthier states and municipalities are net contributors into the fund, with poorer areas being net beneficiaries. This does not create additional opportunities for patronage in poorer areas, however. Rather, the provisions, which essentially place a minimum on the amount to be spent on teacher salaries, may actually have the counterintuitive effect of reducing patronage in other more politically lucrative areas of government. When placed alongside LRF provisions limiting overall spending on salaries, the FUNDEF in effect ensures that a large proportion of total personnel salaries will be paid to primary schoolteachers. Because poor municipalities receive a relatively substantial portion of their overall budgets from the FUNDEF, their opportunities for patronage are squeezed elsewhere by the minimum that must be spent on primary schoolteachers and the maximum that can be spent on personnel as a whole (60 percent of the total budget, per the LRF). The FUNDEF thus can have salutary effects on spending choices beyond education itself.

28. The FUNDEF was modified and renamed Fundeb in 2007. Information is available (in Portuguese) at http://www.fnde.gov.br/index.php/financ-fundeb (accessed August 25, 2010).

29. Technically, the FUNDEF directs 15 percent of the "major taxes" of state and municipal governments into the distribution fund, namely the State Participation Fund, the Municipal Participation Fund, the ICMS, and a handful of other taxes of national scope.

The creation of the FUNDEF converted automatic, unchecked transfers into a system whereby municipal governments were reimbursed on a per-student basis for schooling expenditures incurred. The measure reduced subnational discretion over expenditures by redirecting funds to primary public goods. Quite simply, "this measure represents an incentive for the municipalization of [primary education], since the municipalities will only have access to their resources when they provide for matriculants" (Arretche 2000, 140). A major feature of the reform is that it favors municipalities—not *estados*—as the service provider. Brazilian municipalities and states are not simply a common subnational front opposed to the federal government; it is clear that the center under Cardoso preferred granting funds to the municipalities (cf. Dickovick 2007). This tendency to "avoid governors" is a finding that finds support up into the Lula administration, and across different social sectors, including the conditional cash transfers of the Bolsa Familia program (Fenwick 2009).

Increasing accountability in transfers and a shift toward municipal provision also applies to the health system after 1994, through the full implementation of the Single Health System plan, the SUS (Sistema Único de Saúde). Cardoso inherited legislation designed to transfer responsibilities to SNGs, but the system was not yet in place, and enabling legislation was incomplete until 1996.[30] As a result, much health funding prior to Cardoso's presidency was converted into patronage.[31] The previous system, SUDS (Sistema Único e Descentralizado de Saúde), was designed to promote decentralized health care but was seen by the states and municipalities as an easy route to greater transfers. The previous system also involved the social security bureaucracy (Instituto Nacional de Assistência Médica da Previdência Social, or INAMPS) as a major player seeking to keep expenditure responsibilities within the central government (Weyland 1996).

By contrast with these former systems, the funding mechanisms of the SUS now ensure that local governments are compensated per the amounts and levels of services provided, and are increasingly pressed into higher levels of service. A per capita funding provision (Piso de Atenção Básica) provided incentives to poor localities to integrate into the system. Municipalities were then free to opt into any of three different service provision levels (later

30. The enabling statutes were the Basic Operating Norms (Normas Operacionais Básicas; NOB) of 1991, 1993, and 1996. The 1991 NOB stated that public and private health providers would operate under a single set of rules; the 1993 NOB established the options available to SNGs; and the 1996 NOB triggered municipal adherence to SUS.

31. This discussion of the health care system before Cardoso draws on Weyland 1996.

reduced to two as of 2000), but received more generous transfers with each additional level; this offered incentives for resource-poor *municípios* to assume additional functions (Yunes 1999). The logic also persuaded wealthier municipalities, as SUS transfers for high levels of service came to represent a large percentage of municipal budgets, as contrasted with localities that relied on other transfers, such as the unrestricted Municipal Participation Fund (Garson and Araújo 2001).

The SUS changed the way in which funds for health care were distributed, instituting a program that resembles the logic laid out in the FUNDEF.[32] In fact, the same technical expert, Barjas Negri (who assumed the position of Health Minister when Serra began campaigning for president), worked on the central design features of both programs.[33] The center successfully pressed municipalities to accept the SUS and bypassed the often troublesome bureaucracies at the *estado* level by transferring monies directly into municipal health funds "without the intervention of the State Secretary of Health" (Arretche 2000, 211). One of the keys to federal success in the health area was the establishment of this "fund-to-fund" arrangement, whereby central government transfers to the municipalities bypassed the *estado* bureaucracies entirely; this limited SNG expenditure autonomy at the *estado* level, where overspending was most problematic. Given that discussions over expenditures occurred largely within the national executive branch, and given the close relationship between the president and the Health Ministry in the late 1990s, state governments were unable to generate the traction they could get on revenue issues. In direct contrast with the way SNGs worked through Congress to increase unrestricted revenue transfers, the governors and their *congressista* partners had no effective channels through which to resist implementation of the SUS.[34]

Municipalities did not resist the decentralization push, because the expenditure shift was fully funded. The central government did not rely on unfunded mandates to promote expenditure decentralization; instead, the ministry opted for a reform that would establish a precedent of earmarked funding over the longer term. A key mechanism was the fact that the SUS only reimbursed for existing services, and does not provide funds for the

32. The use of the reimbursement-for-service model did exist before the SUS in Brazil, having made its appearance with the use of contracting arrangements (*convenios*) with private sector service providers in the SUDS/INAMPS era. The SUS used this principle and fully implemented it in the public sector.

33. Interview: José Serra.

34. Interview: José Serra.

future capital expansion of the local health system (Arretche and Rodriguez 1999, 129). Municipalities are thus required to use their own resources for expansion (Arretche and Rodriguez 1999, 129). As former minister José Serra noted, "In the short run, federal resources are funding the SUS. But over the longer term, it is evident that state and municipal financing will represent a larger proportion of health costs. The mayors were amenable to this because they were receiving short-term benefits [in the form of additional health resources]. They know that the one who is going to have to pay more out of their own resources in the long run is some other mayor down the line."[35] Though satisfied with the arrangement, municipalities could not exult that they were extorting money from the center. The SUS was fully funded, but the mechanisms curtailed the flexibility of municipalities because "this form of financing is a limitation on the autonomy of the decentralized units, due to the rigidity it imposes on local provision [adequação local] in the supply of services" (Arretche 2000, 211). In the end, well-structured incentives and federal pressure outweighed the loss of expenditure autonomy. By 2000 over 99 percent of Brazil's municipalities had adhered to the provisions, according to government figures, whereas less than 50 percent of municipalities were adherents in many states in 1996 (Arretche and Rodriguez 1999, 136).

The final piece of the puzzle to increase subnational participation in health funding was a constitutional amendment in 2000 that required SNGs to spend a certain proportion of their resources on health care, just as a previous constitutional provision had done for education. The amendment established that states budget a minimum of 12 percent for the health sector, and that municipalities budget a 15 percent minimum. This amendment had Serra's strong backing, despite his previous resistance to such earmarking at the time of the Constituent Assembly (Serra 2002, 89–90).[36]

The FUNDEF and the SUS have proved popular in public opinion and in the bureaucracies.[37] These administrative reforms dramatically altered

35. Interview: José Serra.
36. The return to democracy in 1988 had technocrats concerned about restricting the flexibility of SNGs (Serra 2002; Interview: Luiz Carlos Bresser Pereira). By the late 1990s many of the same actors were concerned about subnational profligacy. Many Brazilian politicians—including Cardoso—were strong advocates for subnational interests at the end of authoritarian rule in the 1980s but necessarily shifted priorities thereafter, when SNGs compromised fiscal discipline. The reverse holds as well: former presidents such as Itamar Franco and José Sarney battled with the estados while in the presidency only to become thorns in the side of future presidents when subsequently serving as governor or Senator. On career paths in Brazil, see especially Samuels 2003.
37. Interviews: Lucia de Fátima Nascimento de Queiroz, Deildes de Oliveira Prado. See also Araújo and Oliveira (2001) and Garson and Araújo (2001).

Brazil's fiscal federal arrangement: state and local governments that once received money for nothing are now participants in a more prosaic and functional arrangement where they are compensated for the services they provide. Not coincidentally, the areas examined here were administered by techno-political ministers with two features in common: they were from a southeastern (generally São Paulo) background, and they were ideologically committed partners of the president, with each being seen as a possible PSDB successor to Cardoso at one time. The key members of the Cardoso team were characterized by bureaucratic competence and a techno-political outlook on expenditures, with close ties between the president and these ministers that can be traced back to common experiences in political and academic environments (Meneguello 1998, 147–48). Top civil service appointments below the ministerial level also closely followed the interests of the president, as evidenced by the role of Barjas Negri.[38] Indeed, a reputation for effectiveness in running the SUS was even partly responsible for Serra's successful bid for the 2002 PSDB presidential nomination as a possible successor to Cardoso. These simple changes represented a dramatic shift in the incentive structures for SNGs, and enhanced their willingness to assume social service responsibilities.

Of course, changes in Brazil have not taken place across all sectors of the public service. Indeed, advances in Brazil's political economy have been fitful, with probably the greatest changes coming in the areas studied here: finance, education, health, and state reform. In other sectors, Cardoso was forced to distribute cabinet posts to the less fiscally responsible members of his coalition, such as the PFL, and government reinvention lagged in these areas.[39] In fact, the reputation of the Cardoso team was such that Serra's selection as the PSDB 2002 presidential candidate led to cries of outrage from those coalition partners most associated with traditional patronage networks. Faced with the prospective continuation of a Cardoso-style president that could strike a long-term blow to traditional clientelism and *estado* dominance of national politics, the conservative wing of the coalition (the PFL), lambasted Serra as being "very São Paulo" and "anti-PFL" (*Estado de São Paulo*, April 17, 2002).

In highlighting the importance of technocracy at the cabinet level and within the state in reforming public finance and administration, Arretche

---

38. Interview: José Serra.

39. The PFL (Partido da Frente Liberal), nominally a center-right party, was associated with the Northeast oligarchies. It was later renamed the Democrats (DEM).

Table 4.3 Major reductions in expenditure autonomy in Brazil

Mechanism	Year	Change in expenditure autonomy
SUS	1994– present	Implementation of health care decentralization plan provides incentives for SNGs to assume health care responsibilities.
FUNDEF	1996– present	Education decentralization plan provides incentives for SNGs to assume primary education spending.
Fiscal Responsibility Law (LRF)	2000– present	Criminal punishment for subnational politicians who exceed spending limits.

(2000, 53) notes: "[T]he degree of success of a decentralization program is directly associated with decisions to institute operational rules that create effective incentives for [subnational] levels of government. . . . [T]he Constitution of 1988 was not sufficient to make [subnational] administrations decide to use their additional resources to implement programs in specific policy areas. It only meant that local executives had more resources; it did not define *in which policy area* to apply them. . . . [For this] the decisive component is the existence of a strategy efficiently designed and implemented by a higher level of government." In Brazil, a common technocratic vision within the executive facilitated efforts to bring expenditures into line with revenues at all levels of government. With sufficient leverage to appoint copartisan ministers, Cardoso and his executive branch made important changes that state governors, mayors, and congressmen could not easily undermine.

South Africa: Top-Down Management Tools

Low expenditure autonomy contributes to the control of decentralized public finances in South Africa; the macroeconomic difficulties caused by subnational spending in South Africa pale in comparison to the problems in Brazil. Less salutary are the social policy effects of centralized expenditures. While conflicts in other countries have generally been about the levels of revenues, the crux of conflict between national and subnational governments in South Africa is about spending freedom. Most important in recent years have been fights over health matters (especially given the massive disputes over the national AIDS policy created by President Thabo Mbeki). In education as well, conflicts over spending have taken place, with the central government concerned that provinces with weak capacity are incapable of delivering services to all constituents.

Education funding is a useful microcosm of the South African budgetary system as a whole. Public education is funded largely out of the equitable share provision, with provinces receiving substantial distributions to compensate them for the assumption of schooling costs (RSA/NT 2001, 2003). Nonetheless, education policy and costs are still controlled from the top. The cost implications of education provision are essentially dictated at the national level, through two principal mechanisms. First, teacher salaries are bargained for at a national level, especially between the ANC and the country's major teachers' union, the South African Democratic Teachers' Union (SADTU).[40] A vast majority of provincial education budgets are thus controlled through national-level decision making. Second, provincial education departments do not have active retrenchment tools. The only way of reducing educational professionals is through natural attrition; firing can take place only under extremely limited circumstances.[41]

By the letter of the law, the dependence on the equitable share for education funding could mean that the provincial education departments would compete for funds with other provincial departments. Competition is tempered, however, by the fact that minimum educational standards must be achieved, lest the provinces' education systems be overtaken by the national authorities.[42] Given the political cost to the provincial leadership (including possible dismissal of the premier by the president), education standards are actively pursued, as are all other central government directives, and public battles over education are relatively muted.[43] Even so, outputs vary dramatically from one province to another depending on capacity, which is very low in some provinces (such as the Eastern Cape).[44]

40. SADTU is a member organization of COSATU, the trade union federation affiliated with the ANC. SADTU and other unions will be examined in the next chapter.

41. The relative impunity of teachers is extensive and occasionally downright tragic, with some teachers widely reported to have sexually assaulted students, with few or no ramifications for their job.

42. The MinMECs for education formalized the process of meetings in the National Education Policy Act, making this the only department other than the Finance Ministry to institutionalize such meetings (interview: Russell Wildeman).

43. This is relative to health. Conflicts within government are common on education. Under Departmental MEC for Education Helen Zille (Democratic Party), the Western Cape repeatedly fought with the national ministry over policies and over ministerial control of the bureaucracy (interview: Helen Zille). Even in ANC strongholds such as the Eastern Cape, conflicts over bureaucratic power arise: poor school management and performance led the central government to send investigative consultants to recommend overhauling the system, and the province protested central meddling in provincial affairs.

44. A substantial percentage of conditional grants for education ultimately revert to the National Treasury, because provinces do not have the capacity to implement them.

Health policy and funding in South Africa is more complex and controversial in several important ways. Health care funding is more tied to specific, lumpy investments and requires intensive capital expenditures for hospitals, clinics, and equipment; capital needs are exacerbated by particularly severe health care backlogs in the historically underserved black townships and homelands. Apart from personnel, where medical professionals (doctors and nurses, e.g.) in the public sector are part of a single service, much like teachers, health funding has a large component funded through conditional grants, wherein spending is explicitly earmarked for specific projects monitored by the central government.[45] The major shift in health care since 1994 has been the rationalization of hospital services, and a prioritization of primary care, especially in black townships. Blacks gained access to the public hospitals during the post-1994 period, but the spending burden for tertiary and curative care overburdened hospitals.[46] Primary care, which was woefully inadequate, required urgent advances.

Health politics is also much more visibly contested than education and other social services, with national policy under Mbeki receiving vehement public criticism. While a thorough examination of the HIV/AIDS epidemic is far beyond the scope of this analysis, the country's principal public health issue has significant implications for the provinces and has been South Africa's greatest battle over social policy since the end of apartheid. The Mbeki government's HIV/AIDS policy—widely viewed as reactionary and irresponsible—led to substantial intra-ANC splits.[47] A number of upper-level ANC party players, including Nelson Mandela, criticized Mbeki and his policies. Most intriguing was the audacity of provincial premier Mbhazima "Sam" Shilowa of Gauteng, undoubtedly the country's most important province.[48] The conflict reached fever pitch after 2000, with a large coalition within the ANC forming to oppose Mbeki's policy. The rift went public, with open battles between Shilowa and the Mbeki government, especially Health Minister Manto Tshabalala-Msimang. At the opposite end of the spectrum from Shilowa's open defiance, clever SNGs have occasionally been able to sneak antigovernment policies under the radar, suggesting some very limited form of spending autonomy. Western Cape, for instance, quietly began implementing

45. As with education, the private sector covers much of the white minority.
46. Interview: Ingrid Le Roux.
47. The conflict centered on Mbeki's purported belief that the link between HIV, AIDS, and health outcomes was tenuous. Mbeki's ambivalence penetrated his health ministry and resulted in policies that complicated the provision of drugs to reduce transmission.
48. Gauteng includes the country's industrial heart around Johannesburg and Pretoria.

a proactive anti-AIDS program in the late 1990s.[49] By not publicly calling on government to change national policy, the province avoided a confrontation with Mbeki over the policy-setting powers of the provinces. However, Western Cape could defy the central government in ways Gauteng could not, because the province was not ANC-dominated, but an opposition province at the time. Mbeki was not threatened by intraparty opposition and could not pull party levers to control the province. Partisan powers thus mediated negotiations between national and SNG executives.

Limitations on SNGs may be changing, however. Splits such as that epitomized by Shilowa's defiance arise between the center and the provinces over expenditure decisions, and provinces may increasingly raise their collective voice. Conflict between the center and Gauteng may have been a first testing of the waters by provincial ANC elites. Observers both within and outside the ANC have noted that real tests of provincial power will come when ANC provinces stand up to the center.[50] From the provincial perspective, increased expenditure autonomy would be the next logical demand, but incentives for the center to concede this power are still scarce.

In short, the center never gave provinces the same autonomy over expenditures as it did in the area of revenues. Cracking down on expenditures has been easier for the ANC leadership than cracking down on revenues; maintaining and reinforcing central control over spending has proved easier than reversing fiscal decentralization.[51] Earmarking, national performance standards, and preestablished budgets carried over from the apartheid era (including the imperative to integrate homeland governments into the national state structure) have prevented SNGs from transferring funds from one policy area to another.

Comparative Lessons

Most studies of decentralization cannot tell us why centralized governments have had greater success in restricting expenditure autonomy than revenue autonomy. Why did the decline of the NP result in so much less expenditure autonomy than revenue autonomy in South Africa? Why did expenditure

---

49. Interview: Ingrid Le Roux.
50. Interviews: Theo Bekker, Helen Zille.
51. In fact, the ability to control expenditures partially explains the ANC's willingness to accept the division of revenue by equitable share, as it foresaw that top-down central control of public finance could be assured through tight monitoring of expenditures.

autonomy remain so circumscribed when declining governments were forced to (or chose to) concede revenue autonomy? If electoral calculations led presidents to guarantee revenues to SNGs, why didn't they also grant the freedom to spend? Expenditure autonomy is as crucial as revenue autonomy in understanding central and SNG power, and we must answer these questions.

The answer lies in the relevant institutional arenas in which autonomy is negotiated. Accounting for variations in different elements of SNG autonomy requires not only the dynamic political-economic assessment of governmental decline and crisis resolution, but also an examination of how and where negotiations occur: states are more apt to constrain SNGs than legislatures, largely because of the preferences of the actors involved. Presidents and national party leaders have proved more capable of managing their internal coalitions than they have been at ensuring electoral success. The predictor of expenditure autonomy is the strength of the president within the governing coalition. If presidents must distribute cabinet posts to a wide coalition, they are less able to use ministerial levers to control SNG spending. When ministries are controlled by presidential allies, spending will be controlled much more from the top down. Sitting presidents prefer centralized power during their tenure, but when they are in decline and seeking to favor SNGs, they face bureaucratic actors who act independently as well. As presidential power wanes, chief executives lose control over decision making to various actors; among those are bureaucracies that retain numerous tools for the control of subnational expenditures, including placing standards on inputs (requiring amounts to be spent on given sectors), public service outputs (requiring the provision of a given number of services), or service indicators and outcomes (requiring the provision of a certain quantity and quality of public goods). Battles over expenditure autonomy can take place through administrative channels. Central ministries constrain SNGs through policy; expenditure patterns are sticky because bureaucracies play an important static role favoring centralized power, including at those rare moments when even presidents—subjected to the electoral pressures of partisan decline—may not.

While governmental decline and weakness were more limited in their effects due to the institutional arena of contestation, crisis resolutions continued to represent key moments for transforming expenditure rules and outcomes, as it gave presidents the power to overhaul the fiscal federal system by strengthening the president's hand within governing coalitions. In Brazil, Cardoso's surging popularity after the Real Plan brought even traditionally clientelist actors into line behind the president, and moves to require greater public goods provision from SNGs thus met surprisingly little resistance. In South Africa, even minor provincial crises justified the center's tightening of spending controls.

The causal role of decline and crisis holds across South Africa and Brazil, but the outcomes are much more accentuated in the latter. Low expenditure autonomy for SNGs has been the rule in South Africa, and so reversals of autonomy were less apparent on the surface. Because government ministries have been tightly linked to the presidency, they have sought to ensure subnational compliance with national goals. Opposition to presidents within cabinets has been weak. South Africa's story is accordingly one of low overall levels of SNG autonomy, which should temper enthusiasm about decentralizing reforms. The decline of the NP at the national level resulted in some limited increases in autonomy, and the limited nature of crisis meant that South Africa's central government also realized some limited recentralization in this area, but the comparison is one of much less movement than in Brazil. When the center holds power, its need to grab is lessened.

Pre-1994 Brazil is an exceptional case of very high levels of subnational spending autonomy, and the change to post-1994 Brazil is where the largest shifts occurred. The 1988–94 period, when governments relied on tangled webs of patron–client relationships to ensure governability, was the only instance of very high levels of expenditure autonomy in the four countries studied, including the two unitary cases—Peru and Senegal—examined in chapter 6. The weak national executive before the Cardoso years allowed the symbiotic relationship among governors, mayors, and parliamentarians to develop. Governments held themselves together by decentralizing funding and allowing powerful subnational actors to spend monies freely. Coalition "partners" in the cabinet oversaw the political distribution of patronage resources. The Cardoso government reversed this trend with major shifts in the funding of public goods. This coalition placed copartisan ministers in important portfolios that shared several features: they were ideologically committed to responsible fiscal governance, had strong technical backgrounds, and were chosen to monitor important areas in the expenditure equation, with other (more clientelist) coalition partners given access to lesser portfolios.

States matter in intergovernmental relations. Expenditure decentralization is a political issue that resides often in the realm of ministerial and administrative policy-making. Policy decisions in areas such as health and education are not always made through overt bargaining between elected politicians, but are also made by the administrative divisions of the national executive.

As a result, states can more easily bypass legislatures in decisions on expenditures than in decisions on revenues; on average, presidents have more levers with which to control expenditure autonomy than they have to control revenue autonomy. Where presidents can place like-minded technocrats in key economic and social ministries, central government control over subnational spending will be enhanced. The Cardoso government's experience cannot be explained by the usual reference to party variables: Brazilian presidents continue to have weak partisan levers. Moreover, Finance Minister Pedro Malan was not a copartisan of the president, though he was considered a possible presidential candidate to succeed Cardoso on the PSDB ticket. Rather, common technocratic outlook and decision making substituted for partisan levers in the team of Pedro Malan, Paulo Renato Souza, and José Serra in key ministries, and Luiz Carlos Bresser Pereira in the Ministry of Administrative and State Reform. Similarly, ministerial power in South Africa shaped the ways in which subnational governments can spend their revenues. Changes at the top of the state matter.

The intergovernmental division of revenues is insufficient to measure and explain the complexity of intergovernmental fiscal relations. Focusing on revenues alone (or, which levels of government spend how much of total government budgets) would lead to mistaken conclusions. Revenue totals suggest decentralization has given enormous power to SNGs in South Africa, when in fact SNG autonomy is tightly constrained. Yet even revenue and expenditure autonomy together do not conclude a full study of intergovernmental relations. Also needed to round out this examination is a direct look at SNG ability to contract debt and labor, along with central government ability to set hard budget constraints in capital markets and/or control SNG labor markets. I treat these questions in the next chapter, which assesses the "contractual" autonomy of SNGs.

5

—⟞ø⟞ø—

SUBNATIONAL CONTRACTUAL AUTONOMY

Assessments of the economic impact of federalism in the developing world are markedly less optimistic than they once were. Once assumed to be a route to improved governance, federalism is now seen as potentially perilous to macroeconomic stability (e.g., Rodden 2006; Wibbels 2005). The likelihood of "market-preserving federalism" is now adjudged to be low in the developing world (cf. Rodden and Rose-Ackerman 1997; Weingast 1995). Arguments explaining the growing evidence of fiscal federalism's failures in the developing world hinge on one central issue: soft budget constraints for subnational governments. Observers find that the ability of "semiautonomous" SNGs to establish their own contracts—especially in capital markets—has resulted in macroeconomic disasters. The consequences for macroeconomic stability of SNG autonomy to contract debt are thus hotly debated and give reason to discern the causes of this contractual independence.

In this chapter, I demonstrate how crisis and decline affect a third issue area: subnational contractual autonomy, or the autonomy of SNGs to set independent financial contracts. I examine whether SNGs have the authority (de jure) and ability (de facto) to establish their own contracts in several major areas. The first major area of contractual autonomy is a prerequisite for the others: legal or jurisdictional autonomy. Do SNGs have legal independence in their jurisdictions and guarantees that the center cannot intervene directly in SNG affairs? In the absence of jurisdictional autonomy, questions of the semi-sovereignty of SNGs become moot. While studies of genuinely federal countries such as Brazil can safely assume that SNGs have at least some jurisdictional autonomy, this issue must be considered for weakly federal states and for unitary states.

Beyond this legal autonomy come issues related to financial decentralization, and specifically the ability to establish contracts with different sets of private actors, such as creditors and employees. At issue is SNG independence in capital and labor markets. Are SNGs authorized to contract debt, and what sorts of guarantees do central governments provide for subnational debt? And do SNGs control the wage bills for the public officials under their jurisdiction, or are wages and benefits set by the center? The question of SNG roles in capital markets, and the immediately salient issue of the softness or hardness of SNG budget constraints, has taken a prominent place in the literature on intergovernmental relations, especially in Latin America (see, e.g., Eaton and Dickovick 2004; Rodden 2006; Rodden, Eskeland, and Litvack 2003). The role of SNG autonomy in the more overlooked area of labor markets has equally significant implications in these two cases, as shown in this chapter.

The causal argument in this chapter builds on that throughout: governmental decline and weakness lead to increased contractual autonomy for SNGs, and crises of differing intensities make possible decreases in contractual autonomy, yet the consideration of institutional arenas and relevant actors must be extended in one new direction to account for the differences between contractual autonomy and autonomy in the areas of revenues and expenditures. In this area, negotiations between national-level elected officials and subnational elected officials are the central determinants of outcomes, supplanting the executive–legislative relations and intra-executive relations that strongly conditioned revenue autonomy and expenditure autonomy, respectively.[1] As noted in the opening chapter, existing arguments cannot explain why a country would decentralize in one area and not in another. Given generalizable preferences and static actors, we would expect uniform decentralization across issue areas, yet decentralization varies across these areas. Only by incorporating different actors and institutional arenas, we can explain this diversity of outcomes. Success in this area will differ from success in other areas as a result of the changed institutional environment (cf. Mainwaring 1997a). Both Brazil and South Africa increased the contractual autonomy of subnational governments during their transitions to democracy, while on the recentralization side, attempts by presidents to reduce the contractual

1. As noted previously and hereafter, presidential leverage over contractual autonomy may operate primarily in negotiations with elected subnational executives, but legislatures and states do continue to play a role; additional arenas must be added to the model to account for each subsequent area of subnational autonomy as we move from revenues through expenditures to contracts, and outcomes do not depend on a single variable.

autonomy of SNGs succeeded in Brazil only in response to economic crises. Reductions in contractual autonomy were somewhat successful in South Africa, but not as thoroughgoing, and this may be attributed to the limited and localized nature of economic crisis.

In the first section of this chapter, I conceptualize and measure contractual autonomy, using ideal type measures to delineate legal (or jurisdictional) autonomy, capital market autonomy, and labor market autonomy. I also discuss how decline and crisis influence presidential power relative to subnational politicians in intergovernmental bargaining. Three subsequent sections treat legal autonomy, capital market autonomy, and labor market autonomy, in that order. The conclusion links contractual autonomy to previous discussions of revenue autonomy and expenditure autonomy while highlighting the need to keep each distinct.

Explaining Contractual Autonomy: The Inter-executive Arena

SNGs with high levels of contractual autonomy are juridically independent of central governments and have the legal right to enter into independent financial contracts without the approval of the center, especially in capital and labor markets.[2] In capital markets, the key indicator is the extent to which SNGs can enter into independent debt contracts without central government approval. For labor markets, SNGs have higher contractual autonomy insofar as they have the authority to set employment contracts, and hire, fire, and alter the wages of their civil servants. In general, SNGs that are free to negotiate their own contracts have control over their investment and personnel costs, and can resist attempts by central governments to intervene in subnational fiscal management. Some of these issues will be specified in constitutional provisions or amendments, while others are contingent on the outcomes of recurrent political negotiations. We may assume constitutional provisions to have greater weight than ordinary law.

Given these items, it may be said that contractual autonomy comprises three key elements: (1) legal or jurisdictional autonomy, including constitutional independence (most common in federal states) and guarantees of central government nonintervention, or conversely, the legal authorization of

---

2. Also included, though not examined here in detail, may be SNG rights to negotiate directly with the private sector for investment purposes. I would like to thank Adolfo Cespedes Zavaleta for highlighting this possibility with regard to contemporary Peru.

central government intervention and the conditions for it; (2) capital market autonomy, that is, the right to contract or issue debt for capital purposes, as well as the existence or lack of government bailout guarantees; and (3) labor market autonomy, or the right of SNGs to bargain over wages and salaries with public sector employees and their other operations costs. I treat each in turn.

(1) *Jurisdictional (legal) autonomy.* Some legal independence for SNGs, usually guaranteed by the constitution or a foundational law, is a prerequisite for other types of autonomy.[3] It includes some degree of legal independence— whether through constitutional or foundational organic laws—and guarantees of central government nonintervention in affairs under SNG jurisdiction. Jurisdictional autonomy correlates with federalism, of course, since federalism generally implies constitutional rights for SNGs. The considerable legal auto- nomy of Brazil's SNGs, for instance, reflects the country's robust federalism. South Africa's provinces, not traditionally as strong, gained greatly when the constitution established the postapartheid government on federal prin- ciples. Unitary states—like Peru and Senegal treated in the next chapter— obviously leave less authority in the hands of SNGs, but the amount of autonomy afforded to localities and regions can also change over time here, as the 1990s illustrate.

(2) *Capital market (borrowing) autonomy.* Capital market autonomy refers to the ability of SNGs to enter into debt contracts. I assess whether states/ provinces/regions have the legal right to contract or issue long-term debt, what conditions are placed on SNG indebtedness, and whether subnational debt is backed up by central government bailout guarantees.[4] SNGs that have the right to contract debt without implicit central government bailout guarantees score high in capital market autonomy. Scoring even higher, however, are SNGs whose debts are backed up by central government bailouts. In these cases, SNGs are free to borrow (thus internalizing the benefits of credit extension) while externalizing the costs of borrowing (by transferring the cost of risk to central governments). I consider these cases of "extreme" capital market autonomy in table 5.1 below. That is, the highest form of autonomy in capital markets is the ability of an SNG to enter into a contract without concern over whether it can meet its obligations. Scoring low are SNGs that

3. In fact, it may be argued that juridical/legal autonomy is a prerequisite for the revenue and expenditure autonomy outlined in previous chapters.
4. Several existing studies examine the question of subnational borrowing, with particular emphasis on the need for hard budget constraints for SNG (Rodden, Eskeland, and Litvack 2003; Ter-Minassian 1997). I refer to these in the empirical sections.

may only contract debt under tightly circumscribed rules or that do not have that right or power at all.

Capital market autonomy is distinct from the access to revenue treated in chapter 3. Debt financing must be viewed differently from tax revenue, because it does not reflect income, but rather a liability. As significantly, it is possible for SNGs to have considerable autonomy with respect to IGTs or tax capacity, but no ability to incur debt. This empirical distinction—highlighted by the South African case—has substantive significance for development and investment. The extension of credit to SNGs creates opportunities for lumpy fixed investments that tax revenues cannot generate; simultaneously, capital market transactions by SNGs can create financial and fiscal problems beyond those that can be generated by short-term overspending. In the case of Brazil especially, reductions in capital market autonomy are of great consequence even when revenue distribution is not permanently changed.

(3) *Labor market (wage) autonomy.* Surely, the more understudied area of contractual autonomy is the set of rules governing labor markets. Analogous to capital markets, the highest level of SNG autonomy is the ability to set contracts while passing the costs to the center: SNGs with "extreme" autonomy can hire personnel on a patronage basis, with the center picking up the tab. Below this extreme, SNGs that have the right to bargain directly with their civil service over wages and salaries have relatively high degrees of labor market autonomy. SNGs in countries where the central government sets the wages, salaries, and benefits of all civil servants have less autonomy in this area. We may also subsume questions of control over certain operations costs into this category, though most such costs are adequately captured under the discussion of expenditure autonomy.[5] SNGs prefer to make autonomous decisions regarding their costs of operation, and any such decisions imposed by the center necessarily reduce this autonomy in a contractual sense.

Labor market autonomy is distinct from spending autonomy much as capital market autonomy is distinct from revenues, despite the obvious links between personnel costs and overall expenditures. Spending autonomy refers to the ability of SNGs to make funds fungible; SNGs with the ability to maneuver funds from one line item to another, or from one public spending sector to another, have greater degrees of spending autonomy than those

---

5. The ability to establish independent contracts for non-personnel operations costs will rarely be of great empirical significance. Any SNG that does not have control over its own operations costs—such as contracting for the purchase of materials—likely does not even have any legal autonomy whatsoever. This would mean the SNG is a local representative of the central state, and would make questions about autonomy irrelevant.

Table 5.1 Subnational contractual autonomy: Ideal type measures

Degree of autonomy	Ideal typical features
Extreme	Central government inability to control SNGs High access to capital markets with central government bailouts Subnational labor patronage with central government guarantees
High	Secure (constitutional) legal autonomy over jurisdiction Authorization to issue and contract debt; access to loans Decentralized wage bargaining
Medium	Conditional legal autonomy Restrictions on debt issuance Centralized wage bargaining with some subnational latitude
Low	No legal autonomy; legal autonomy revocable No authorization to contract debt; no access to loans Centralized control of all public service labor market

SNGs without this ability. This understanding of spending autonomy says little, however, about ways that central governments can control cost drivers by imposing strict standards on how public servants are paid. An example is South Africa, whose provinces have some expenditure autonomy in a purely legalistic sense (i.e., there are no explicit prohibitions on transferring funds across line items) yet are hemmed in on their spending by standards that require fixed numbers of employees and specific wages. The weakness of South Africa's provinces must be understood with reference to their inability to set their own labor contracts. By contrast, one may consider SNGs with spending autonomy *and* labor market autonomy, such as states and localities in the United States, that would have much fuller control over spending.

Thus, contractual autonomy clearly links to the study of revenue and expenditure but is conceptually and empirically distinct.[6] With respect to fiscal decentralization, financial flows from debt increase cash flow in the short term, but are not the equivalent of tax revenues. Borrowed funds represent long-term liabilities on the government balance sheet, not assets. Similarly, on the expenditure side, I focus here on the issue of control over spending cost drivers, especially the wage and salary costs of the civil service; I am no longer addressing whether SNGs choose to spend money on social welfare versus patronage networks, but whether they can set their own payrolls. In table 5.1, I offer the measures of contractual autonomy and give several indicators, all of which are statutory in nature. Even more than expenditure

---

6. Clearly, labor costs are a category of expenditure, while the financial flows resulting from loans represent short-term positive cash flows.

autonomy, contractual autonomy provides a clear example of why intergovern-mental outcomes must be seen not only as fiscal quantities, but as a set of institutions that constrain political behavior.

I build here on the prevailing arguments and assumptions employed previously. Governmental decline makes presidents more vulnerable to bottom-up proposals from subnational politicians, and also increases the strategic value of top-down political solutions whereby the president's party benefits in the future from increased power at the subnational levels. As with the other issue areas, the contractual independence of local and regional governments varies inversely with presidential power. My assumptions about the preferences of the different actors involved parallel those in the previous chapters. SNGs prefer to increase their own autonomy. Ideally, they would like the aforementioned "extreme autonomy" that comes with the ability to enter into contracts, freely combined with central government guarantees to fund those contracts. On the other hand, presidents generally prefer to exert greater power over SNGs and wish to reduce subnational contractual autonomy.[7]

In this light, presidential initiatives to expand subnational autonomy are responses to political weakness, rather than demonstrations of strength, while reductions in SNG autonomy are the converse. In seeking to reduce subnational autonomy, presidents may on some occasions give SNGs greater latitude to reduce their financial commitments, while preventing any expan-sion in financial obligations. In capital markets, this could take the form of a legal no-bailout clause or other credible commitment not to bail out SNGs, as these constrain SNG behavior. Similarly, in labor markets, presidents may give SNGs greater power to fire civil servants, because this will reduce rigidities in subnational contracts that may (depending upon the polity) place undue fiscal pressure on the center.

On issues of contractual autonomy, presidents frequently exercise their power in a relatively less institutionalized arena, engaging in open negotiations with subnational elected executives; this enhances volatility in outcomes. Subnational financial contracts may directly implicate the finances of the central government, and this necessitates central government interactions with juridically independent subnational decision makers, but the institu-tions governing these inter-executive negotiations are less established than the legislatures and states with which presidents interact to shape revenue

---

7. Other preferences remain the same as in chapters 4 and 5. National parliamentarians' preferences will depend upon whether the structure of representation means legislators represent subnational interests or national party interests. State bureaucracies—especially ministries of finance—will usually side with the president in fiscal matters.

autonomy and expenditure autonomy, respectively.[8] Correspondingly, the outcomes of these negotiations are highly variable, though governmental decline and the resolution of economic crisis remain reliable predictors.

Contractual autonomy increased in both Brazil and South Africa at moments of central government decline. Both shifted from unitary states to more federal systems with the transitions to democracy in the 1980s and 1990s, and the Constituent National Assemblies of 1987–88 and 1994–96, respectively. These constitutional assemblies gave *estado*/provincial and municipal governments guarantees of autonomy.[9] Though the jurisdictional independence of Brazil's SNGs is secure, reversals of contractual autonomy were also significant. Brazil's SNGs saw their autonomy reduced from 1994 to 2002 after the Real Plan ended the hyperinflationary crisis. In a more limited fashion, South Africa's ANC seized on small provincial crises to assert authority over provincial premiers and impose central government restrictions on borrowing.

The institutional arena of contestation matters, as the party system contributed in a particular way to recentralization in this area of autonomy: the low autonomy in this area in the South African case is because the ANC's intraparty negotiations strongly favor the president relative to subnational politicians. Only by incorporating an understanding of the arenas can we explain why the center in South Africa was able to recentralize actively in this issue area, while it could merely "hold" power in other areas. Even more than the tight earmarking of expenditures detailed in the previous chapter, the lack of contractual authority for South Africa's provinces is the clearest indication that these SNGs are not truly autonomous political bodies. Centralized wage bargaining and centrally imposed "gentlemen's agreements" limited provincial freedom to borrow, and together constitute crucial constraints on subnational action. Also, the central government can and does intervene directly in affairs of provincial jurisdiction, as happened on a handful of occasions in the late 1990s. While the transition from apartheid

8. Of course, executive–legislative relations and central state institutions—which took center stage in chapters 3 and 4, respectively—continue to matter here, because laws transforming contractual autonomy are ultimately passed through either the legislature or through administrative and regulatory channels. Subnational elected officials are the principal—but not the only—interlocutors for presidents in the area of contractual autonomy. Yet legislatures and the national executive branch play a lesser role here, and direct negotiations between national and subnational executives are central. Strong presidential powers within the executive and vis-à-vis the parliament will favor the center, though patterns of behavior are less standardized.

9. The Constituent Assemblies in both countries enshrined the rights of municipalities in the national constitution—a rare victory for local governments that was nearly unique in the world in 1988.

resulted in increases in the contractual autonomy of the provinces and municipalities, the central government in South Africa since apartheid has used
provincial financial difficulties as a pretext for broad reductions in subnational autonomy. The indicators of low autonomy are the provinces' low degrees
of control over capital, labor, and the central government's ability to cross
jurisdictional boundaries and arrogate provincial powers to itself.

Legal Autonomy (and the Federalism Question Revisited)

Federalism clearly implies meaningful jurisdictional autonomy for SNGs and
some freedom for SNGs to establish their own contracts. Indeed, federalism
itself has been viewed by Riker (1964) and followers as an intergovernmental
contract that emerges from a process of "coming together"; this makes SNGs
the *objects* of a certain contractual autonomy. While recognizing that not all
federations emerge as the result of a Rikerian bargain, Rodden (2006, 32)
notes that federalism implies a set of "contractual relations between central
and subnational governments." In following this process-oriented definition,
I intend to examine contractual autonomy in two senses: it implies the existence of a contract between levels of government, and it implies that SNGs
have some ability to form their own contracts in private markets. Under
federalism, then, SNGs also become the *subjects* of contractual autonomy,
able to establish their own contracts semiautonomously from the center in
ways SNGs cannot in more unitary states.

In adjudicating among various possible definitions of federalism, the
question of institutional arrangements also emerges. Wibbels (2005), for
instance, argues that federal systems are those in which SNGs are represented
at the national level in the legislature and have their own elected legislatures. A related institutional arrangement of significance is constitutional
guarantees for SNGs, which constitute the most obvious elaboration of an
intergovernmental contract. Such contracts are evident in both the Brazilian
and South African constitutions, with both ensuring SNGs considerable legal
autonomy, but the processes giving rise to these charters differed. The more
bottom-up process of democratic transition in Brazil clearly provided greater
bargaining power to SNGs, while the more top-down process in South Africa
created additional provinces and endowed them with increased powers. We
would expect the more robust federal system in Brazil to have higher overall
levels of legal autonomy than South African SNGs.

Jurisdictional Autonomy in Brazil

The decentralization of contractual autonomy in Brazil, especially in the wake of the 1964–85 military government's efforts at centralization, was dramatic. Brazil's 1988 constitution afforded unique protections to both states and municipalities, and the central government has not sought to reverse the fundamental gains of 1988. Most federal constitutions specify certain exclusive powers that are the domain of the central (federal) government, while reserving any unspecified powers to the constituent members of the federation—the states or provinces. In Brazil, the federal constitution reserved considerable powers for the states (including revenue guarantees), but also stated that the localities (*municípios*) are constituent members of the federation. The central government has relatively weak constitutional prerogatives. The Constituent Assembly, which was heavily influenced by local elites, buttressed the jurisdictional independence of the *estados* and the *municípios* by creating electoral rules that give legislators strong incentives to cultivate local followings, and designed the Senate to represent the *estados* and the Chamber of Deputies to have strong links to localities (Samuels and Abrucio 2000; Souza 1997).

Indeed, there is even substantial evidence of the power of Brazilian *municípios.* Indicative of the politically "bottom-up" nature of Brazil's federation is the possibility of "seceding" from a municipality. Cities in the 1990s had extraordinary liberty to alter their own formal structures, including subdividing existing local governments and reconstituting them as new municipalities. With relative ease, subdivisions of existing municipalities could vote to form their own local government. Especially in poorer rural areas, incentives to subdivide were strong because federal grants to municipalities are generous. Accordingly, municipalities—especially small, rural ones—proliferated in Brazil, with approximately 1,500 municipalities created after democratization, an increase of nearly 50 percent. From 1984 to 2000, the number of municipalities in Brazil increased from just over 3,000 to 5,507.[10] For the most part, these municipalities had small tax bases and required massive subsidization from the central government, through the Municipal Participation Fund (Maia Gomes and MacDowell 2000). Only later did the central government under Cardoso reduce the incentives for municipal proliferation by better earmarking revenue transfers. That is, the right of localities to secede was constrained not through legal limitations, but through changes examined

10. Maia Gomes and MacDowell (2000) place the number of municipalities in Brazil in 2000 at 5,507, while Rodden (2003) places the figure at 5,559.

Table 5.2 Creation of municipalities in Brazil, by population size (1984–1997)

Population size	< 5,000	5,000–10,000	10,000–20,000	20,000–50,000–	50,000–100,000	100,000–500,000	Total
# new *municípios*	735	360	234	61	11	4	1,405

source: Maia Gomes and MacDowell (2000, 11).

in the two previous chapters. This maneuvering on the part of the federal government further demonstrates the inter-connectedness of the three issue areas of fiscal autonomy.

Jurisdictional Autonomy in South Africa

South Africa's provinces and municipalities received ample consideration in the writing of the 1994 and 1996 constitutions, though their ability to resist central government intrusion has been quite limited in practice. The transition from apartheid and the constitution of 1996 greatly strengthened the provinces and South Africa's black townships and former homelands. The Constitutional Assembly agreed to the creation of nine provinces, up from the original four. More subtly, the municipalities were explicitly "elevated" to become a constitutionally protected level of government. The 1996 constitution and the Constitutional Assembly went to great lengths to stress the interdependence of the different governments and even rejected the notion that government was arranged hierarchically in layers or tiers, instead preferring to enshrine a principle of "cooperative government" between three "spheres" of government that are "interdependent and inter-related" (Atkinson and Reitzes 1998; Levy and Tapscott 2001, 1, 4). The provinces were assigned a substantial number of responsibilities, as detailed in the previous chapters, and retained many residual powers (Murray 2001, 69–70). South Africa's localities, meanwhile, were thus not the legal creations of the provinces, and this reduces the power of the provinces to interfere in local affairs (cf. Ahmad 2003, 348; Levy and Tapscott 2001).

Despite the great effort to ensure cooperation among the three "spheres" of government, section 100 of the constitution gave the central government clear priority over the provinces and cities. Increasingly, observers recognize that South Africa does not rest firmly on federal principles, but on a more traditional hierarchical system of government in which the "higher" level can intervene in the affairs of the "lower" level with relative impunity. This important constitutional provision empowers the central government to step into provincial affairs in the event of mismanagement.

Top-down politics allowed the ANC central leadership to adopt a set of measures that reconfigured SNG according to the center's interests, even prior to crisis. First, the central government initiated a process of re-demarcating the boundaries of South Africa's local governments (Cameron 1997); this created larger units that are more likely to "go ANC." In contrast to Brazil, where subnational power and perverse incentives led to a dramatic increase in the number of municipalities throughout the 1990s, South Africa's re-demarcation process reduced the number of localities there from more than eight hundred to fewer than three hundred. Members of the demarcation boards were drawn from all levels of government; nonetheless, the predominance of ANC members at the national and local levels, combined with strong discipline within the party and a variety of powers conferred to national ministries and review boards, made for a situation that greatly favored the interests of the center, while inevitably sacking some local-level ANC officials.[11]

Second, the center has established precedents that strengthen its right to intervene in subnational affairs in circumstances where SNGs do not perform up to standard; this enabled the president to exert greater authority over subnational officials. The center is empowered (by section 100 of the constitution) to take extraordinary measures to intervene in provinces under certain circumstances, as happened in the late 1990s with provincial overspending and mismanagement. Disputes over finances in several provinces constituted a set of localized crises that provided the president with an opportunity to constrict borrowing power (to be discussed in the next section), while mismanagement in service provisions gave an opportunity to impose new personnel and standards in low-performing sectors such as the Eastern Cape's education department.

Most governmental responsibilities in South Africa are concurrent between the center and the provinces, and national legislation dominates in these matters. Moreover, "[e]ven in matters of 'exclusive' provincial responsibility, the national government may intervene and pass legislation that gives it a certain degree of control" (Murray 2001, 69–70).[12] Similarly, the provinces have legal backing of section 139 of the constitution, which allows them to step in and intervene in municipalities as necessary (Murray 2001, 71). These sections 100 and 139 of the constitution in effect trump the rhetorical emphasis

11. Cameron (1997, 10–11) notes that the Minister for Provincial Affairs and Constitutional Development (later broken up into the Ministry of Provincial and Local Government and the Ministry of Justice and Constitutional Development) held increasing powers in these matters. Unresolved matters were referred to the national demarcation board, which had the final say.

12. Murray goes on to dispute the notion that the center will necessarily dominate indefinitely, noting that the courts may have some role in supporting provincial interests.

given to intergovernmental cooperation and establish a cascading system of hierarchical rights in South Africa.

The greatest weapon of Thabo Mbeki as an ANC president, however, was his power as party leader to view provincial ANC officials as direct subordinates. This feature of South Africa shows the importance of a historically informed approach that elaborates on the different arenas of deliberation. Historically, the strong centralization of partisan powers in the ANC emerged from South Africa's apartheid era and the ANC's militarized response to the regime, as suggested in chapter 2. In South Africa, this historical fact of the president's dominance of the ANC, combined with the ANC's dominant party status after democratization, reduced the "game" between national and subnational actors to an intraparty negotiation. In 1997, as president-elect of the ANC, Mbeki demanded of his party the right to nominate premiers, the executives at the provincial level. This right was coupled with section 100, which held that the president could appoint an administrator in cases of provincial mismanagement, to give Mbeki virtual control over the appointment and dismissal of premiers. He soon extended this direct control not only over premiers, but also over the hiring and firing of specific provincial ministers (Members of the Executive Council, or MECs).[13] With this sort of authority over the ANC's elected officials in the provinces, the president can reward those loyal to the center and punish those who take contrary stands; this reinforces top-down governance in the country as a whole, with even ANC provincial veterans in powerful Gauteng province asserting that it would be foolish for any subnational official to contradict the president.[14] The legal autonomy conferred to provincial officials has less value in an atmosphere where a single dominant party controls provincial premiers from the national capital. In the inter-executive arena, an ahistorical approach could not inform us about why the center can hold power in South Africa; by contrast, attentiveness both to the country's history and to the particular arena of deliberation enables a fuller understanding of the reasons why certain elements of SNG autonomy are more restricted than others.

Capital Market (Borrowing) Autonomy

Financial decentralization, which corresponds to increases in contractual autonomy, resulted in the Borrowing Powers of Provinces Act in South Africa,

13. A subsequent incident was a debate over whether Mbeki instructed the premier of the Eastern Cape to dismiss three top officials.
14. Interview: Theo Bekker.

and the establishment of considerable borrowing power for each of Brazil's *estados*. In Brazil, autonomy took on a form that proved particularly destructive to the national economy: *estado*-owned banks with soft budget constraints that were empowered to loan to the *estados* themselves. While South Africa may be viewed as having established moderate borrowing autonomy, Brazil's states had an extreme version of this autonomy. But in both countries, capital market actions by SNG were later restricted after economic crises. The extent of recentralization was much higher in Brazil, in correspondence with the more expansive nature of the hyperinflationary economic crisis there.

Capital Market Autonomy in Brazil

In terms of borrowing, the years following the 1988 enactment of the constitution saw governors and state elites channel their political power through the Federal Congress to ensure themselves a virtual license to print money via subnational access to capital markets. A favorite maneuver by SNGs in the early 1990s was to "pass on up" (*jogar para cima*) subnational deficits for the central government to rectify, typically through the use of bailouts for *estado*-owned banks. *Estado*-owned banks throughout the country would provide soft loans to *estado* governments; when *estados* were unable to meet debt obligations, they would routinely request federal funds to keep the *estados* and their banks afloat, using the threat of risk to the national credit rating and/or the leverage of subnationally beholden federal legislators to demand executive action. Brazil's *estados* forced central government bailouts for their spending on several occasions (Rodden 2003, 229–31). As Rodden (2003, 225) notes, "owing largely to the politics of federalism, the Brazilian federal government has had weak or inadequate tools with which to curb the borrowing activities of the states." As one Ministry of Finance official noted, this turned a Brazilian saying on its head: "The traditional saying is 'I owe you, I don't deny it, and I'll pay you as soon as I can.' This became 'I owe you, I don't deny it, and I won't pay as long as I can avoid it.'"[15]

Institutional and legal changes after 1994 altered the situation. Following the Real Plan and the establishment of the aforementioned Social Emergency Fund (FSE), the federal government began to chip away at the subnational roots of economic instability. Specifically, the central government entered directly into negotiations with individual *estados*. The Cardoso government

---

15. Interview: Jorge Kahlil. The Portuguese expressions: "Devo, não nego, e pago quando puder" and "Devo, não nego, e não pago enquanto puder."

agreed to a one-off assumption of state and municipal debts in return for the liquidation or privatization of banks owned by the states (Fleischer 1998, 132). This bargain was a crucial piece in a slowly assembled answer to fiscal instability. The assumption of debt was costly, but the exchange was ultimately favorable for the center, as it removed a primary institutional source of soft budget constraints. The first major success came with the cleaning up of the state bank of the large (and famously clientelistic) northeastern state of Bahia (Mainwaring 1997a, 104). By 1999 Cardoso's administration had successfully negotiated the closure of twenty-four banks, which removed the ability to "print money" from nearly all of Brazil's states (cf. Dillinger and Webb 2001).

Whereas the intergovernmental arena long favored SNGs, Cardoso's success with economic reforms turned the tables and allowed the president to use the centralized authorities such as the Central Bank and the Ministry of Finance to demand fiscal reform from individual states (Montero 2004, 144–45). As witnessed with respect to spending autonomy, the condition of state finances also facilitated institutional change. Cardoso's macroeconomic management disciplined his coalition on matters of fiscal federalism by making antireform votes untenable for influential subnational actors.[16] Also useful was broader public support; Yoshiaki Nakano, São Paulo state's reformist Minister of Finance at the time, noted that the string of moratoria in the 1990s led to a swing in public opinion against the municipalities and state governors, and in favor of the federal bureaucracy.[17]

Crucially for the link between crisis and recentralization, a second Brazilian crisis (of much smaller magnitude) served to consolidate the Cardoso reforms. In January 1999 Itamar Franco, former president (at the inception of the Real Plan), assumed the governorship of the powerful state of Minas Gerais and promptly declared a moratorium on the state's debt payments to Brasilia. In the wake of the 1997 East Asian financial crisis, this was widely interpreted in international circles as the last straw that forced the Brazilian government to devalue and eventually float the real, whose value collapsed by 40 percent. The central government covered the Minas Gerais debt to protect the national credit rating, but simply withheld an equivalent amount in federal transfers due to the state (Dillinger and Webb 1999, 33). From the perspective of the governors, this attempt by a powerful governor to procure a bailout backfired badly. Unlike earlier bailouts, the *estados* ultimately gained nothing but

16. Interview: Erika Amorim Araújo.
17. Interview: Yoshiaki Nakano.

instead gave an additional impetus to the passage of further laws restricting SNGs, this time in the form of the powerful Fiscal Responsibility Law (LRF). As with the crisis of the early 1990s, Cardoso crafted an institutional response to address the risk; while the hyperinflationary nature of the earlier crisis made for more dramatic changes in the form of the Real Plan, the passage of the LRF after 1999 showed how the center could consolidate its hold on the fiscal system.

Brazil's Fiscal Responsibility Law of 2000 included provisions limiting the capital market flexibility of the *estados*. Alongside statutory limitations on payroll expenditures and budgets (and punishments for SNG executives who do not abide by these rules), the LRF gives the federal government the right to strike down as invalid any *estado* debt obligations that push the total debt beyond a percentage of the *estado*'s revenues; the specific percentage was to be set by the president. The LRF also forbade the central government to bail out other levels of government, and specified that the central bank is not authorized to swap subnational debt for federal debt (Rodden 2003, 239).[18] It further affirmed that the central government could simply deduct the *estado* debt obligations from transfers to the states when *estados* failed to repay. This principle, established in the lead-up to the passage of the LRF, altered the calculus of SNGs in considering state debt defaults.

The 1999 flotation of the real thus provided a confirmatory echo on the link between crisis resolution and recentralization, which was originally seen in 1994. In Montero's (2004) formulation, a key in the intergovernmental arena is whether SNGs can act collectively to either enforce their policy preferences or veto reforms that reduce subnational autonomy. Before the Real Plan, subnational executives were capable of coordinating against the fiscal interests of the center, and national executives were incapable of sanctioning SNGs, creating an "all-on-one" dynamic. The Real Plan both strengthened presidential powers to sanction SNGs and reduced the abilities of SNGs to coordinate, by exposing subnational finances and facilitating an increased role for the Central Bank and Ministry of Finance in intergovernmental relations. The response to the crisis of 1999 highlighted two new facts: states such as Minas Gerais now acted on a "one-on-one" basis against the center (rather than in coordination with other states); and the central government now had the ability to sanction individual states (cf. Montero 2004, 153–57). The result was not only that Brasília "broke even" with Minas Gerais, but

---

18. As Rodden (2003) and Samuels (2003) note, this provision is among the least convincing provisions, as politics are likely to determine future proclivities for bailouts.

rather that the state's fiscal profligacy gave impetus to further recentralization in the form of the LRF; as a Senate budget expert noted, the inability of the subnational–congressional nexus to hold created an opportunity in which support for the LRF from the entrepreneurial and middle classes (along with implicit support from the dominant Globo media conglomerate) could prevail.[19]

By hardening budget constraints, Cardoso's reforms reduced SNG autonomy considerably from the extreme levels present before 1994 (Rodden 2003). The success of the Real Plan altered the calculations of the actors in intergovernmental bargaining: legislators, SNG officials, and the executive. The end of inflation exposed *estado* finances, making them vulnerable to efforts by the center to regain control. In addition, the political calculus after the Real Plan was decidedly progovernment. Coalition partners continued to expect patronage, but politicians increasingly saw benefits from supporting fiscal responsibility.[20] The *estados* and *municípios* still contract debt, but only under certain specified limits, and without the expectation of bailouts.

The LRF and related reforms—particularly the elimination of the *estado* banks and the increased requirements in financial reporting—constitute a sequenced set of centralizing reforms. Equally important is the staying power of the reforms. Some argue that the Cardoso reforms are temporary, and that Brazil's political culture will ultimately dictate a return to bailouts (cf., e.g., Rodden 2003; Samuels 2003). Currently, however, the LRF eliminates states' access to extra-constitutional revenue sources (especially the soft loans from state banks) and represents a federal commitment to replace bailouts for SNGs with deductions from transfers. Without a strong party system to facilitate change, Cardoso leveraged his crisis resolution opportunity and operated in direct negotiations with subnational officials and with his broad congressional coalition to reduce *estado* borrowing power. With regard to staying power, the reform sequence pushed even Brazil's famously parochial legislators in the direction of supporting more programmatic and policy-based agendas, as noted in previous chapters, rather than relying on patronage resources (which have declined) as the basis for electoral campaigns.[21]

Capital Market Autonomy in South Africa

Contractual autonomy for SNGs also decreased over time in South Africa's capital markets, as the ANC national government progressively constricted

---

19. Interview: Robison Gonçalves de Castro.
20. Interview: Erika Amorim Araújo.
21. Interview: Erika Amorim Araújo. See also Hagopian, Gervasoni, and Moraes 2009.

SNG borrowing powers. Initially, in 1996, provinces gained the right to issue debt within the bounds set by the Minister of Finance (later National Treasury), in the Borrowing Powers of Provincial Governments Act.[22] The intention of the NP and its allies at the establishment of provinces was clearly to have strong entities capable of independent policy-making and endowed with generous revenue sources and fiscal independence, to include borrowing capacity. This act conferred upon provinces the right to contract debt, including in international markets. According to the Borrowing Powers Act, the minister had the right to set debt limits for each province, but would not guarantee provincial loans.

By the time the Borrowing Powers Act was passed, however, the ANC had consolidated its political position at the center and was represented in government in seven of the nine provinces. As provinces began overspending their budgets in 1996–97, the ANC central government moved swiftly to curb SNG indebtedness (see Wehner 2000b, 71, table 13). The Ministry of Finance secured a so-called "gentlemen's agreement" or "policy understanding" with the provinces at a budget council meeting in early January 1997 (Ahmad 2003, 331; Van Zyl 1998, 32; Wehner 2000b, 70). The provinces, which were relatively flush with funds for capital expenditure, acceded to the demands of the center not to borrow. According to Ahmad (2003, 331), the failure to secure such an agreement would have represented a moral hazard for the center: if the provinces have very few own-source revenues from taxation, then provincial autonomy in borrowing would be perceived as an implicit bailout guarantee from the center. The center's reaction was deemed a necessity, as one interviewee noted: "The executive decisions came right at the top. Mbeki and his guys decided early on that they would play by the rules of financial markets. And it took political strength to do that. It might have lost them some support, but it was much better to do the restructuring on [South Africa's] terms than to face an IMF structural adjustment down the line."[23] The "gentlemen's agreement" proved successful from the center's perspective.[24] The provinces, having foregone their borrowing privileges, resorted to a variety of short-term measures to support their deficits, including costly bank overdrafts, delayed payments to creditors, and withholding raises and pension contributions (Wehner 2000b, 70). The Ministry of

22. The text of the Borrowing Powers of Provincial Governments Act is available at http://www.info.gov.za/gazette/acts/1996/a48-96.htm (accessed July 29, 2010).

23. Interview: Martin Wittenberg.

24. Some might consider the so-called "gentlemen's agreement" a "gentleman's agreement," emphasizing that Thabo Mbeki pushed most for such an arrangement.

Finance threatened to crack down on these activities as well (Van Zyl 1998, 33), and the provinces soon brought spending into line with their budgeted revenues.

The center leveraged provincial deficits to delimit privileges, under section 100 of the constitution, which empowers the center to intervene in provinces under certain circumstances. (As noted previously, this happened in four provinces between 1997 and 1999.) The center took such a hard line that provinces were underspending their budgets by 1999, thereby obviating the need to borrow. Additionally, as one observer noted, the provinces have little incentive to seek out debt on their own; even if revenues were short, the provinces would prefer to coordinate borrowing through the central government, which can secure better rates in capital markets due to its better creditworthiness.[25]

The "gentlemen's agreement" held for several reasons. Along with the political power of the president, one factor is that provinces were flush with funds for capital expenditure. Apart from borrowing for capital projects, the constitution states that provinces may borrow only for very short-term "bridging" expenditures designed to carry over from one fiscal year to another, and not for current and recurring expenditures. For capital investment loans, provinces must in effect establish that a capital need has gone unmet, such as a shortage of schools or hospitals, lest they be subject to central government intervention in their fiscal affairs. Under the center's stringent expenditure guidance, the question of borrowing thus became moot.

During the brief period of provincial overspending in South Africa, the center drafted the Public Finance Management Act (PFMA) and passed it in 1999. While less dramatic than Brazil's LRF in reducing borrowing autonomy, the PFMA illustrates an overarching finding from the South African case: central governments are capable of holding power even after seemingly dynamic decentralization processes, and even without substantial recentrali-zation. The PFMA aimed to improve expenditure management by requiring provincial governments to submit periodic reports to the center, and estab-lished the National Treasury as the body ultimately responsible for all revenues and expenditures. (The PFMA was later complemented by a partner bill, the Municipal Finance Management Act of 2003, which aimed to modernize budgeting practices at the local level.) Among other stipulations about the management of expenditures, the PFMA stated that provinces were not permitted to contract debt in foreign currency, and that any access to foreign capital markets would be subject to central government approval, though

25. Interview: Hildegaard Fast.

the central government still could not provide guarantees on these loans. This limited SNGs to domestic capital markets. Moreover, SNGs faced a strict no-bailout clause rooted in the constitution and the PFMA. The PFMA was seen by many in the public finance community as a long-awaited statutory codification of the 1997 "gentlemen's agreement" that controlled borrowing, and as a necessary credible commitment not to bail out "profligate" provinces.[26] As late as 2005, the center held a dim view of provincial borrowing, noting that provinces have limited tax authority and little need to borrow. In a presentation, the National Treasury noted that "we are open to giving more tax and borrowing powers in the future, but need to ensure expenditure efficiency first."[27]

Labor Market (Wage) Autonomy

The freedom of SNGs to establish their own contracts is not limited to capital markets, but also extends to human resources contracts: SNGs with hiring and firing (or retrenchment) power are more autonomous than SNGs without such authority. This is especially relevant in South Africa, where central government control over the labor decisions of SNGs places a substantial restriction on their autonomy. It is the inability to contract independently of the center that makes South Africa's provinces weak; this clearly builds on the findings of the previous chapter, wherein the provinces had little autonomy over their expenditures. In Brazil, very high levels of SNG labor market autonomy further complicated macroeconomic governance, and reductions in this autonomy proved an important piece of resolving the fiscal-federal crisis there.

Labor Market Autonomy in Brazil

From 1988 until the Cardoso administration, Brazil's *estado* and municipal governments had "extreme" levels of autonomy in labor markets: the SNGs could hire while the central government would guarantee the positions and privileges of subnational civil servants. Cardoso succeeded in reducing the labor market autonomy of the SNGs only toward the end of his term. The situation even through much of Cardoso's administration presented a dilemma

26. Interviews: Tania Ajam, Iraj Abedian.
27. See "Fiscal Responsibility in South Africa," available at http://siteresources.worldbank.org /PSGLP/Resources/SouthAfrica.pdf (accessed August 25, 2010.)

to the federal government: the federal constitution "defines the rights of public sector employees at all three levels of government. Governments could neither dismiss redundant civil servants nor reduce salaries in nominal terms. Public employees were granted the right to retire after only 35 years of employment (fewer for women and teachers) and with a pension equal to their exit salary" (Haggard and Webb 2004, 256). The 1988 constitution established a full-salary pension program for all civil servants, and the rules extended to subnational civil servants, as the constitution unified public employment under a "single juridical regime" that covered all public sector labor relations (Mora and Varsano 2001, 17). This constituted a long-term fiscal liability for all levels of government, as it essentially subsidized subnational patronage networks.

However, the Brazilian central government later reduced labor market autonomy by giving SNGs additional responsibilities with regard to cutting wages and salaries (Falleti 2005, 336). In response to the deficits brought on largely by *estado*-level patronage spending, the center transferred responsibility for firing subnational civil servants. In education, for instance, this included the responsibility to hire and fire teachers, as well as the determination of wages (Falleti 2005, 334). Requiring greater labor market responsibility from the *estados* and *municípios* was a crucial piece of a central government program to return the country to fiscal balance and reduce the overall power of the SNGs. Clearly, this closes the circle on subnational autonomy in the area of education. While the FUNDEF provisions, highlighted in chapter 4, required a fixed percentage of expenditures be spent on basic education, this transfer of labor market authority required SNGs to balance their spending.

To be clear: the interpretation in this instance is that contractual autonomy *decreased,* rather than increased when SNGs took on a new authority, for reasons shown in table 5.1. Under the previous public sector labor market regime, the Brazilian central government essentially guaranteed generous terms of civil service employment while leaving hiring decisions to the *estados.* After the change, the costs of subnational hiring have been increasingly internalized by SNGs. The analogy to capital markets is that Brazil's central government "hardened the budget constraint" in the area of subnational hiring. The center's decision to subnationalize hiring and firing constituted a reduction in SNG ability to spend with impunity. This is a move from "extreme autonomy" for SNGs to merely high or medium autonomy. Brazil's states can no longer play a patronage game in which the central government picks up the tab for subnational contracts. In cross-national perspective, Brazil remains decentralized on this measure, since SNGs contract their own labor; it is the reduction in autonomy over time that is noteworthy.

Labor Market Autonomy in South Africa

Centralized wage bargaining is arguably the institution upon which all SNG autonomy hinges in South Africa. In contrast to Brazil, South Africa shows that the center's appropriation of the right to hire and fire can constitute a reduction in autonomy relative to the alternative. The central government negotiates nearly all public wages—including the wages of provincial employees. This fact underpins the argument in the previous chapter that provinces have very little control over their expenditures. Personnel costs, which regularly account for over half of provincial spending, are essentially dictated by the central government. Collective bargaining negotiations between very robust unions and the national ANC leadership set public sector wages. The most important of these unions, federated under the Congress of South African Trade Unions (COSATU), include the National Education, Health and Applied Workers Union (NEHAWU), the South African Democratic Teachers Union (SADTU), and the South African Municipal Workers Union (SAMWU), which together account for approximately five hundred thousand public sector workers.[28]

Approximately 60 percent of provincial budgets, on aggregate, go to wages, salaries, and benefits for labor. Ahmad (2003, 336) notes that annual wage and salary increases represent provincial obligations over which the provinces have no vote; in fact, due to the centralized nature of the bargaining, the provinces are sometimes even left unaware that certain increases or personnel obligations have been mandated. In short, centralized wage bargaining "in effect locks in the expenditure commitments of the 'unconditional' grants provided by the center. In fact, approximately 80 percent of the funds in health, education, and welfare is already spoken for in terms of personnel costs even before reaching the provinces" (Ahmad 2003, 335). Teacher's salaries constitute about 85 percent of provincial education spending.[29]

28. According to the respective organizations, in and around 2009, the NEHAWU represented more than 200,000 members, SADTU more than 240,000, and SAMWU about 136,000 (see http://www.nehawu.org.za/about/index.asp, http://www.sadtu.org.za/, http://www.cosatu.org.za/show.php?include=docs/cosatu2day/2009/pr1217a.html; accessed September 1, 2010).

29. Interview: Helen Zille. Similarly, social security transfers—also determined by center, but at one time administered by the provinces—represented 88 percent of payments in the welfare sector (Van Zyl 1998, 32). As noted previously, South Africa now tallies social security payments as central government expenditures in national accounts.

At the time of transition to democracy, the principal political parties (the NP, the ANC, and the IFP) reached an agreement to incorporate the bureaucracies of the former black homelands inherited from apartheid; this fixed the number of permanent public servants (Lodge 1999, 15–16). The prevailing rights of bureaucracies in former homelands and preexisting white localities made the dismissal of state employees exceedingly difficult.[30] Simultaneously, the center developed standards for provinces in terms of inputs, mandating a minimum number of personnel, via pupil–teacher ratios for instance. These numbers of personnel and input standards are combined with centrally determined wage rates to virtually fix a total wage bill for the provinces. Since South Africa's unions bargain directly with the central government, and since hiring and firing are essentially controlled from Pretoria, the provinces have minimal discretion over the vast majority of their budgets. Centralized bargaining dates back to apartheid, when provinces did not control their personnel, but the pattern has been reinforced by the ANC.

Provincial governments have responsibility for a wide range of public services and would be quite autonomous in their spending, were they free to hire, fire, and reshape their work forces, yet South Africa's central government has routinely claimed the right to intervene in provincial administration, and not only in the cases of provincial crisis mentioned above. The central government can summarily dismiss teachers and other public servants, for example, though this usually requires some justification.[31] Provinces, on the other hand, are essentially unable to fire or retrench their employees, apart from egregious instances of abuse (and even in some of these cases): the dismissal or firing will often come from the relevant central government ministry.

In keeping with the prevailing claims about recentralization, this low autonomy in the labor market has existed since the transition from apartheid, but it should be noted that local crises did stimulate reductions in autonomy. The intervention on the part of the national government is usually contingent on disastrous performance, as has been the case in the Eastern Cape and the Northern Province especially.[32] Provinces, not the central government, generally continue to administer staff on a daily basis; the center only steps in and provinces are "forced to cut spending" where local crises of overspending occur (Naidoo and Pintusewitz 1998, 37). Even in the context of strong national control over expenditures and personnel, local mismanagement

30. Interview: Chris Tapscott.
31. Interviews: Helen Zille, Duncan Hindle.
32. Interviews: Russell Wildeman, Duncan Hindle, Charles Simkins.

is uniquely capable of justifying substantial central government intervention; absent a systemic crisis, the center cannot make sweeping changes in the provincial personnel it controls.

Comparative Lessons

The major shifts in contractual autonomy in Brazil and South Africa in recent years have included the elimination of the state banks and the passage of the LRF in Brazil and the exercise of presidential authority over borrowing, provincial leadership, and certain provincial jurisdictional issues in South Africa. Most major shifts since democratization have moved in the direction of central control, and some of the most aggressive moves have come in this issue area. Presidents have had relative success in reversing contractual autonomy. In Brazil and South Africa, the initial enhancement of contractual autonomy took place in the context of a Constituent National Assembly. Reductions in contractual autonomy, on the other hand, once again came with the resolution of economic crisis, and the scope of the reduction in subnational autonomy reflects the scope of crisis: in South Africa, the center's ability to remove contractual authority from a province is legally contingent on economic mismanagement in that province. Again, in Brazil, reductions in contractual autonomy occurred as a result of Cardoso's resolution of the hyperinflationary crisis. In Brazil, the Real Plan was only the first step in an arduous and methodical process of limiting subnational autonomy across the board.

In South Africa, the central government has had some success in recentralizing in this arena, where localized crises translated directly and powerfully into bargaining leverage relative to subnational politicians. Moreover, it is important to note that presidents with strong party powers relative to SNG politicians have greater leverage in this institutional arena than elsewhere, since the negotiations with SNG politicians are the most direct in the area of contractual autonomy. This certainly holds in South Africa under the ANC: reductions in SNG contractual autonomy in South Africa have often been intraparty affairs. The central government did step in and assume responsibility for provincial issues in the wake of a localized crisis on a handful of occasions, but the biggest changes in South Africa took place largely in intraparty negotiations, with the "gentlemen's agreement" reducing borrowing autonomy and the assertion of presidential control over the premiers representing an assault on the provinces as independently elected bodies.

A final note concerns the center's role in granting states/provinces/regions greater "freedom to fail," and whether we should view this as an increase or a decrease in subnational autonomy. South Africa and Brazil (until recently) both had centralized control over wage bargaining, but the effect was quite different, and for a very simple reason. In South Africa, the central government in effect sets the wage rate *and* the number of provincial employees, just as we will see the unitary cases of Peru and Senegal did with respect to their regions in the next chapter. In Brazil, the central government sets wages and salary guarantees for laborers, but SNGs essentially set the number of employees. This created a massive moral hazard in Brazil, with the *estados* having no incentive to restrain hiring in the context of central government bailouts. In the context of the Fiscal Responsibility Law, however, the *estados* now have strong incentives to trim hiring, plus the legal prerogative to reduce staff; this guts the subnational patronage networks that had prevailed before the Cardoso era. In Brazil, then, the decision to decentralize the right to fire employees did not represent an increase in subnational autonomy, but instead took SNGs from an extremely high level of labor market autonomy to a more intermediate level.

In both cases, strong presidential leverage relative to subnational politicians was the key to reductions in contractual autonomy. This power was some-times mediated through political parties (South Africa), and was sometimes exercised in relatively direct negotiations without partisan influence playing a major role (Brazil). Subnational politician strength is a result of a national-level party leadership in decline, and SNG weakness is directly attributable to some level of economic crisis, be it systemic or localized. Even where presidents have weak partisan powers (Brazil), they can centralize when they have the exceptional leverage provided by crisis; even where presidents have stronger partisan powers, they can only centralize in a limited fashion in response to limited crises (South Africa). More than partisan powers, crisis provides the most analytical leverage on these outcomes.

In conclusion, the question of contractual autonomy further shows that political-economic change triggers changes in SNG autonomy, but these changes are propagated by negotiations between differing sets of actors and are mediated through various institutional environments. By definition, the legis-lature and the state continue to have important roles in the ultimate passage and administration of legislation about contracts; but, more importantly, decisions about contractual autonomy often result from direct negotiations between executives at the different levels of government, as with the elimina-tion of state banks and provincial borrowing in Brazil and South Africa.

The numerous changes in contractual autonomy reflect the unstable nature of interactions in this particular institutional arena. Being largely a function of direct negotiations among executives at different levels of government, contractual autonomy is not heavily mediated through established (and relatively predictable) institutional channels such as legislatures and states. It is therefore prone to volatility, especially at the early stages of democratic consolidation when debates over the extent of federalism are still far from settled. Still, the success of presidents and governors (or provincial premiers) has as a predictable factor the waxing and waning of presidential power. As with the other areas of subnational autonomy, I have argued (contrasting South Africa's weak federalism with Brazil's more robust form) that this logic is not contingent on a particular form of federalism. In the next chapter, I build and extend this argument's generalizability by assessing variations in all three forms of subnational autonomy in two unitary states.

6

—⟨0∕0⟩—

SUBNATIONAL AUTONOMY IN UNITARY STATES

The literature on federalism is thriving. Recent contributions have high-lighted particular dynamics likely to emerge when SNGs are "semi-sovereign," have elected legislatures and territorial representation at the national level, or have constitutional guarantees (Rodden 2006; Wibbels 2005). While federalism merits the significant attention it is receiving from scholars, it is also possi-ble to overstate its significance by assuming—explicitly or implicitly—that federalism's formal institutions determine intergovernmental relations; in this, the incorporation of unitary states here reflects the preoccupation in Gibson (2004, 6–9), who notes that federalism has some independent causal power as an institutional arrangement, but that its effects are ambiguous and must be tested carefully rather than assumed.

Federal and unitary states echo common themes with regard to the causes of subnational autonomy, and extending the argument to unitary cases allows us to place federalism itself in comparative perspective and to ask how and when federalism matters.[1] Treating unitary cases independently provides a test of the argument's generalizability while enabling the differential treat-ment federal and unitary cases demand. The conclusions with regard to federalism's importance are ambiguous: federalism does shape the extent of decentralization, but federal cases also share many dynamics with unitary states where the political bases of SNGs are much weaker. Absent this explicit comparison, the convergence of literatures on decentralization and federalism runs the risk of squeezing out examination of unitary cases; an ironic twist, given that decentralization as a policy reform has recently been

---

1. Of course, several scholars have successfully treated both federalism and unitarism in a single context (cf. Diaz-Cayeros 2006; Eaton 2004a; Montero and Samuels 2004).

trumpeted as a corrective to centralized states. The unitary cases here—Peru and Senegal—also extend the analysis into lower-income countries in francophone Africa and the Andean region of Latin America, showing that the logic extends not only beyond federal states, but also beyond middle-income polities.

Top-down decentralization predominates in unitary states, with processes in both countries taking on electoralist characteristics. In Peru, the major attempt to decentralize was based on the calculations of a declining governing party that it would fare best at subnational levels, while in Senegal the governing party combined more uncertain electoral calculations with an effort to shore up its national legitimacy as electoral uncertainty increased, leading to a timid decentralization push. Recentralization occurred with the resolution of economic crises in Peru, while attempts at centralization faltered in the absence of economic crisis in Senegal.

The organization of the chapter echoes the development of the argument in the previous three chapters. I first explore the preliminary question of the legal (or jurisdictional) autonomy of SNGs. The bulk of the chapter comes in three subsequent sections in which I examine the three areas of autonomy—revenue autonomy, expenditure autonomy, and contractual autonomy—in succession. For each of these three sections, I offer subsections on the Peruvian and Senegalese cases. The chapter concludes with a set of comparative lessons.

Jurisdictional Autonomy in Unitary States

Some degree of legal independence for SNGs is a prerequisite for other forms of autonomy, and the mere existence of this jurisdictional autonomy is more contested (on an ongoing basis) in unitary states than in federal states. Whereas federal states typically have protections for SNGs written into national constitutions, unitary states offer much softer guarantees. In unitary states, SNGs are generally empowered by ordinary law, which is more easily reversed than constitutional provisions. In both Peru and Senegal, declining governments sought to create and empower regional governments. These decentralizations took place due to declines in party popularity under the Parti Socialiste (PS) in Senegal and under the Alianza Popular Revolucionária Americana (APRA) in Peru. Central governments that replaced these declining parties subsequently sought to weaken the legal authority of these newly created SNGs, or even disband them entirely, but a central government's ability to undercut SNGs was contingent upon the resolution of crisis.

Alberto Fujimori's success in eliminating Peru's regions depended on his successful reckoning with economic crisis in the 1990s, while Abdoulaye Wade's attempts to reconfigure Senegal's SNGs faltered in the face of public resistance.

Jurisdictional Autonomy in Peru

In Peru, the greatest changes in regional autonomy have taken place at the level of juridical recognition, with the fate of the regions vacillating dramatically since 1980. The constitution of 1979 ordered Peru's central government to establish regional governments but also required a National Regionalization Plan and a presidential order as enabling legislation.[2] Fernando Belaúnde Terry's (1980–85) Acción Popular government took little action with regard to the regions and only advanced as far as creating departmental development corporations in its five years in power (Schmidt 1989, 213–14). These organizations were seen as precursors to regions but remained delegated entities of the national government. In the initial years of his first presidential mandate, APRA president Alan García (1985–90) also showed little enthusiasm for giving the regions legal autonomy (Kim 1992, 251; Schmidt 1989, 215). When García first took action, it was not to establish the regions as intended in the constitution, but instead to transfer functions to a set of "microregions" that would also remain under presidential control as deconcentrated bodies of the central state (Kim 1992, 252).

APRA's dramatic decline at the national level changed the calculus, as shown by O'Neill (2005). Since APRA had a strong regional base and a weakening grip on national power, García's attitude toward regional government changed dramatically in the late 1980s. After a failed bank nationalization attempt and the collapse of the economy, García recognized that his APRA government was doomed to lose the 1990 presidential election but retain strong power bases at more local levels. García accordingly rushed through regional legislation in 1988 that established twelve regions, each with elected leadership. The regions became legally autonomous with elections held in 1990, but their independence would last for less than two years. The weakness of the national executive triggered the decentralization attempt,

2. Party politics at the time of Peru's CNA and thereafter offered the opposition little to stand on in facing a centralizing president. Unlike in Brazil and South Africa, Peru's CNA gave limited attention to regionalism and subnational groups. Democratization was led by elites, with strong presidentialism the outcome of the negotiations (Cameron 1997). Peru's proclivity for strong presidentialism enabled Fujimori to turn his strong position into a dictatorial regime with surprising ease. In this context, another Constituent Assembly called by Fujimori in 1993 to write a new constitution offered little to SNGs.

but the very crisis that was at the root of political decline also served as the basis for subsequent recentralization.

Alberto Fujimori's election to the presidency in 1990 came at the peak of the economic crisis, with hyperinflation running at over 7,500 percent. Fujimori's orthodox resolution of this crisis—the so-called "Fujishock"— paved the way for his wholesale elimination of subnational autonomy. The most significant change in subnational politics under Fujimori was the disbanding of the regions, which took place with the *autogolpe* of 1992. As part of a brazen attempt to centralize power, Fujimori replaced the elected regional governments with appointed administrations, the Consejos Transitórios de Administración Regional (CTARs). With this authoritarian overhaul, Fujimori placed considerable powers under the Ministry of the Presidency, which was assigned the task of coordinating the CTARs (Planas 1998, 569). By definition, these CTARs could have no real jurisdictional autonomy, as they were deconcentrated entities wholly under central control. Control over wages and capital remained entirely within the central government, and more particularly the ministries most linked to Fujimori himself.

Fujimori's unilateral decision to disband the regions contrasts with the negotiated changes in the Brazilian and South African recentralization processes, and it is an obvious indicator of one area in which federalism does matter, since it depended on the preponderance of presidential power relative to subnational elected officials. Fujimori consolidated this imbalance by replacing the bicameral legislature with a unicameral legislature with a single national district; this precluded allegiance to localities or regions on the part of the new legislators when a Fujimori-dominated Congress passed a new constitution in 1993. Local governments, meanwhile, retained some legal authority, but only over the small number of services they ran, including user fees for utilities, basic civil registries, and the management of public spaces and markets.

After the fall of Fujimori in 2000, it was in the area of legal autonomy that the decentralization and regionalization process under Alejandro Toledo (2001–6) advanced furthest. Upon assuming the presidency, Toledo announced a decentralization scheme to restore the regions, in an attempt to break with the Fujimori legacy and strengthen his party base. The Toledo government established a legal set of norms for decentralization, and the reinstallation of regions under Toledo restored the *sine qua non* factor for other forms of subnational autonomy.

Soon, however, Toledo's government suffered an embarrassing rout in regional elections at the hands of a resurgent APRA; this altered Toledo's incentives and calculations. Almost immediately after the opposition demonstrated its dominance in the regions, Toledo began backpedaling on decentralization promises, and he halted the decentralization process by withholding power in the areas of revenue and expenditure.[3] Regional governors, while elected, were left with a very unclear mandate, and even less budget capacity, and SNGs continue to be constrained in the capital and labor markets. Militating against greater devolution of fiscal power were the continued presence of entrenched bureaucratic interests, executive control over the commission responsible for decentralization, and the weakness of the president's party at the regional level, as discussed below. Yet without a successful economic program to reinforce his newfound centralizing tendency, Toledo was required to move ahead with some stated plans for decentralization. With little room to recentralize, attempts to limit subnational autonomy thus came in other areas, especially with regard to enforcing expenditures from the top, much as occurred previously in South Africa.

Jurisdictional Autonomy in Senegal

Senegalese regions and localities were on shaky legal ground in the 1990s, but decentralization created vested interests that are slowly improving their ability to resist central government encroachment. Jurisdictional independence in rural areas came later than for urban *communes* such as Dakar, as most of Senegal's territory was not incorporated into local governments until Léopold Sédar Senghor's PS passed a law creating rural *collectivités locales* in 1972. Regional governments were then established by the PS as its electoral hegemony faded in the early 1990s, with a Regionalization Law in 1992 and regional elections in 1996. Senegal's unitary structure provides for relatively little SNG autonomy at either the local or regional level. Regions have both an elected council and an arm of the state in the form of an administrative governor. The central state arm has the greater tasks in governance than the elected councils, since the governors coordinate various levels of bureaucracy and approve budgets, whereas councils have only minimal discretion over a small amount of funding.[4]

After Senegal's *alternance* of power with the defeat of the PS in 2000, the newly elected Abdoulaye Wade administration of the Parti Démocratique Sénégalais (PDS) moved to end lingering PS power by eliminating local

---

3. Interviews: Gabriel Ortiz de Zavallos, Felipe Reátegui.
4. Interview: Khalifa Guèye.

government autonomy. On November 11, 2001, a young PDS parliamentarian introduced a law that summarily dismissed all elected local councilors, citing the need to "shake up the system."[5] Wade's party replaced local councilors with appointed managers, including a large number of PDS copartisans.[6] Opposition politicians, particularly those removed from their mandates, cried foul, as did a consortium of the major international donors, who indefinitely suspended new aid inflows to local governments for decentralization projects; this represented a considerable loss considering that several donors supported local governance projects in Senegal to the tune of over $100 million in the early years of the Wade administration.[7] Wade thus allowed the election of new local officials to proceed, ending the crisis; aid disbursements resumed, with most representatives asserting this was a minor setback (*petit recul*), but ultimately an unsustainable move.[8]

Ominously for regional elected officials, the PDS government later floated a proposal to eliminate the eleven elected regional governments entirely, in favor of thirty-five elected provincial governments that would be "closer to the people."[9] The proposal was to reduce the regions to deconcentrated extensions of the center while electing officials to the smaller "provinces." Even those in favor of the change expressed uneasiness about Wade's provincialization initiative and wondered aloud about the intentions of the government. Such was the case with a former Ministry of Economy and Finance official, responsible for an internally commissioned study on Senegalese local finance: "The administration floated a proposal, a major *projet de texte,* claiming to promote decentralization. The goal was to replace the regions with a larger number of smaller departments. This would be a real decentralizing change, but it has since been put on ice [*au frigo*]. The question is, do you judge the administration on the text, or on the fact that they put it on ice? Their intentions are difficult to read."[10]

Ultimately, the Wade government withdrew the proposal. Senegal is thus a crucial "negative case," since the central government made attempts to reduce contractual autonomy, even in the absence of crisis, and failed. Wade's efforts in Senegal were transparent in their objectives, and their ultimate reversal

5. Interviews: Seynabou Ba, Christian Fournier. The law was held up by the Constitutional Court in December ("Rétrospective 2001," *Le Soleil,* January 7, 2002).

6. Of course, Wade's defenders insisted that the replacements were not partisan in nature, but this seems unlikely.

7. Interviews: Seynabou Ba, Christian Fournier, J. Guy LaRochelle.

8. Interview: Seynabou Ba.

9. Interview: Khalifa Guèye.

10. Interviews: Papa Ndiaye, Macoudou Guèye.

supports the argument that recentralization is conditioned on the resolution of significant national crises. The decision to suspend all local officials represented a unilateral move with obvious partisan implications, a bold maneuver to remove incumbent PS politicians in advance of an election. A lack of opposition in the cabinet and in the legislature gave Abdoulaye Wade exceptionally high within-coalition power as well as strong leverage relative to a legislature dominated by his coalition, making Wade's reversal all the more telling. Wade's initiatives to replace local officials with appointed partisans and to eliminate the regions were both truncated, even in a system with only weak partisan alternatives; the resistance from numerous public actors in the face of recentralization attempts proved decisive. This is stunning, from a purely institutional perspective, given Senegal's lack of constitutional protections for SNGs and its historical legacy of centralism. The failed attempts to centralize show that SNGs can successfully defend their autonomy even in comparatively centralized unitary states; the center's aims were countered and ended by adverse reactions domestically and internationally that supported existing decentralized structures. Recentralization was unsuccessful and most resisted where crisis conditions were absent. Even the progovernment *Le Soleil* newspaper ultimately touted Wade's move away from the unpopular initiatives, suggesting the end of the provincialization initiative proved Wade's lack of dogmatism in the face of public pressure.[11]

A similar interpretation applies to the Senegalese senate. This institution was abolished by the Wade administration under the new constitution in 2001, but it was later restored in 2007. The senate represents subnational governments and presents additional electoral opportunities for rank-and-file members of the governing party and coalition. The reestablishment of the senate is thus another instance where political decentralization to subnational governments created vested interests that counter recentralization efforts.

Revenue Autonomy

While both Brazil and South Africa decentralized revenues during constituent assemblies and transitions to democracy, this is not the only path to revenue decentralization. In the case of ordinary legislation, bargaining between different legislators and between the legislative and executive

---

11. Mamadou Sèye, "Editorial: La morale du dire," *Le Soleil* online, http://www.lesoleil.sn /article.php3?id_article=12714 (accessed July 29, 2010).

branches can lead to increased revenue autonomy when presidents weaken. This happened in both Peru and Senegal. Decentralization took place as a result of a decline in a governing party's popularity under the PS in Senegal and under the APRA in Peru. The 1979 Constituent National Assembly in Peru nominally increased revenue autonomy. Senegal did not have a Constituent Assembly in the period in question, having instead witnessed a long and slow transition to greater democracy. On the flip side, with respect to recentralization, the resolution of a hyperinflationary crisis in Peru triggered central assertion of revenue control, while in Senegal the story was "no crisis, no centralization."

Revenue Autonomy in Peru

The revenue autonomy pendulum has swung little in Peru, with the center having dominated. Pressure for strong regions surged at the time of the 1979 constitution, but even this was insufficient to transform the country's centralized structures. The Belaúnde Terry government never moved competencies to the regions, as the constitution had established. Regionalization was also on the back burner for much of García's APRA presidency, until 1988. At that time, García foresaw that his mismanagement of the political economy in the late 1980s made APRA a near-certain loser in the upcoming national elections of 1990. After overspending and nationalizing the banking system, García watched as Peru veered quickly into hyperinflation and APRA's national party leadership faced the decline of the party as a whole.

Whereas other Peruvian parties (including Belaúnde's AP) were largely individual electoral vehicles, APRA had a stronger historical base in the regions, particularly along Peru's relatively wealthy and commercial north coast. The obvious political solution, for García and APRA at the end of his term in the late 1980s, was to create and fund regions, as a matter of political expediency rather than ideological conviction. The dénouement was the party's miserable performance in the 1990 national election; as predicted, however, APRA commanded most regional level governments, having been the only party capable of mobilizing a mass base on a national scale. The eventual winner of the presidency in 1990, Alberto Fujimori, led only a hastily constructed party and took advantage of the partisan vacuum left by APRA's national-level collapse to consolidate power. García's plan to devolve up to 60 percent of revenues to the regions—which would have brought Peru into line with the most federal of states (such as Brazil) in terms of decentralization—was summarily eliminated.

After Fujimori's successful resolution of economic crisis in 1990 and 1991, Peru became hypercentralized in 1992 and years thereafter. Unlike the Brazilian case, where the centrifugal fiscal power of SNGs necessitated simultaneous efforts to recentralize and resolve the economic crisis, the Peruvian case exhibited a more sequential relationship between crisis resolution and subsequent recentralization. After taming hyperinflation, Fujimori first halted the devolution of power to the regions and municipalities that García had envisioned in the death throes of his presidency. Rather, Fujimori created, almost without resistance whatsoever, institutions for the central management of revenue in and after 1992. Alongside his centralization of power through the dismissal of the legislative and judicial branches, Fujimori moved to shift revenues from various ministries to his own Ministry of the Presidency and its attendant agencies. Alongside these machinations, Fujimori created a unicameral legislature elected in a single-national district, which reduced any legislative incentive to undertake projects of localized benefit and further dampened initiatives to promote revenue decentralization.

Executive prerogatives, already generous by 1980, were reinforced by constitutional changes in the 1990s. In 1992, as Fujimori dismissed both the legislative and judicial branches of government in his *autogolpe*, he also moved to consolidate presidential domination of Peru's politics. This domination came partly through the creation of a set of "superministries," most notably the Ministry of the Presidency, which coordinated many of the portfolios formerly held by ministries such as Health and Education, and which were staffed at the upper levels by Fujimori's most loyal supporters. Fujimori also made extensive use of the Consejo de Ministros, another superministry that served as the principal information channel between the cabinet and the president. These efforts were consolidated with a series of legal modifications to the 1993 constitution (itself essentially formulated by Fujimori's political team) that concentrated budgeting and fiscal power in presidential hands.

The Fujimori regime replaced Peru's twelve regional governments with twenty-five departments controlled from the center; this elimination of the legal independence of regions by extension eliminated revenue autonomy. With specific regard to revenue control under Fujimori, a principal function of the Ministry of the Presidency became the coordination of the newly appointed regional administrations (the CTARs). This reversed García's decentralizing reforms of 1988 and took the entire sum of regional budgets under the wing of the Ministry of the Presidency.

The weaknesses of Fujimori's populist, no-party strategy became clear at the local level as his preferred candidates fared poorly in local elections despite the president's enduring popularity and a resurgent economy. Without a credible party machine, Fujimori lacked coattails. The result was an about-face with regard to local government. Previously content to eviscerate national and regional institutions, Fujimori turned his centralizing attentions to the municipal sphere after his failure in the 1993 local elections, though only about 5 percent of government revenues were collected there (Araoz and Urrunaga 1996, 97–98). A new Municipal Tax Law (Legislative Decree 776) ordered new property and sales tax rates in cities throughout the country, and shrank municipal budgets by 79 percent (Kay 1996, 71). To substitute for locally generated revenues, Fujimori created a centrally controlled program to transfer funds to Peru's municipalities—the Municipal Compensation Fund (Fundo de Compensación Municipal, or FONCOMUN)—that was guided by a formula, with distributions based on the population and poverty indices in different municipalities; amounts scarcely surpassed 4 percent of the total government budget.[12] In most cases the FONCOMUN only served to finance the basic recurrent expenditures of the municipality (Ortiz de Zevallos and Pollarolo 2000b, 20–21). These funds were most significant for the poorest municipalities, where property taxes were unviable and the FONCOMUN thus largely substituted for own-source revenue. Politically, the measure was an attempt to counter the growing political influence of provincial mayors, especially the popular mayors Ricardo Belmont (Lima) and Daniel Estrada (Cusco), both of whom Fujimori saw as prospective presidential challengers.

With the passing of the Fujimori era, Peru saw some renewed hope for decentralization under Alejandro Toledo, but steps toward subnational revenue autonomy were fitful at best. Toledo was particularly keen to make a strong political gesture by returning to a system of government where regions mattered; he promised regionalization in his inauguration speech, against the cautioning of advisors who suggested he might be moving too quickly.[13] Decentralization remained a political strategy, though the impulse was not as narrowly electoral as in other moments in Peru: with a weak regional base, Toledo had a reduced incentive to send resources to the regions, but did seek to boost the legitimacy of his government through a clear break with Fujimori's rule.[14] The reinstatement of elected regional governments in

12. This percentage is calculated on 1997–2002 data from the Ministry of Economy and Finance (Ministerio de Economía y Finanzas, Transferencias Del Gobierno Nacional, http://www.mef.gob.pe/DNPP/transferencia_gobnac.php; accessed September 2, 2010).

13. Interviews: Pedro-Pablo Kuczynski, Gabriel Ortiz de Zavallos.

14. On decentralization as legitimation strategy, see Rodriguez 1997.

2002 returned Peru to the pre-Fujimori era. Subsequent breaks included the deactivation of the Ministry of the Presidency and the establishment of semiautonomous regional budgets.[15]

After these elections, however, the narrowly partisan objectives of García's and Fujimori's terms returned with a vengeance. APRA's surprising victory in a plurality of the regions, combined with a terrible performance for Toledo's Perú Posible party, gave Toledo a political disincentive to support the regions. Just as Fujimori moved to starve the municipalities of resources after his electoral defeat at the local level in the early 1990s, Toledo began to backtrack on the transfer of funds to the regions.[16] Notwithstanding Toledo's initial changes, the government retained control over the vast majority of resources and opted to transfer certain investment funds and competencies to localities in a face-saving attempt to circumvent the regions.[17]

Revenue Autonomy in Senegal

The years after Abdou Diouf assumed Senegal's presidency in 1981 were years of increasing pressure on the governing PS (Galvan 2001; Hesseling 1985). Diouf inherited a party whose national executive leadership had held a domi-nant role in executive–legislative relations since the early 1960s, but Diouf's control over the PS increasingly depended on the accommodation of growing numbers of party elites; the president's power was undisputed in formal terms but quite circumscribed in practice. In addition, as Senegal's democracy grew increasingly competitive, the PS watched its national electoral future grow more uncertain. Calls to decentralize served multiple electoral functions: it served to satisfy PS cadres by increasing their electoral opportunities, and it constituted an attempt to increase the party's legitimacy, as was the case when Mexico's dominant party, the PRI, chose to decentralize (cf. Rodriguez 1997).

15. On the deactivation of the Ministry of the Presidency, see RP/MP 2002. At this time, Fujimori's major social fund, FONCODES (to be discussed subsequently), was transferred from the defunct Ministry of the Presidency to the Ministry of Women's Issues and Social Development.

16. Interviews: Franz Portugal, Ivan Aldave.

17. Interview: Franz Portugal. Even were a president committed to regional government, it is unclear that the structure of the state would allow for rapid decentralization. Bureaucratic actors (especially the Ministry of Finance) continue to shape budgetary politics, and Peru's central govern-ment, which has not yet transferred any significant funds to the regions, is virtually unbounded in its ability to reschedule transfers without interference from the regions. As importantly, the use of those revenues scheduled for transfer is predetermined through specific expenditure requirements. These will be considered in the subsequent section on expenditure autonomy (interviews: Franz Portugal, Rafael Valencia Dongo).

In April 1992 Diouf's government initiated a regionalization program designed to convert the country's appointed regions into autonomous SNGs.

Diouf's 1990s decentralization and creation of regional governments, and the electoral aims of reform evoke the similar electoral calculations made by García in Peru: "In contrast to the party's [PS] uncertain success in the country's larger cities, control over this stratum of government is assured insofar as regional voters will come overwhelmingly from rural areas—creating hundreds of elected positions for PS rank-and-file" (Marks 1996b, 141). Finally established as elected SNGs by PS government legislation in 1996, the regions were designed to depend entirely on the central government with no independent taxation authority. While endowed with guaranteed transfers for recurrent expenses, they are not fully independent (with regions having both a weak elected council and a strong arm of the state in the form of an administrative governor).

The Fonds d'Equipement des Collectivités Locales (FECL, or Local Government Capital Fund), which existed throughout much of the Senghor and Diouf presidencies, was one of the largest sources of SNG funding, but its effectiveness was limited. This funding, earmarked for capital expenditures, was made available to local governments on a *concours* basis, meaning local governments applied for funding, with decisions about disbursement being left to the discretion of a small committee comprising central government officials.[18] No statute guarantees local governments any recourse or appeal.[19] Perhaps not surprisingly, the distributions seemed to be conditioned on intraparty politics, with those subnational politicians who held leverage within the PS receiving the lion's share of disbursements (Marks 1996a, 57–62).[20]

In 1996 a new set of Decentralization Laws established new transfers for SNGs at the local level, along with giving some marginal autonomy to the regions. The laws created a Decentralization Fund—Fonds de Dotation de la Décentralisation (FDD)—intended for distribution to all local governments and in amounts more substantial than the FECL. The FDD was coupled with the legal dispositions of Law 96-07, which made local government responsible for the provision of basic services in nine major social service areas, including health and education (RS/MI 1996). Unlike the FECL, which is

18. Interviews: Moctar Gaye (#1, #2).

19. Interviews Moctar Gaye (#1, #2).

20. The progression of the FECL from 1993 to 1996 shows some increase from 3.4 percent to 7.8 percent of the total of overall local budgets, and this slight increase in discretionary funding continued to 2002. However, the fragility of this source is demonstrated by its volatility, with no transfers being made whatsoever in 1990–91, a substantial recovery in 1991–92 and another precipitous decline in 1993 (Marks 1996a, 26).

intended for capital investment, the FDD is designed to finance the day-to-day functioning of local government services.[21] Yet even now, the majority of spending on these social services takes place at the national level, as civil service personnel (including teachers) continue to be paid and overseen by the state.[22] In addition, while evidence is thin as to which municipalities receive FDD funds, it is significant that the fund passes through the same bureaucratic machinery as the FECL. The formulae for the division of FDD revenues are opaque, leaving room for considerable central government discretion over even these automatically transferable revenues.[23]

Beyond transfers from the center, Senegal's SNGs have only limited revenue from own-sources. Tax collection in Senegal is dominated by the central government, which collects tariffs, business taxes, and a value-added tax (Ndir et al. 1999). Local level tax bases are quite limited and vary depending on the type of local government. Urban *communes* collect property taxes, though amounts are substantial only in Dakar (Marks 1996a). User service fees (such as trash collection and fees for utilities) constitute another major source of income. Meanwhile, ever since the rural communities were created in 1972, they have relied largely on the *taxe rurale,* an annual 1,000 CFA franc (approximately $2.00) head tax that generates only very limited funds, and user fees for the use of public property such as market space. Limited tax bases mean that the rural community revenues cover only the basic operating costs of the local council, which include simple civic obligations and record-keeping, but not the salaries of teachers and health care workers, nor capital investment, which comes largely from the FECL or from international donors. Meanwhile, the eleven regions have no tax authority (*assiette fiscale*) of their own and rely completely on central government transfers.[24] Regional budgets are entirely funded by the Decentralization Fund.[25] Indeed, the relative weakness and superfluous nature of the regional governments resulted in the later drive toward provincialization that would suppress the elected status of the regions.[26]

The FDD revenues transferred in the 1996 reforms were insufficient to realize such functions as health and education investment, and though both revenues and expenditures were supposed to be decentralized in 1996, the

21. Interview: Moctar Gaye (#2).
22. Interviews: Seynabou Ba, Moctar Gaye (#1, #2).
23. The official responsible for the management of the FDD says that the budgets are based almost exclusively on the previous year's budget (interview: Moctar Gaye [#1]).
24. Interview: Moctar Gaye (#1).
25. Interview: Moctar Gaye (#1).
26. Interviews: Khalifa Guèye, Macoudou Guèye.

vast majority of Senegal's finances remain in the hands of appointed administrators, including departmental prefects and *arrondissement* subprefects,
and not in the hands of elected local officials. In short, Senegal has created
a set of underfunded mandates coupled with central government control
over most funds. As one Senegalese functionary confessed succinctly, "the
state has decentralized more problems than solutions."[27]

These changes under Diouf's government in the 1990s, then, are best seen
as a middling attempt at decentralization, albeit a notable one in a country
where most local governments are under-resourced and weak in capacity. From
a partisan perspective, Abdoulaye Wade's current (2000–present) government,
comprising his PDS party and several others in his Sopi (Change) coalition,
likewise had few incentives to move decision making from the bureaucracy
to local government. First, Wade's coalition is more secure at the national
level than at the local level, where the opposition can fare better in first-past-
the-post elections in rural strongholds. With the city of Dakar uniquely
capable of producing its own revenue (and likely being the loser in any
redistributive revenue transfers), even the biggest local vote source for
Wade's coalition had relatively little incentive to push for the decentralization of resources.

The aforementioned reduction in jurisdictional autonomy under Wade
was temporary, and did not result in a modification of the FDD. The sudden
suspension of several hundred elected local officials meant that for a six-month
period, the revenues transferred to the localities were in the hands of state
appointees rather than elected officials. A subsequent round of elections
restored local government to management by elected officials, but the centralizing attempt was clear, with a former Ministry of Economy and Finance
official noting that Wade retained a will (*volonté*) to centralize, and that the
new constitution of January 7, 2001, was very presidentialist.[28] The PDS lacks
incentives to decentralize further, and localities remain marginal players in
Senegalese governance, despite the FDD. The creation of the FECL and the
FDD are minor increases to subnational revenue autonomy in a country
where SNG revenues remain quite restricted.

Expenditure Autonomy

The differences between the administration of health and education provisions in Senegal and Peru versus those in contemporary South Africa are

27. Interview: Amadou Bocoum.
28. Interview: Papa Ndiaye.

relatively minor.[29] In none of these countries has the principle of centralism in expenditure control been challenged. Both Peru and Senegal represent sustained low levels of expenditure autonomy, with reductions nonetheless occurring even from low levels in Peru when President Alberto Fujimori asserted strong-armed control over his own government in response to hyper-inflationary crisis. In the latter case, the two key independent variables follow one another in rapid succession, as political decline and economic crisis went hand in hand; while the decline of APRA (from 1988 to 1990) drove decentralization, the economic crisis behind the decline also created the opportunity structure for Fujimori to recentralize upon its resolution.

Expenditure Autonomy in Peru

The transition from Alan García to Alberto Fujimori in Peru was also a transition from a hasty decentralizer to a hypercentralizer, a shift explicable only through the lens of the economic and political crisis facing Peru in 1990. García and APRA created regions and gave them initial revenue flows, and crafted initial plans to decentralize expenditures as well, but he never accomplished the transfer of spending authority before they were voted out of office in 1990. On the contrary, the economic crisis initiated under García and the one major institutional innovation made at the time—the creation of the Ministry of the Presidency—instead laid the groundwork for centralization of power via the construction of vertical state–society relationships.

The early years of the Fujimori regime put to rest any hopes for expenditure decentralization, as several important institutions were subsumed into the Ministry of the Presidency, including FONCODES (Fondo Nacional de Compensación y Desarrollo Social, or National Fund for Compensation and Social Development), the internationally acclaimed "social fund" designed to provide public goods in the short term to mitigate the shocks of structural adjustment. Fujimori set aside substantial funding for FONCODES, which in 1993 alone accounted for more than the combined budgets of all local governments (Planas 1998, 570). Fujimori then used those resources to target the rural and peri-urban economies most essential to his future (Schady 1999). Despite rhetoric promising a "decentralized" approach, FONCODES was located at the president's right hand, representing what one observer called

---

29. This is not to say there is no difference in the end result. Education standards and quality vary considerably from country to country, and within countries. The minimal difference is with respect to the organization of the sectors: in both countries, the national government controls social expenditures.

"executive philanthropy bankrolled by a liberal state" (Kay 1996, 56). Initially, FONCODES was explicitly a part of the president's personal regime, with Luz Salgado, the secretary-general of Fujimori's Cambio 90/Nueva Mayoría movement, as its titular head (Kay 1996, 78).[30] Fujimori boasted that his programs offered direct relationships between president and presided, without the annoyance of institutional intermediaries; the slogan at ribbon-cuttings for FONCODES projects was "direct democracy, without parties" (Kay 1996, 56).[31]

The Ministry of the Presidency, including FONCODES, became a massive, centralized bureaucracy, soon characterized as a "resource glutton" (*recursofágia*). A principal function of the ministry became the coordination of the newly appointed regional governments—the CTARs—that replaced the elected regional governments following the *autogolpe* of 1992. Other institutions soon fell under the ministry's purview. In 1993 the government increased business sector "contributions" to the quasi-presidential National Housing Fund (Fondo Nacional de Vivienda, or FONAVI). Due to an almost total lack of opposition in the Congress, an additional $180 million per year was placed under the direct control of the presidency (Kay 1996, 80). The various agencies in the ministry also crowded out investment elsewhere. Losses in municipal revenues were supposedly compensated for via central government spending through agencies such as CORLICA (Corporación de Desarrollo de Lima y Callao), which sidelined the municipalities of Lima and Callao (Planas 1998, 570–71). Fujimori's agencies even ran roughshod over grassroots and civil society organizations, such as local mothers' clubs (*clubes de madres*), "popular cafeterias" (*comedores populares*), and the "glass of milk" (*vaso de leche*) programs in low-income neighborhoods.[32]

Under Fujimori, the education and health ministries lost resources to the Ministry of the Presidency. In education, initiatives to devolve some limited authority were announced on four occasions (Ortiz de Zevallos and

30. Eventually, international donor organizations arranged for the exit of Salgado from the post, but Fujimori's intentions were clear.

31. In fact, projects initiated by the social fund almost directly reflected the logic behind its creation. In most cases, the only contribution of communities was in the initial phases of project proposals, with the execution and financing of projects flowing directly from the national government to the target community. Even in the initiation of projects, the FONCODES staff came to dominate in many cases, being responsible for an estimated 36 percent of proposals, according to one survey (Kay 1996).

32. See Planas 1998, 570–71. Other similar clientelist agencies were either created in the ministry or absorbed into it. Among these were the Programa Nacional de Asistencia Alimentaria (PRONAA), Programa Nacional de Agua Potable (PRONAP), the embattled Fondo Nacional de

Pollarolo 2000a, 16). These took a variety of forms, from Chilean-style privatization to local pilot projects to enhanced authority for subregional "educational service units," but none came to fruition. Education remained highly centralized, with investments from FONCODES and the presidency uncoordinated with the Education Ministry (Tanaka 2002, 12–13). The only authority conferred to local entities were minor decisions about curricula and school calendars, and even these were largely subverted by bureaucratic resistance (Ortiz de Zevallos and Pollarolo 2000a, 17–19). Fujimori also announced in 1999 that health expenditures would be devolved to localities (Ortiz de Zevallos and Pollarolo 2000d). Here too, decentralization was more promise than reality; the centrally appointed CTARs retained control over most health monies. Centralization in health was partially mitigated by functioning Local Health Committees (Comités Locales de Administración de Salúd), which were present in many of Peru's localities (Ortiz de Zevallos and Pollarolo 2000d, 16). These committees retained operational autonomy, but had no secure funding base; they are of a "quasi-private" nature, and had ambiguous links to municipal governments (Ortiz de Zevallos and Pollarolo 2000d, 26–27).

After Fujimori's departure, Toledo renewed the discussion about decentralization (specifically regionalization) and held regional elections in the twenty-five departments in 2002, but later used all tools at his disposal to tightly limit any sort of autonomy to the regions after his APRA opponents dominated regional elections. Toledo's principal means of limiting regionalization was tight restrictions on expenditure autonomy, rather than attempting to stall revenue transfers. The 2003 budget, for instance, offered nearly 22 percent of the consolidated national budget to the regions, a substantial sum for a recently restored level of government.[33] However, the detailed budgeting for the regions was laid out in seven lengthy annexes to the national budget, comprising a total of 238 pages.[34] Budgets were detailed down to the line item for each sector in each region. The modality for distributing resources to the regions, therefore, was almost exactly the same as that used to fund the CTARs that were fully under the control of the presidency.[35] Regions

---

Vivienda (FONAVI, which underwent a tax-and-budget scandal and was partly replaced by a parallel organization, MiVivienda), and the Corporación de Desarrollo de Lima y Callao (CORLICA, later split into CORDELIMA and CORDECALLAO).

33. The proposed budget for the regions in 2003 was 9.6 billion soles (approx. $3 billion), out of a total consolidated budget of 44.5 billion soles.

34. These annexes are available from the MEF's Dirección General del Presupuesto Público at http://www.mef.gob.pe/DNPP/estadistica.php (accessed September 2, 2010).

35. Interviews: Felipe Reátegui, Ivan Aldave, Efraín Gonzales de Olarte.

thus had elected governments, but no more discretion over their funding than a "deconcentrated" bureaucracy belonging to the state. Sectorally, programs to decentralize education and health care remained on the back burner.[36]

Even those sympathetic to Toledo's initial decentralizing objectives, including his first Minister of Economy and Finance, advised that his pressure for quick regional elections could be a political mistake and should be approached more slowly and with more caution.[37] To be sure, Toledo's approach to regionalization required significant backpedaling as APRA's surprising success left him clamoring for ways to control the damage to his government's interests.[38] Toledo's unidimensional decentralization reflected less profound incentives for devolution: without the electoral advantage at the subnational level (or with uncertainty about electoral prospects at that level prior to elections), decentralization is likely to be much less transformational. Having conceded revenue autonomy, Toledo used the lack of expenditure autonomy for the regions to reduce them to a marginal role.

Chief among Toledo's tools in controlling expenditure was the National Decentralization Council (Consejo Nacional de la Descentralización, or CND). This council was officially responsible for proposals about the future of Peruvian intergovernmental relations and comprised representatives of the national executive, the regions, and the municipalities. However, the CND came under fire from a wide range of actors for overrepresenting the interests of the national executive, where both the president and the Ministry of Economy and Finance are represented, giving Toledo a virtual veto over proposals.[39] Decisions made in April 2003 to route certain funding provisions to the municipalities instead of to the regions were a first step in Toledo's efforts to marginalize the regions after APRA's victories (Dickovick 2007).

36. Interviews: Gabriel Ortiz de Zavallos, Felipe Reátegui.
37. Interviews: Gabriel Ortiz de Zavallos, Pedro-Pablo Kuczynski.
38. Toledo's decision to dismantle Fujimori's president-dominated clientelism had implications for his political success. Fujimori's dominance of organizations such as FONCODES, FONAVI, and CORLICA gave him a massive electoral tool in both the sierra and the capital. After barely winning a 1995 constitutional referendum allowing him to run for a second term of office, his credit-claiming campaign enabled him to pick up votes in the subsequent presidential election (Schady 1999). Toledo's failure in regional elections, on the other hand, was in part attributable to his inability to build such a base of popular support after he decided to "slowly deactivate" the Ministry of the Presidency (RP/MP 2002).
39. Interviews: Franz Portugal, Rafael Valencia Dongo. Of the nine members of the council, five are seen to represent the interests of the center, including two representatives from the Ministry of Economy and Finance. The regions send two representatives, as do the municipalities.

Expenditure Autonomy in Senegal

Senegal's SNGs continue to measure very low on expenditure autonomy, and even during the decline of the PS the central government bureaucracy held onto decision-making power, despite the 1996 Decentralization Laws that purported to give Senegal's regions and local governments their first taste of significant spending responsibility by designating nine major public services, including health and education, as responsibilities of the *collectivités locales*.[40] Before 1996 local governments were responsible only for the most skeletal municipal services. Small local tax bases meant supplemental investment and expenditures were very low, with only Dakar and a handful of secondary cities investing in municipal public works (such as sewer systems, roadways, and other infrastructure), and even these investments often came from funds disbursed ad hoc at the discretion of the national government. The scope of the transfers after 1996 remained quite limited. Three facts illustrate Senegal's weak expenditure autonomy. First, the central government, itself squeezed for revenue, conceded that it could not fully fund the decentralization initiative; the change was thus tantamount to an unfunded mandate (Ndir et al. 1999, 19–21).[41] Second, the funds designated for use by SNGs were generally earmarked for expenditure on specified line items.[42] And third, personnel remained under the purview of the central state, as will be discussed later under contractual autonomy.[43]

The first and most obvious constraint on expenditure autonomy in Senegal's decentralization is that the 1996 reforms are best interpreted as an offloading of social spending responsibilities in the form of unfunded mandates (cf. Vengroff 2000).[44] The acts clarified the division of responsibilities, but SNGs facing major unfunded mandates clearly have low spending autonomy, particularly under resource constraints and when personnel make up a large portion of spending.[45] As a comprehensive 1999 World Bank review of Senegal's subnational finances found: "The expenditure analysis shows that the

40. The areas are Public Land (Domaines); Environment and Natural Resource Management; Health, Population and Social Welfare; Youth, Sports, and Recreation; Culture; Education; Planning; Land management, Zoning, and Local Development (Aménagement du territoire); and Urban Development and Housing (Urbanisme et habitat). See République du Sénégal, Ministère de l'Intérieur 1996, 111–12.

41. Interviews: Mamadou Moctar Fall and Amadou Bocoum.

42. Interview: Moctar Gaye (#1, #2).

43. Interview: Seynabou Ba.

44. Interviews: Amadou Bocoum, Christian Fournier.

45. An additional constraint on SNGs comes in the form of a list of "compulsory expenditures," which take up 80–90 percent of aggregate subnational budgets. These compulsory

SUBNATIONAL AUTONOMY IN UNITARY STATES

SNG constitute a very low proportion of the public expenses and that the level has not increased in recent years despite the transfer of new functions. The largest expenditure share is general public service, of which administration constitutes the major share" (IBRD/DANIDA 1999, 19). The general public services referred to here are not the teachers and health care workers that form the majority of public personnel, but the much smaller number of administrative staff required to manage municipal affairs, such as clerking, public registers, and fee collection. The so-called expenditure decentralization in 1996 thus applies only to capital investments (through the FECL) and maintenance and recurrent expenditures (through the FDD), and not to the lion's share of expenditure (and patronage opportunities) taken up in staff.

Beyond the fact of unfunded mandates—and the question of central control over civil servants to be discussed shortly—a second limitation on spending autonomy is the centralized control of spending priorities in the major social service areas—such as health and education—ostensibly under SNG purview. The 1996 laws had relatively little impact on patterns of education and health provision, despite the nominal transfer of social service responsibilities to localities. Decisions on the relative budgets of the different sectors are made at annual meetings—the so-called Conférence Nationale des Collectivités Locales (CNCL)—that bring together the president, the Interior Ministry representatives for local government (from the Direction des Collectivités Locales, or DCL), and line ministry officials. At the CNCL, national political decisions are made on the distribution of resources by sector, based on executive policy priorities.[46] Budget proposals are the prerogative of the executive, with the legislature having only a marginal role.[47] After dividing the budget across spending priorities, transfer amounts for each SNG are drawn up in the Ministry of the Interior's Decentralization office.

Education expenditure is a prime example of how sectoral distributions to SNGs are controlled from the center.[48] All local communities receive

---

expenditures, however, do not seem to be meaningful constraints because the lists are quite extensive in nature. Compulsory expenditures, for instance, include the payment of permanent local staff, all investment expenditures approved by the local council, and maintenance and supply expenditures (IBRD/DANIDA 1999, 252–53).

46. Interview: Moctar Gaye (#1).

47. Interviews: Moctar Gaye (#1), Papa Ndiaye.

48. Interviews: Moctar Gaye (#1, #2). Major differences between health and education come in the structure of subnational administration. Each sector has its own map of territorial subdivisions, and these do not overlap. Thus, the health ministry administers health districts that do not correspond to education districts. Health districts are somewhat anomalous, while education districts correspond to Senegal's political map.

transfers for education spending. Central government officials consider education to be more "deconcentrated," and more centralized than health (i.e., controlled by the central state on the ground), insofar as the central ministry has tight control over school operations.[49] The management and construction of schools takes place according to a national education plan (*carte scolaire*) written by the central government. The FDD funds transferred to localities are supposed to be determined by the costs of the maintenance, functioning, and materials for the schools, again from a national plan, though the disbursement of FDD funds is less than transparent.[50] Emblematic of the centralized nature of the arrangement is that the Ministry of Education had a standing point person for decentralization (a technical advisor), but none of the other institutions linked to decentralization professed to have any contact with this official.[51]

The decentralization of health care tells a story similar to that in education; again, centralism prevails. Health care in Senegal is run on a different map from other major public services; health funds are not distributed to all rural communities under the auspices of the FDD, but only to the urban communes.[52] Moreover, health districts do not correspond to administrative districts.[53] These health districts often are smaller than the communes, but are managed at the commune level, where each health district is overseen

49. Interviews: Moctar Gaye (#2), Papa Ndiaye.

50. Central state payment of salaries in education and health care can also mask certain transfers to some communities. Some communities receive generous endowments of salaried human resources, while other communities are relatively understaffed with human resources. State placements of *fonctionnaires* are in-kind transfers to local governments, and the distribution of these transfers remains at the discretion of the center. State personnel expenditures increase in response to the amount of established physical infrastructure. For example, communities that build schools are those most able to lobby successfully for increased numbers of teachers. These communities thus receive greater resources from the center. Also influential is the government-run AGETIP (Agence d'Exécution des Travaux d'Intérêt Public; or Public Works and Employment Agency), a labor-intensive public works program that subsidizes up to 90 percent of projects in communities. The result is likely to be regressive: poorer communities receive lower public support than do better-organized, wealthier communities. Foreign aid and central government capital investment (through the FECL mentioned in chapter 4) serve as partial correctives, as some of Senegal's poorer provinces receive greater infrastructure support from foreign donors. Interviews: Abdoul Wahab Ba, J. Guy LaRochelle, Seynabou Ba, Biram Owens Ndiaye.

51. This lack of communication with the appointed officials in the Education Ministry held both within other government bodies (most notably the DCL in the Ministry of the Interior) and among other technical experts in the Dakar donor community.

52. FDD budgets for the local communities are different for the urban communes and the rural communities. Transfers to the communes comprise education, health, and youth programs. In rural communities, local governments receive transfers for education, youth programs, and culture. Interview: Moctar Gaye (#2).

53. Interview: Moctar Gaye (#2).

by a state-appointed head doctor (*médecin-chef*).[54] The health map thus comprises so-called "federated entities"—local structures under the auspices of the health district—linked to the center through funding distributions. As such, the center still funds health expenditures line item by line item.

Contractual Autonomy

Contractual autonomy is likewise fragile in Peru and Senegal. In unitary states where subnational politicians are historically weak and have little bargaining power, we would expect to see very little movement in the direction of devolving contractual authority to SNGs. This is true even when central governments have top-down incentives to create and empower SNGs, and even when some revenue decentralization emerges from executive–legislative bargaining. The finding that contractual autonomy was exceptionally limited in unitary states furthers the argument that institutional arenas matter for decentralization and recentralization. Whereas national parties and executive–legislative relations have at times pushed revenue decentralization, subnational politicians have not been sufficiently coordinated to demand concurrent autonomy in the areas of borrowing and contracting power.

Contractual Autonomy in Peru

Peru's national government has consistently dominated wage and capital contracts since 1980. Again, the Alan García interlude in the late 1980s constituted a brief exception: García created legally independent regions in 1987–88, but the disastrous economic performance of his administration rendered irrelevant the right to borrow, and regional labor costs were essentially fixed for the short time the regions existed. Contractual autonomy thus increased even less than revenue autonomy under García's administration from 1985 to 1990.

Throughout the 1980s and the 1990s, capital market access for Peru's regions was limited at best. Nominally, Regionalization Laws (the Plan Nacional de Regionalización and the Ley de Bases de la Regionalización) promulgated by García and APRA foresaw the establishment of regions with financial authority. The Regionalization Law did not specify the access the regions

54. For example, the budget transferred to the city of Rufisque would include funding for the large health *centres* and the smaller health *postes* not only in Rufisque city, but also in the surrounding towns of Sangalkam, Bargny, and so forth. Interview: Moctar Gaye (#2).

would have to the open capital markets, but did provide for the creation of a development bank (*banco de fomento regional*) in each region, whose governing board would have a majority of representatives from the regional governments (Zas Fris Burga 1998, 245). The economic crisis of the late García administration, and especially the bank nationalization, triggered capital flight and turned the national government into a poor credit risk. In these circumstances, Peru's new regions had no prospective creditors, making borrowing impossible.

In terms of labor contracts as well, the García efforts were made between 1988 and 1990. The laws creating the regions stipulated that personnel in a number of areas would be transferred to the regions, and that the regions would have control over these staff (Zas Fris Burga 1998, 246–47).[55] The extent to which the regions would be able to exercise authority over schoolteachers and health personnel, among other personnel, remained unproven, as the brief period of regionalization only allowed for limited transfers in certain areas before being reversed. García's original plan called for increasing revenue transfers to the regions, including a minimum increase of 2.5 percent per year up to the point where the regions would receive 60 percent of total revenues (Kim 1992). The intention was thus obviously to transfer the responsibilities for human resources to the regions, though it remained unclear whether the ability to set wages would also be decentralized or if the civil service would retain a national character.

The first two Fujimori years also saw little activity in regional finances, and beyond the statutory law establishing the regional banks, there is little evidence that they were funded or even endowed with an administration. By 1992 the elimination of the regions and their replacement with the administrative CTARs ended the possibility of capital market autonomy. Meanwhile, Peru's cities retained nominal autonomy in the credit markets, but in reality this is compromised by the weak financial power of nearly all cities except for the capital; since municipalities rely on unstable central government transfers and on weak tax bases for revenue, most are not able to use the capital market autonomy extended in theory to all cities, with Lima being the exception.

Fujimori's *autogolpe* also ended labor market autonomy through the centralization of many public service functions, including education and

---

55. This included personnel in agriculture, health, education, justice, labor and social development, energy and mines, industry, domestic commerce (*comercio interno*), tourism and national integration (*turismo e integración*), housing and construction, fishing, transportation and communication, and the National Statistics Institute.

health care, while the control of capital flows (including international donor support) was centralized via Fujimori's Ministry of the Presidency and chan-neled through top-down agencies such as FONCODES. Regional personnel were brought under the central administration in the CTARs, with the Ministry of the Presidency taking over responsibility for the vast majority of the personnel formerly attributed to the regions. Municipalities retained greater control to hire and fire their own staff, but only in the limited number of service areas under municipal control.

Under Toledo, the regions regained their jurisdictional independence, but faced difficulties in reestablishing autonomy in both capital and labor markets. After his loss to APRA in the regional elections, Toledo aimed to limit regionalization: the central government did not take measures to increase the capital autonomy of the regional governments. In fact, the original idea to capitalize the *bancos de fomento* was lost during the Fujimori years, and the transfer of capital assets to the regions remained uncertain at best, with only certain regional development projects being transferred to the regions on an ad hoc basis ("CND propone siete grandes proyectos para el desarrollo," *El Comercio,* January 5, 2002). The Toledo government and several Peruvian scholars correctly argued that readying the regions for capital market access would take time even in the presence of political incentives to regionalize.[56] Yet the government failed to pass enabling legislation, leading other observers to attribute Toledo's inaction to a concern that the APRA-dominated regions not be allowed to develop fiscal independence from the center.[57]

Regional governments under Alejandro Toledo did not recuperate the freedom to set their wages and numbers of staff. As the vast majority of educa-tion and health services are provided by the central government or the private sector, the newly empowered regions did not control their own labor, just as they did not control their capital flows. The first laws put into place to promote regionalization were passed literally on the very eve of regional elections, when it became clear that Toledo was bound to lose. As leading APRA congressman Cesar Zumaeta argued, Toledo and Perú Posible would "await the results of the regional elections, and since [Toledo's party] Perú Posible [was] going to suffer a real electoral failure this Sunday, they will begin to calculate what exactly they will transfer in January and what they won't" ("Gobierno y APRA se responsabilizan mútuamente por falta de ley de regiones," *La Gestión,* November 17, 2002). Zumaeta and other congress

56. Interviews: Ernesto Herrera, Gabriel Ortiz de Zavallos, Rudecindo Vega.
57. Interviews: Franz Portugal, Ivan Aldave.

members decried Toledo's wait-and-see attitude, saying it allowed him to pick and choose what "assets and liabilities" would be transferred to the regions depending on electoral results. Toledo's failure in regional elections removed any impetus to transfer personnel responsibilities to the regions, and aligned his preferences with "elements of the bureaucracy" that were most resistant to regionalization (Rafael Valencia Dongo, "¿Alto a la descentralización del Perú? Marchas y contramarchas," *El Peruano*, February 18, 2002). Toledo's ability to control the speed and extent of the process was solidified by the national executive's majority on the aforementioned Consejo Nacional de la Descentralización.[58] This entrenchment of bureaucratic interests, facilitated by Peru's top-down processes of state formation, showed the lingering power of the state in allowing the center to hold power through decentralization processes.

Contractual Autonomy in Senegal

Autonomy in capital and labor markets remains low in Senegal, and efforts by the center to suspend the legal structures of SNGs were not so much reductions in autonomy as symptoms of the fact that this autonomy remains as low as ever. Subnational borrowing is strictly overseen by the center. A 1999 World Bank review of subnational financial autonomy in Senegal outlines the legal empowerment of Senegal's SNGs but notes the practical constraints that largely invalidate this power:

> The SNG are quite free to borrow from the banking and capital market. However, this possibility is subject to prior approval by the central government through its local level representative when the borrowings reach CFAF 100 million [approx. $170,000] and when they result from a loan agreement through international cooperation. This provision, which restricts the binding force of these decisions taken by the SNG, represents progress compared to the situation that prevailed before 1996, since control is no longer exercised by the central authority *but rather by the State's representative at the local level* (governor, prefect, or sub-prefect). (Ndir et al. 1999, 29, emphasis added)

The sanguine reaction to the change does not obscure the fact that the change simply shifts responsibility for monitoring borrowing from the central

---

58. Interview: Ivan Aldave.

government in Dakar to the central government agent outside the capital. This is a deconcentration, rather than a devolution, of power. State representatives have numerous prerogatives with respect to subnational loans, with the center (acting through deconcentrated officials at the regional level and below) retaining the right to view borrowing schedules a priori, and to approve any guarantees offered on the loans.[59]

Moreover, the structure of revenue distributions does not allow SNGs to generate the revenues necessary to repay loans. Since the annual FDD distributions are entirely for use on current expenditures, and the FECL capital fund is an unstable discretionary source of revenues, SNGs would have to rely on own-source tax revenues to repay any debt obligations. But the regions have no tax authority, and most local governments have little such capacity. For the biggest exception—Dakar—the legal restrictions on borrowing come into effect. The theoretical right to enter into capital market contracts is thus largely irrelevant; only guaranteed transfers of funds for capital investment or the transfer of tax authority will increase SNG borrowing autonomy. This suggests the interconnectedness of areas of subnational fiscal autonomy. While distinct, each area of autonomy constitutes a part of a whole fiscal system, and a lack of autonomy in one area can moot an otherwise high level of autonomy in another area; in this case, the lack of revenue autonomy can render de jure borrowing autonomy irrelevant.

In terms of labor market autonomy, SNGs are similarly circumscribed. Senegal operates with a single, unified national civil service, meaning labor market autonomy for SNGs is all but nonexistent. Public sector workers in Senegal—including teachers and public health workers—are part of the state and do not respond to the directives of decentralized officials on a day-to-day basis. Municipalities can hire their own staff, but do so only on thin budgetary margins. The central government continues to control the majority of spending on social services at the subnational level, largely via control over civil service spending.[60] Personnel still paid by the state form a large percentage of total expenditures. Staff are assigned by the central government, even in the expenditure areas that nominally are the responsibilities of the regional and local governments.[61] Teachers, health workers, and other state officials have their salaries paid by the center, and patronage opportunities thus remain at the national level. The PS used this patronage extensively to

59. Interview: Moctar Gaye (#1).
60. Interviews: Seynabou Ba, Biram Owens Ndiaye.
61. Interviews: Seynabou Ba, Christian Fournier, Biram Owens Ndiaye.

shore up support, even as it was in decline (see Galvan 2001, 60; Marks 1996a, 40–41), and the PDS had no incentive to abandon this power thereafter.

State control over personnel expenditure includes national civil servants, as well as locally assigned "communal civil servants" that the center places at the disposal of localities, and which represent a large percentage of local officials in most SNGs. By controlling communal civil servants, the central government extends its control over any patronage opportunities to be gleaned from the distribution of salaried positions:

> Communal civil servants are apt to occupy the permanent adminis-
> trative and technical jobs of the communes. They are appointed by
> the State, but they are under the direct authority of the mayors under
> whom they fulfill their duties. They may be posted to other local
> authorities, if need be. . . . All important decisions belong to the
> central government. Indeed, the decision by which an official is appointed
> in the body of the communal civil servants, sanctioned, transferred,
> dismissed, or retired, is taken by the State. The local authority man-
> ages but does not administer the communal civil servant. (Ndir et al.
> 1999, 277)

Even more stringent limitations are placed on the management of local government employees in rural areas. Urban *communes* and the regions are at least nominally eligible to recruit and maintain their own supplementary staff, based on own-source revenue, though this practice is limited by the lack of funds; meanwhile, recruitment in most local governments—that is, in the *communautés rurales*—remains entirely under the purview of the state. Rural communities are not permitted to recruit their own staff, but instead must depend on state appointees (Ndir et al. 1999, 280).[62]

The lack of local control over staff is even more pronounced in Senegal for two additional reasons. First, state personnel resist proposed assignments (*affectations*) in many cases, particularly to rural areas.[63] Many national *fonc-tionnaires* are assigned to posts throughout the country, with the express

---

62. Municipalities were always able to manage their own staff, but this only corresponded to even smaller staffs than those observed in Peru, for instance. Whereas municipalities in Peru and middle-income unitary states often have some meaningful property tax base and take up functions such as public sanitation, localities in very low-income states like Senegal often rely on head taxes (the *taxe rurale*) and have functions limited to such minor items as the creation and maintenance of civil registries.

63. Interview: El Hadj Sidy Niang.

purpose of supporting SNGs at several levels, including the regions.[64] While postings ultimately are under the control of the center, state personnel resistance represents an additional layer of complication for local and regional governments looking to secure human resources. Second, the center actually reduces subnational budgets to cover the cost of posting national personnel. A fixed 8 percent of the Decentralization Fund is withheld from SNGs to compensate the center for services provided by national personnel, and the regions have little or no say over the posting of these personnel.[65]

Comparative Lessons

The most substantial and apparent lesson from the Peru–Senegal comparison is the confirmation of the argument that decentralization can be traced to the decline or weakening of executive powers, and recentralization to instances of crisis resolution; the cross-regional comparison extends the argument beyond the bounds of federal states and to lower-income countries, suggesting its applicability to a range of circumstances in the developing world. Federalism matters in specific and limited ways in shaping subnational autonomy. The scope of subnational autonomy is, by definition, lower in unitary states than in federal states where regions are fiscally sovereign or semi-sovereign, to use Rodden's (2006) terminology. Federalism shapes the broad parameters of decentralization insofar as decentralization in unitary states is likely to be top down, unlike robust federal countries such as Brazil where strong subnational actors can drive decentralization from the bottom up. The instances of decentralization here resemble the experience of South Africa's weak form of federalism; there, the National Party opted to decentralize when facing defeat, just like García's APRA and Senegal's PS. South Africa sits across the federal–unitary divide from Peru and Senegal, yet the cases share many characteristics. Federalism is not—on its own—an explanatory variable for the dynamics of intergovernmental relations. On the contrary, the dynamics leading to higher levels of subnational autonomy may be similar across federal and unitary states, even if federalism correlates with overall levels of decentralism.

64. Interviews: Fall et al.

65. The FDD is divided into three parts: 82 percent to cover the functioning of the nine expenditure areas transferred to the SNGs; 10 percent for the administration of the regions, including regional salaries; and 8 percent reserved for the services of central government personnel (interview: Moctar Gaye [#1]).

Much as the decentralization story in Peru and Senegal echoed that in South Africa, so too did recentralization continue to be a function of the resolution of economic crisis in unitary states. The resolution of macroeconomic crisis in Peru (especially hyperinflation) facilitated recentralization in unitary states just as it did in Brazil's federal system. Senegal confirms that recentralization, when attempted by presidents, is unlikely to succeed in democratic contexts in the absence of crisis. On the other hand, Senegal shows the limitations central governments can place on SNGs via strict controls on expenditure autonomy and contractual autonomy, even after SNG revenues have been increased. The existence of decentralization with a lack of recentralization, as in Senegal, does not mean that central states are weak relative to SNGs; rather, it means that central states have institutionalized ways to withhold power from SNGs. Even in an age of decentralization, the center can hold.

With regard to institutional arenas and the three areas of subnational autonomy, we find that the two unitary cases further reflect the South African experience in particular. Subnational autonomy increased most in the area of revenues, and not as much in the areas of expenditures or contracting autonomy. This can be attributed to the strength of presidents' interlocutors in various bargaining arenas. Revenues, which are primarily shaped in executive–legislative negotiations, represented an area where presidential copartisans had reason to demand decentralization. Increasing subnational spending autonomy, by contrast, requires taking some authority from central states; with states resisting such decentralization, presidents had less need to enhance subnational power on this measure. Similarly, regional politicians were quite weak in both Peru and Senegal and remain so to this day; the principal claimants for contractual autonomy thus scarcely registered. Even when enthusiasm for decentralization is high, central governments find numerous ways to limit reforms, and under crisis conditions, central states can occasionally even find ways to reverse devolution.

7

—⟨𝕠𝕠𝕠⟩—

WHEN THE CENTER HOLDS:
CONCLUSIONS AND IMPLICATIONS

Why do central governments decentralize power? And under what conditions
can they reverse the decentralization of power? After beginning this analysis
with these two questions, I have examined why fiscal relations between
different levels of government change over time, using evidence from four
countries in the developing world that represent a wide range of experiences
with subnational autonomy: Brazil is a case of quite high autonomy and "robust
federalism," with South Africa being a "quasi-federal" state with moderate
subnational autonomy, and Peru and Senegal being more historically centralized unitary states. Subnational fiscal autonomy in these countries has varied
over time in recent years primarily because of changes in the political economy,
not due to static institutional factors. Central governments in all four countries
decentralized power to some degree, but only in the cases of Brazil and
Peru did central governments succeed in recentralizing on a national basis.
The two African countries (surprisingly) recentralized much less, with South
Africa making only limited recentralizing reforms and Senegal failing to
recentralize even when attempts were made. Two dynamic shifts in the political
economy—electoral decline and economic crisis—triggered these changes
in fiscal relations. Decline and crisis shift the balance of government power
by respectively decreasing and increasing the political power of presidents,
who represent the interests of the center. In this final chapter, I address several theoretical conclusions, and examine the implications of the findings.

The Political Economy and Institutions of Subnational Autonomy

This book draws heavily on two major literatures: political economy and
comparative institutionalism (with an emphasis on presidential powers and

on federalism). Explanations drawing on these two areas have also interacted throughout the argument. Changes in the political economy drive large "macrolevel" shifts in decentralization and (re)centralization. These changes are then mediated through different institutional arenas depending on the relevant issue area, be these subnational revenues, subnational expenditures, or subnational contracts.

Comparative political economy emerges clearly in the treatment of the two independent variables: electoral decline and economic crisis. Central governments decentralize power and correspondingly increase subnational fiscal autonomy, when suffering electoral weakness at the national level. In times of decline, presidents (who under normal circumstances represent central interests more than other political actors) are more vulnerable to bottom-up pressures from subnational actors within their own governing coalition. Simultaneously, as Kathleen O'Neill (2003, 2005) and others have noted, the national-level decline of a president's party increases the attractiveness of top-down solutions whereby presidents choose to strengthen subnational governments in order to develop or strengthen regional bases for the future. This twofold logic favoring decentralization is found in decentralizing moments in all four countries, even though institutional environments—including electoral rules, presidential authority, political party systems, and degrees of federalism—varied dramatically. In Peru and Senegal, decentralization occurred when parties anticipated defeat in regularly scheduled national elections, while in Brazil and South Africa, decentralization occurred at Constituent Assemblies when departing presidents were especially weak.

Whereas decentralization depends in political decline, recentralization is a function of the resolution of macroeconomic crisis. More precisely, presidents who resolve hyperinflationary crises gain unprecedented leverage over subnational governments and are able to recentralize power. Interestingly, recentralization after crisis occurs even in the two weaker party systems (Brazil and Peru), whereas in the absence of crisis, even dominant governments in strong party systems (South Africa and Senegal) could not recentralize. This evidence shows that the need to build on comparative static models that predict stable political party institutions drives differences in centralism and decentralism. Additional observable implications reinforce the argument: I have shown that even small, localized fiscal crises in the South African case also generate a centralizing dynamic, but one that is correspondingly weaker than the dynamic created by larger systemic crises.

Comparative institutionalism emerges as central to the argument insofar as battles over subnational autonomy play out in different institutional arenas for different issue areas. The three outcomes of interest are affected through different political mechanisms. Revenue autonomy, examined in chapter 3, is affected most directly by the president's power relative to the legislature. Governing parties facing national defeat increase revenue autonomy across the range of countries. The decline of sitting governments can take place in the realm of everyday politics, or at more particular foundational moments, as in the case of regime change at the Constituent National Assembly in South Africa. The analysis extends existing arguments about the secular decline of parties into a more general argument about why subnational revenue auto-nomy increases as governments weaken. In these moments, presidents must accommodate legislators in their own parties, in order to strengthen the party for the future; as the party's hold on national government weakens, the balance of power in the governing party shifts toward legislators (who increasingly look to SNGs for their political futures) and away from the president. On the flip side of these declines are the occasions when presidents that successfully managed economic crisis (in Brazil and Peru) were able to assert their authority over the legislature. In doing so, they were able to recentralize revenues. Again, the broader political economy triggers change: absent crisis, even presidents with exceptionally high legislative backing (Senegal and South Africa) were surprisingly weak willed in reducing revenue autonomy.

Subnational expenditure autonomy (assessed in chapter 4) depends not only on executive–legislative relations, but rather varies inversely with the strength of the president in controlling the executive. This is because states have greater authority in implementing expenditure rules than in shaping revenue flows. For this portion of the argument, it is crucial to emphasize that presidential control over the executive branch is not constant over time. Presidents in Brazil and Peru increased their authority over their own branch of government after resolving their respective economic crises. After defeating hyperinflation—the key indicator for a macroeconomic crisis—the Brazilian and Peruvian presidents asserted (in authoritarian fashion in Peru's case) greater powers of appointment over their cabinets, relative to their prede-cessors. Such presidents, who can place like-minded loyalists to prominent cabinet posts, are better able to control subnational expenditures (and reduce subnational expenditure autonomy) in those sectors. Elsewhere, African central states generally retained power over expenditures throughout this period. In both Senegal and South Africa, power was transferred directly from one strong government to another. Presidential control over the cabinet, ministries, and state bureaucracy was not compromised. As a result, no signi-ficant devolution of expenditure autonomy occurred. Clearly, the overall level of decentralization was less significant in the area of expenditure than in the area of revenues; accounting for this necessitates the understanding of various institutional arenas offered here, to complement the extant arguments in the decentralization literature about party politics.

Finally, contractual autonomy (i.e., the independence of subnational governments in setting their own contracts in labor and capital markets) is partially affected by executive–legislative relations and by intra-executive considerations, but also by its own particular dynamic, as is shown in chapter 5. Here, government decline and economic crisis also shifted presidents' power in their direct negotiations with subnational politicians. Beyond the legislature and the executive, presidents also negotiate directly with governors, mayors, and other subnational government officials. In ways similar to those shown above, decline weakens presidents in bargaining processes and leads to greater concessions, such as the funding of state banks and increased latitude for provinces and municipalities in debt issuance. Crisis resolution, on the other hand, allows presidents to eliminate state-level banks, impose conditionalities on provinces, reduce borrowing privileges, reform subnational hiring and firing practices, and even directly subsume regional officials into the national executive.

Particularly in the study of concepts as complex as decentralization, there are multiple ways of interrogating case countries. I have opted for a dynamic treatment of changes over time, as contrasted with comparative static snapshots. In order to give a brief consideration to this sort of static cross-national perspective, we can line up the cases as follows in table 7.1 for the present day.

In such a cross-national approach to explain current levels of subnational autonomy, the outcomes here would correlate highly with prevailing sets of political institutions, as found in Garman, Haggard, and Willis (2001). In Brazil, for instance, high levels of subnational autonomy would coexist alongside federalism and electoral rules that favor local elites; similarly, in Peru, centralization correlates with traditionally weak links between subnational officials and the national Congress. The analytical puzzles, in this perspective, are historical: why do countries develop trends in centralism or decentralism the way they do? These outcomes, and the institutions that appear to be their proximal causes, lend themselves to a longer-term historical analysis, of the type presented in chapter 2. Such an approach sets the broad parameters of the cases, enabling us to understand how each comes "up to the starting line" and enabling an explanation that focuses on the question of shorter-term variations. The historical approach of chapter 2 enables us to disentangle where influential institutions come from, while also bracketing

Table 7.1 Centralism and decentralism in the case countries: Comparative statics

Autonomy	Brazil	Peru	Senegal	South Africa
Revenue	High	Low	Low	High
Expenditure	Medium	Low	Low	Low
Contractual	Medium	Low	Low	Low

this discussion and enabling the subsequent analysis that relies not on comparative statics, but on comparative dynamics.

An alternative way of examining the cases would be to look at a single moment of change and to maximize variation in these outcomes across the three areas. Focusing for the moment just on revenues and expenditures (and leaving aside contractual autonomy briefly) an example of this approach might fit the cases as in table 7.2 below. Using one moment from each country, we could fill the range of possibilities in the decentralization or centralization of revenue and expenditure. We could then examine whether the changes devolved revenue and expenditure concurrently ("equilibrating") or not, as well as which level of government gains from the reform in terms of power shifts.

Attention to which level of government is favored by centralization and decentralization is crucial for illustrating that not all forms of decentralization favor SNGs, nor do all forms of centralization favor the center. For instance, the two principal cases of centralizing reform in this study took quite different forms. Brazil's Cardoso *decentralized* expenditures under democratic auspices while Peru's Fujimori *recentralized* expenditures in an authoritarian fashion, yet in both cases, the president's responses to crisis provided governing opportunities that enabled the center to delimit what SNGs can do with their money.

However, this figure too offers only a partial view of the story of intergovernmental relations, because it begs prior questions about the origins of institutions. Of course, this does not obviate the need for explanations of how institutions perpetuate patterns once these are established. In South Africa, for instance, a strong national party with top-down discipline, a strong Parliament without district allegiances, and a weak upper chamber (the NCOP) will tend to perpetuate strong central control over subnational autonomy, while legal precedent and the "stickiness" of decentralization protect subnational revenues. In Brazil, by contrast, a very strong Senate and district-based lower chamber of the Parliament, and a weak party system mean that presidents will still require regional support for many initiatives even with enhanced legal backing; subnational autonomy has been reduced somewhat but will

Table 7.2 Centralization and decentralization in the case countries: Recent reforms

Revenue	Expenditure	Equilibrating?	Change favors?	Example (Country-Year)
Decentralized	Centralized	No	SNG	Brazil 1988 (not after 1994)
Centralized	Centralized	Yes	CG	Peru 1992
Centralized	Decentralized	No	CG	Senegal 1996
Decentralized	Decentralized	Yes	SNG	South Africa 1996

remain strong. Institutions similarly matter in Peru and Senegal, where weak parliaments, executives with strong powers, and governing parties with weak links to local districts will prevent any major increases in subnational fiscal autonomy in the short term. A major implication of this research is not to expunge institutional explanations, but rather to note that these are limited in their causal power and must be complemented with historical process-tracing of the origins of change.

The Argument in the Cases and Beyond the Cases

In examining three distinct areas of decentralization, along with the converse process of (re)centralization, I have forwarded an argument that is broadly compatible with certain of the existing literatures on decentralization, though I also have aimed to add texture and conceptual development by considering revenues, the decentralization of expenditure rules, and the underexamined elements of contractual autonomy. With regard to recentralization, I have aimed to demonstrate that the reversal of reform can prove politically distinct from the enactment of initial reform (cf., e.g., Pierson 1996). Understanding recentralization as a converse of decentralization will be increasingly essential as the prospect arises in more countries.

The findings here support the rationalist-institutionalist vein in studies of decentralization, though I focus less on actors' decisions and more on the consequences of political-economic changes and institutional design. Among the rationalist-institutionalist writings on decentralization, the arguments here echo the findings of the likes of Kathleen O'Neill, Kent Eaton, and Victoria Rodriguez. Indeed, Peru is one of the Andean cases O'Neill uses to demonstrate that decentralization is driven by parties with declining national power and robust regional power, and O'Neill's (2003, 2005) findings are essential building blocks for my argument. The Peruvian APRA under Alan García exemplifies the declining national party with a strong subnational base.

South Africa similarly supports O'Neill's conclusions, with minor modifications. The puzzle in South Africa was why the incoming ANC, a party destined to be hegemonic and whose *weaknesses* lay in regional opposition, would permit decentralization. Yet the transition shows that decentralization was not the choice of the ANC, but was rather the principal compromise necessary to effectuate the transition itself. The National Party was willing to accede to ANC predominance at the national level, provided the ANC would devolve substantial authority to those levels of government where the NP could build a political future. Combined with the ANC's imperative to adopt a technocratic approach to the transition, the correlation of political forces dictated some decentralization. South Africa's decentralization was in fact pushed through by parties whose political future lay at the subnational level, most notably the NP, as O'Neill's argument predicts.

For the Brazilian case, understanding changes in the 1980s requires a greater focus on bottom-up dynamics. Here Kent Eaton's (2004a) work is essential. The changes at the Constituent National Assembly of 1987–88 came as a weak president caved to strong pressures from subnational actors (cf. Martinez-Lara 1996). The relative coordination of these subnational actors in Brazil is quite different from the top-down calculations made by APRA or the NP. Historical weakness at the center was the distal causal factor for electoral rules that favor subnational elites; these rules in turn are a proximal causal factor for decentralism. Moreover, the sequence of the transition to democracy favored subnational governments, as their 1982 election prior to the election of the president (which followed only in 1985) gave them a coherence at the Constituent Assembly that few other forces shared. Again, Brazil's long historical trajectory based on "bottom-up" federal dynamics undoubtedly favored such an outcome.

Senegal in the 1990s witnessed a dominant but weakening party decentralizing in order to shore up its flagging support, echoing similar findings for the likes of Mexico (cf. Rodriguez 1997). National elites at the head of a long-governing party—the PS in Senegal, like the PRI in Mexico—sought proactively to shore up their legitimacy and electability by conferring some limited autonomy to subnational actors. Top-down logics intertwined with bottom-up logics in Senegal: the PS leadership needed to accommodate growing numbers of the party's disaffected rank and file, and thus had an additional reason to open SNGs up to elections. While Peru was a case of straightforward electoral calculation by the national governing elite, and

Brazil was a case of superior subnational power, Senegal suggests that top-down logics can work alongside bottom-up ones.

Decentralization in relatively centralized states, both unitary and federal, can thus often be explained by the electoral motivations of governing parties at the center, but the cases here illustrate the need to broaden the view of electoralist motivations. Divergent cases support a range of calculations by partisans and presidents as causes for decentralization, beyond the narrow focus on a governing party's calculations about its relative power at central and subnational levels. By permitting variations in specific paths to decentralization while retaining a common origin, an understanding of processes of governmental decline and weakness improves empirical fit for a wider range of cases.[1] To be sure, shifting from narrow arguments about relative partisan strength to broader arguments about presidential weakness sacrifices some of the elegance of a highly parsimonious explanation for the improved fit it offers. Yet the broader conception of motivations for decentralization also, crucially, enables the argument to explain a wider range of cases, including robust federal systems with undeniable bottom-up dynamics and cross-regional applicability (such as to African cases).

The argument regarding recentralization also draws empirical support from beyond the four cases directly examined. With respect to scope conditions for the argument that recentralization is a consequence of crisis and its resolution, it is important to recall that the present argument is about recentralization after decentralization, though I have also documented the number of ways central governments can retain authority even in the presence of decentralization. Some prior degree of decentralization is a necessary prerequisite for the argument that economic crisis resolution leads to recentralization. As such, the argument does not address stasis in highly centralized countries where no decentralization has been undertaken. It may be that one can extend the argument to say the logic of crisis and its resolution will facilitate central authority generally, but I have not offered a full examination of these linkages. For example, Zimbabwe is perhaps the most significant case of hyperinflation in recent years, but the present argument for recentralization is not expected to hold there, since Zimbabwe has had neither

1. The need to loosen the strictures of the electoral calculation argument can be illustrated by cases beyond the four chosen here. Venezuela provides an example. In this case, O'Neill's (2005) own account of mid-1990s decentralization introduces multiple political parties—including both Acción Democrática (AD) and the Comité de Organización Política Electoral Independiente (COPEI)—and even newly crafted negotiating institutions such as the Comisión Presidencial para la Reforma del Estado (COPRE, the Presidential Commission on State Reform) as actors driving a nuanced decentralization process.

any significant prior fiscal decentralization nor a turnover in government from the Mugabe regime that initiated the crisis. Barring these, further "centralization" of power in the executive may occur in a case like Zimbabwe, but this does not signify change in the intergovernmental relations that are the subject of the present argument.

While decentralization is a prerequisite for meaningful recentralization (as conceptualized here), the pressing causal issue is whether economic crisis is a necessary and/or sufficient condition to explain successful fiscal recentralization. While comprehensive testing of the argument on other cases may generate new conditions and revised probabilistic explanations, the present argument does offer initial insight into how decentralizing and recentralizing moves unfold in cases beyond the four examined here. One example is contemporary Venezuela under President Hugo Chávez, a case where recentralization efforts have advanced modestly, but where eradicating the fiscal autonomy of SNGs has also proved elusive even for a powerful president.[2] While a full treatment of the Venezuelan case is not possible here, two facts are especially salient. First is the sequence of centralization efforts under Chávez. Venezuela approached the hyperinflationary threshold at the end of the Rafael Caldera government from 1996 to 1998, reaching a peak of approximately 100 percent per year in 1996 (International Monetary Fund 2008). While the inflationary situation was not as dire as in Peru under García's first administration, certain parallels between the cases are striking, as Venezuelans came to find themselves operating in the "domain of losses," to use Weyland's (2002) term, and increased their tolerance for higher-risk reforms to rectify the political economy. Weyland (2002, 244) further specifies parallels, as Venezuelans (like Peruvians in 1990) elected a "radical antisystem outsider" who proceeded to arrogate power to the office of the presidency and undertake recentralizing efforts. In the decade following their respective elections, each leader then continued on similar paths of increasing authoritarianism, which included efforts to undercut the mayor of the capital city—one of the country's leading subnational elected officials—in each case. How far Chávez can eventually push recentralization in Venezuela is uncertain, and it remains possible that overt fiscal recentralization may arise as part of a path-dependent, contingent sequence that differs from that outlined for Peru, but it is striking that Chávez's efforts at recentralization (both political and fiscal) emerged

---

2. I am thankful to Jonathan Eastwood for his helpful comments on the Venezuelan case, including the need for close attention to the areas where Hugo Chávez has succeeded in recentralizing authority since attempted constitutional reforms in 2007. The usual disclaimer applies that any errors of interpretation are my own.

in the wake of economic crisis, and that success has been somewhat slower and more uncertain on fiscal issues than in Peru, where economic crisis was more acute.

For the second way in which the argument aids in interpreting the Venezuelan case, we turn from the "macro" argument about political economy to the "micro" argument about institutional arenas and how these matter. Among the many areas where Chávez has endeavored to centralize authority, his success has perhaps been most checkered in recentralizing fiscal power from state and municipal governments. As late as 2004, after dramatic changes to legislative, judicial, and party systems, Cruz (2004, 198–201) found that decentralization "continue[d] to enjoy a high level of support," even among Chavistas in the National Assembly, since these needed to retain constituent support, and even as Chávez himself sought a variety of paths to reduce or eliminate SNG powers. Setbacks to Chávez in efforts to eliminate subnational autonomy directly continued up through the failed 2007 referendum, in which Chávez sought (among other expansions of his powers) the right to appoint SNG officials. Consistent with the experiences of executive branches in the other cases here, Chávez has responded to the thorny challenge of intergovernmental relations by looking beyond fiscal recentralization to a variety of other approaches to reassert central power. In particular, Chávez has sought to marginalize states and municipalities by reshaping the institutional arena via alternative providers of public goods directed by the presidency, such as via local *misiones* and the national development fund FONDEN (Corrales and Penfold 2007, 106; Myers 2009, 317). Nonetheless, in a descriptive survey of Chávez's efforts to increase his powers across several issue areas, Myers (2009, 312–18) shows how the Venezuelan president had removed most political veto points in the legislature, the judiciary, and elsewhere in Venezuelan society through a restructuring of executive action, but can only document more limited success in eliminating regional government as a veto point.

Venezuela from the mid-1990s to the present seems to provide initial evidence (from beyond the cases selected) to support two of my central contentions. The first is the assertion that executives may work from a menu of governing options at their disposal in holding fiscal power, as outlined especially in chapter 4. That is, "the center can hold" in a number of ways. The other finding emerges directly from the causal argument regarding centralizing dynamics: fiscal decentralization is quite "sticky" once established, and efforts at recentralization are likely to have only limited success (of the kind seen in South Africa) if not sequenced after significant economic crises. High levels of contestation over recentralization in Venezuela can be understood through the optics of an otherwise strongly positioned executive lacking the extraordinary justification that deep economic crisis offered to recentralization efforts in Peru and Brazil. Together, these observations suggest that while central governments have numerous instruments for holding fiscal power and increasing their own autonomy of action through new institutional mechanisms, they have less leverage to reduce the fiscal power of SNGs once decentralization has occurred. To be sure, Venezuela's future path is uncertain, and direct fiscal recentralization remains an apparent objective for the president and an open possibility; recent attempts to further centralize power show this continues to advance on a piecemeal basis. The hypothesis generated by the present argument, however, is that Chávez will continue to be more successful in creating new central institutions to circumnavigate states and municipalities than he will be in directly recentralizing revenues from SNGs. Should Chávez succeed more convincingly in direct recentralization, this will necessitate further explication of the sequences linking economic crises and recentralization, most particularly in cases where regimes move in increasingly authoritarian directions and where presidencies have successfully dismantled other governing institutions.

The findings from the cases examined also have implications beyond the study of decentralization. First, I have sought to explain short-term, within-country variations. My analysis explains why patterns of change vary across countries *and* over time, with time being the most crucial source of variation. In the broadest sense, I argue that institutional theories must be supplemented in order to explain such processes of intertemporal change. Drawing on the criticisms made by Robert Bates (1988), I have problematized the origins of the political institutions that govern fiscal relationships within countries. As a result, my conclusions go beyond comparative statics, as suggested above: the central question is not why Brazil is more decentralized than Senegal (a historical question treated in a necessarily brief fashion in chapter 2), but rather, why both Brazil and Senegal (and Peru and South Africa) changed their intergovernmental systems when they did.

Purely institutional analyses might consider these changes in the political economy to be "exogenous shocks," but these shocks must be at the heart of studies that require dynamic causes for fiscal relations. Institutions do matter, but they are often *intervening* variables that mediate shifts in the political economy and translate them into outcomes. One of the major implications of this study, therefore, builds on work by scholars such as Haggard and Kaufman (1992, 1995), who place political economy at the core of their analyses, yet remain attentive to the ways in which institutional environments condition outcomes. Such lessons transcend the specific content area addressed. In this regard, what holds for democratization holds for decentralization and recentralization.

Among the institutions that shape decentralization and recentralization, federalism looms large. Federal states are seen by some scholars as a brand of states apart from unitary states; the emphasis on federalism in the literature is well-deserved, as recent work has amply demonstrated (Diaz-Cayeros 2006; Gibson 2004; Rodden 2006; Wibbels 2005). Most obviously, the questions of subnational autonomy are typically most salient as the degree of federalism increases. In addition, it goes without saying that federalism correlates heavily with the institutional designs that shape SNG autonomy. Any study of decentralization or recentralization would neglect the "front-and-center" nature of federalism at its peril. And the benefits of taking federalism seriously are not just in costs avoided: existing debates on the measure and causal role of federalism are themselves rich and varied, providing important theoretical underpinnings for studies of central–subnational politics.

Acknowledging federalism's obvious salience, I argue that it is of ambiguous importance for decentralization and recentralization. Ambiguous because federalism matters for some aspects of intergovernmental relations, but not others. It clearly matters for the overall level of decentralism, for instance. Country trajectories make clear that partisan politics are not the whole story, but rather that deep historical legacies are perpetuated through time. Long-term trends are strongly conditioned by historical developments: the more historically decentralized country (Brazil) remains the more decentralized today, and so on. The amount of independent revenues transferred to SNGs in unitary countries will likely never match that in Brazil, and this can be traced to long-run paths and sequences that contemporary developments in political economy cannot explain. Similarly, federalism entered into my argument in shaping the particular sequence linking crisis resolution and recentralization, with high levels of SNG autonomy in federal Brazil requiring the central government to *simultaneously* address economic crisis and fiscal federalism, whereas the recentralization in unitary Peru came *sequentially* after the economic crisis was fundamentally resolved. In these ways, federalism sets the empirical backdrop for a given case and may be expected to shape the details of fiscal change, since federalism (as an institutional arrangement) clearly vests SNGs with greater negotiating powers than in unitary states.

Being a product of long-run historical conditions, however, federalism as a variable is ill equipped to explain short-term dynamics, and a country's federal or unitary status does not alter the fundamental causal arguments here. Top-down decentralization occurred in both federal and unitary states, for instance, though bottom-up decentralization seems likelier to happen in federal states alone, given that subnational power is needed to make "decentralization from below" happen. Across the spectrum of four cases that range from robust federal systems through weak federal systems to centralized unitary states, decentralization happened for similar reasons of governmental decline and weakness. Similarly, as noted, recentralization in the wake of crisis happens in both federal and unitary cases, with federalism influencing only the different particular sequences linking the two variables. In terms of recentralization, the two unitary cases notably represented the two most different outcomes: the most complete recentralization and the case of failed attempts at recentralization. Meanwhile, Brazil recentralized more than South Africa despite a bevy of institutional variables—linked to federalism—that would predict the contrary.

Bureaucratic Centralization and Extreme Decentralization

Some of the most pressing questions on the topic of decentralization and intergovernmental relations are not about causes but about consequences. In this study, I have not intended to express a normative preference for decentralization, and I do not assume that more decentralization is better. Rather, the normative appeal of centralization varies by case, and with the degree of federalism. In Brazil, for instance, enhanced central control of SNG spending was viewed as desirable and even necessary by international capital markets and most observers. Simply put, Brazil is historically too decentralized. Extreme decentralization compromised macroeconomic stability and effective service provision in social policy, and perpetuated local and regional oligarchies. In unitary states with legacies of centralism, by contrast, tight central control can signal a fearfulness of devolution that raises legitimate concerns about excessive central power. Some countries (Senegal, and especially Peru) are historically overcentralized. Yet not all decentralization processes are advantageous, even in highly centralized states: decentralization processes in Peru and Senegal did little to enhance subnational autonomy.

Political scientists, policymakers, and other observers of governance have expressed a variety of justifications for decentralization. First is an assumption that decentralized government is "closer to the people," and one key corollary holds that decentralized government will thus be more progressive and participatory. For some, decentralization can signify deeper local democracy based on increased grassroots mobilization. A second corollary for others is that SNGs will exhibit higher levels of state efficacy and effectiveness than central governments, since decentralization can trim bloated central states. Empirical evidence on the "failure of the centralized state" (cf. Wunsch and Olowu 1990) is seen as tantamount to a need for decentralization; theoretically, decentralization promotes fiscal federal ideals wherein local jurisdictions can approximate market-based competition by offering different clusters of public goods and taxation rates to current and prospective inhabitants. Decentralization thus enables high-performing SNGs to distinguish themselves from others, and facilitates better matching of societal demands with public supply of goods, whereas centralized governance fails to do so. A third purported advantage of decentralization is the concern that subnational government in the developing world is historically underdeveloped, and that continued centralization due to low local capacity will create a vicious circle that will only lead to fewer options in the future. And fourth is the argument that decentralization improves political socialization, with stronger local government serving as the basis for future national leaders in politics and society. Though not an exhaustive list of the reasons for decentralization, these arguments are probably the most significant, with the first two being the most prominent in the literature. In brief, with SNGs being "closer" to the people than central government, increasing the scope of SNGs relative to the center will improve local access to political decision making, and improved responsiveness and accountability, as local elected officials face incentives to reply to local demands.

Decentralization and recentralization may each be optimal policy under different fiscal circumstances. Rapid centralization may go hand in hand with strong central government capable of resolving economic crises, but this need not necessarily lead to the construction of even-handed relations between central and subnational governments. Conversely, while the weakening of presidential partisan powers promotes decentralization, weak party systems do not necessarily engender the consolidation of good governance. In short, the root causes of decentralization have ambiguous effects on governance. The appropriate changes to improve an intergovernmental fiscal system depend heavily on a country's political context at given historical moments.

Adherence to the principles of fiscal federalism may thus be more appropriate than unconditional support for decentralization. Early normative arguments in favor of decentralization were drawn from economic theorems, of which the theorems of fiscal federalism (Oates 1972) and the efficiencies generated by jurisdictional mobility (Tiebout 1956) were paramount. This fiscal federal logic is supported by the cases here, if precisely because the country cases (like most) fail to fit the ideal type. Generally, the unitary cases (Peru and Senegal) would benefit in terms of social service provision from strengthening SNGs at the expense of the center, since the fiscal predominance of the center is not in question, while the more federal cases (Brazil and South Africa) benefit in terms of fiscal stability from strengthening central power at the expense of SNGs. The experiences of Brazil (1988–98) and South Africa (1995–97) demonstrate that subnational profligacy can be more destructive than the centralization of power. In strongly federal countries, where central governments struggle with powerful regional elites, there are good reasons for reformers to argue that recentralization can improve equity, service provision, and political modernization. The initial problems with the provinces in South Africa were turned around largely because the central government recognized decentralization's dangers. Additionally, the fiscal federal framework—in its ideal form—can also limit or control potentially destructive fiscal competition between SNGs. Similarly, central governments must play the lead roles in laws on the establishment and demarcation of municipalities and regions. Focusing on strengthening SNGs can be disastrous where the center is too weak even to regulate interjurisdictional competition.

An additional conceptual implication matters for political scientists and practitioners: support for local government does not equal decentralization. "Decentralization" should exclusively denote increases in subnational autonomy, as devolved *from central government to subnational government*. By contrast, a number of donor agencies have promoted governance projects as "decentralization" that primarily involve direct transfers from donors to local governments, or support for institutional development of SNGs. The essence of decentralization must be a *political* process of change by which power and/or resources are moved from the center to those levels of government beyond the center. Far from denying the center a major role in the process, this justifiably places intergovernmental relations—and not simply the empowerment of SNGs—at the heart of decentralization. National governments must be viewed as "central" players in decentralization schemes, in order to ensure improvements in the all-important linkages between levels of government. Improving decentralization involves greater incorporation of central governments, not less.

Following the fiscal federal logic laid out above, it will often prove advantageous to strengthen the capacity of ministries of finance to manage intergovernmental financial relations, while strengthening the policy powers of subnational officials (both elected and appointed) in social service areas. South Africa succinctly illustrates why: technocrats in the National Treasury have very successfully coordinated fiscal relations, but central ministry dominance in health was disastrous in the face of the AIDS epidemic, in large part because the center precluded local-level flexibility in treatment. Enhancing finance ministry monitoring of subnational spending is of particular importance in more federal states, where subnational fiscal profligacy can have deleterious effects on the national macroeconomy; subnational flexibility in implementing social policy solutions is equally necessary.

Strengthening the national bureaucracy in finance and subnational bureaucracies in social service sectors fits with the principles of fiscal federalism and offers opportunities to fulfill the ideal of subnational experimentation, with the center setting the framework for questions of national importance while allowing subnational government greater flexibility in the provision of public goods in order to respond to the needs and demands of differing constituencies. More generally, the recommendation for supporters of decentralized governance is to shift the conceptual view of the policy terrain. A *relational* view of intergovernmental finance, as opposed to a focus purely on the performance and needs of SNGs, will allow for improved communication between levels of government. Rather than simply aiming to reform and strengthen subnational government, policy advocates should aim to reform and strengthen linkages between central and subnational government (cf. Burki, Perry, and Dillinger 1999).

Negotiating the terrain between excessively centralized politics and excessively decentralized politics also means viewing subnational autonomy across all the issue areas examined here, and not only one area (such as revenues). Future analyses of decentralization must consider treating revenue and expenditure as distinct (yet interrelated) elements of a national fiscal system. Decentralizing expenditures without decentralizing revenues can lead to bureaucratic centralization, while the inverse can lead to excessive decentralization. This book suggests a way to approach these various elements, in the hope of producing both improved analyses and improved policy.

Beyond Decentralization: When the Center Holds

One of Peru's foremost commentators on centralism and decentralization argued that the concept of decentralization has been "prostituted" by national

governments for decades (Planas 2001, 51). And indeed, rhetoric and excitement about decentralization has far outpaced real reforms in many countries.
One of my claims is that the center holds onto far more power than genera-
tions of would-be decentralizers would wish. Decentralization is more complex
and contested than is often assumed in certain policy circles, where it is
argued to be a "win-win" proposition. In some cases, decentralization has
meant less than full transfer of authority to subnational governments, while
in other cases decentralization has created "more problems than solutions,"
to return to the telling quote of a Senegalese official.

Decentralization remains open for debate, and its causes are only beginning
to be firmly established in comparative perspective. Yet, simultaneously, we
must begin to reckon with the implications of a recentralizing "reverse wave"
that may be taking shape in many of the cases where decentralization was
most assertive. Despite a recent growth of scholarly contributions, this reverse
wave remains the understudied area of intergovernmental relations. The
central aims of this analysis are to improve the reach and depth of our
understanding of decentralization and its causes, as well as those of its
converse, (re)centralization. We need explanations of both when the center
concedes power to SNGs, and when the center holds onto power and resources;
I have argued that such explanations require an analysis of both the political
economy and prevailing political institutions. Among these institutions,
federalism has an ambiguous place: it clearly matters—as a defining concept,
a cause, and an outcome—but it does not alter the causes of decentralization and recentralization.

A continued focus on decentralization, federalism, and now recentralization is growing even more pressing. As most studies of decentralization
have noted, the contributions of this field are not limited to debates within
comparative politics; rather, fundamental normative issues about the quality
of governance are at issue here. Knowledge of intergovernmental politics,
across a wide variety of political systems, will offer greater wisdom in making
policies governing subnational autonomy.

APPENDIX: INTERVIEWEES (BY COUNTRY)

Brazil

Amorim Araújo, Erika. Economist, Banco Nacional de Desenvolvimento Econômico e Social (BNDES). Rio de Janeiro, August 7, 2001.

Arretche, Marta. Professor of Political Science, UNICAMP. São Paulo, June 29, 2001.

Blumm, Maria Helena. Ministry of Health. Brasilia, August 9, 2001.

Bresser Pereira, Luiz Carlos. Former Minister of Finance and Former Minister of Public Administration and State Reform (Administração Pública e Reforma do Estado). São Paulo, August 8, 2001.

Gonçalves de Castro, Robison. Technical advisor, Federal Senate. Brasilia, August 10, 2001.

Graeff, Eduardo. Special Advisor to the President. Brasilia, August 10, 2001.

Guimarães, Maria do Carmo. Professor of Political Science, Universidade Federal da Bahia. Salvador, August 2001.

Kahlil, Jorge. Technical advisor, Ministry of Finance. Brasilia, August 10, 2001.

Mendes, Marcos. Economist at the Central Bank of Brazil, former Economist at the Brazilian Senate, Debt Specialist at the National Treasury. São Paulo, June 28, 2001.

Moraes, Filomeno. Professor of Political Science, Universidade de Fortaleza. Fortaleza, August 30, 2001.

Nakano, Yoshiaki. Former Secretary of State for Finance, São Paulo State. São Paulo, July 24, 2001.

Parente, Josênio. Professor of Sociology, Universidade Federal do Ceará. Fortaleza, August 29, 2001.

Prado, Deildes de Oliveira. Director, Regionalization Program, Ministry of Health. Brasilia, August 10, 2001.
de Queiroz, Lucia de Fátima Nascimento. Technical expert, Ministry of Health. Brasilia, August 10, 2001.
Serra, José. Former Minister of Health, Former Minister of Planning, Former Presidential Candidate (PSDB). Princeton, N.J., July 27, 2003.
Souza, Celina. Professor of Political Science, Universidade Federal da Bahia. São Paulo, July 11, 2001.
Spink, Peter. Director, Programa de Gestão Pública e Cidadania, Fundação Getulio Vargas–São Paulo (FGV). São Paulo, June 27, 2001.

Peru

Aldave, Ivan. Banco Central de Reserva del Perú. Lima, April 9, 2003.
Anonymous. CARE-Perú. Lima, June 20, 2000.
Arenas, Freddy. Technical consultant, Regiduria de Transito de la Municipalidad Provincial de Chiclayo. Chiclayo, July 20, 2000.
Aspajo, Francisco. General Manager, Instituto de Desarrollo del Sector Informal (IDESI). Chiclayo, July 21, 2000.
Balbi, Carmen Rosa. Political Scientist, Pontificia Universidad Católica del Perú (PUCP). Lima, July 1, 2000.
Carpena de Doig, Angelica. Municipal Manager, Regiduria de Transito de la Municipalidad Provincial de Chiclayo. Chiclayo, July 20, 2000.
Dongo, Rafael Valencia. Congressman. Lima, April 11, 2003.
Flores, Flavio, and Forrest Metz. Consultants, Instituto del Desarrollo del Sector Informal (IDESI). Lima, June 28, 2000.
Gonzalez, Pepe. Manager, Camara de Comercio y de Producción de Lambayeque. Chiclayo, July 20, 2000.
Gonzales de Olarte, Efraín. Professor of Political Science, Pontifícia Universidad Católica del Perú. Princeton, N.J., October 20, 2001, and Lima, April 15, 2003.
Grompone, Romeo. Sociologist, Instituto de Estudios Peruanos. Lima, June 20, 2000.
Guerrero, Elsie. Director of Commercialization, Municipalidad de Lima. Lima, July 3, 2000.
Haak, David Sulmont. Sociologist, Pontificia Universidad Católica del Perú (PUCP). Lima, June 26, 2000.
Herrera, Ernesto. Congressman, Perú Posible. Lima, April 10, 2003.

Hurtado, Daniel. General Manager, Centro de Servicios Empresariales (CESEM). Chiclayo, July 21, 2000.

Kouri, Henry. Mayor, Pimentel (Lambayeque department). Chiclayo, July 21, 2000.

Kuczynski, Pedro-Pablo. Former Minister of Finance, Alejandro Toledo government. Miami (via telephone), March 17, 2003.

Melendez, Rosa Ivonne. Regional Manager for Investment Promotion, Lambayeque department. Chiclayo, July 19, 2000.

Mendoza, Waldo. Ministry of Economy and Finance. Lima, April 11, 2003.

Mesones, Carlos Balarezo. Regional Director, Ministerio de Industria, Turismo, Integración y Negociaciones Internacionales, Lambayeque department. Chiclayo, July 25, 2000.

Noblesilla, Fernando. Deputy Mayor, Municipalidad Provincial de Chiclayo. Chiclayo, July 24, 2000.

Ortiz de Zavallos, Gabriel. Director/President, Instituto Apoyo. Lima, April 17, 2003.

Portugal, Franz. Advisor to Congressman Cesár Zumaeta. Lima, April 10, 2003.

Reátegui, Felipe. Banco Central de Reserva del Perú. Lima, April 9, 2003.

Rosa, Felix de la. President, Concejo Transitorio de Administracion Regional, Lambayeque department. Chiclayo, July 19, 2000.

Ruiz Hui, Manuel. Banco Central de Reserva del Perú. Lima, April 10, 2003.

Tanaka, Martin. Sociologist, Instituto de Estudios Peruanos. Lima, July 11, 2000.

Torres, Mario. Banco Central de Reserva del Perú. Lima, April 10, 2003.

Torres, Pablo. Director of Informal Commerce, Municipalidad de Lima. Lima, July 3, 2000.

Vega, Rudecindo. Former official, Ministry of the Presidency, Advisor to President Alejandro Toledo. Lima, April 10, 2003.

Webb, Richard. President, Banco Central de Reserva del Perú. Lima, April 9, 2003.

Senegal

Ba, Abdou Wahab. Decentralization Project Manager, USAID. Dakar, October 30, 2001.

Ba, Omar. Technical expert, Direction d'Expansion Rurale, Government of Senegal. Dakar, October 30, 2001.

Ba, Seynabou. Decentralization Expert, ENDA–Tiers Monde, European Union Cooperation. Dakar, June 11, 2002.

Bocoum, Amadou. Local Finance Analyst, Direction des Collectivites Locales. Dakar, October 29, 2001.

Cissé, Malick. Inspector, Direction de l'Administration Générale et de l'Equipement. Dakar, July 4, 2002.

Diouf, Awa Ndiaye. Editor, *Echos des Collectivites Locales,* USAID/DGF-FELO. Dakar, October 31, 2001.

Djibo, Ibrahima. Associate Resident Representative and Adjunct Director of Programs, UNDP-Senegal. Dakar, October 29, 2001.

Fall, Amadou Lamine, Abdourahmane Diop, Adama Fall, Moctar Diallo, Amadou Yahole, and Salimata Boye. PADMIR-Kébémer Technical Assistance Unit, United Nations Capital Development Fund. Kébémer, November 1–3, 2001.

Fall, Boubacar. Assistant Resident Representative, United Nations Capital Development Fund–Senegal. Dakar, October 29, 2001.

Fall, Mamadou Moctar. National Program Coordinator, PADMIR program, United Nations Capital Development Fund. Dakar, October 29, 2001.

Faye, Gilbert. Sub-prefect, Ndande, Louga Province. Ndande, November 2, 2001.

Fournier, Christian. Regional Expert on Decentralization, West Africa Region, United Nations Capital Development Fund. New York, October 26, 2001, and Dakar, June 5, 2002.

Gaye, Ibrahim. Professor/Researcher, Ecole Nationale d'Economie Appliquée. Dakar, October 30, 2001.

Gaye, Moctar. Assistant Director, Direction des Collectivites Locales. Dakar, (#1) July 2, 2002, and (#2) July 4, 2002.

Gueye, Francois, Ousmane Gueye, Khady Diop, and Maggatte Fall. Centre d'Extension Rurale Polyvalent, Louga Province. Kébémer, November 2, 2001.

Guèye, Khalifa. Director, Direction des Collectivites Locales. Dakar, October 29, 2001.

Guèye, Macoudou. Director, National Tax Service. Dakar, June 26, 2002.

LaRochelle, J. Guy. Director, Programme d'Appui aux Elus Locaux. Dakar, June 28, 2002.

Lo, Henri Papa. Professor, Department of Environmental Engineering, Université Cheikh Anta Diop de Dakar. Dakar, October 29, 2001.

Ndiaye, Biram Owens. Former Prefect, and Coordinator, Decentralization Project, Canadian Development Assistance Program. Dakar, October 31, 2001, and July 3, 2002.

Ndiaye, Papa. Consultant, Ministry of Economy and Finance. Dakar, June 10, 2002.

Ndiaye, Tahibou. Directeur de Cadastre, Direction Generale des Impôts. Dakar, June 18, 2002.

Niang, El Hadj Sidy. Coordinator, Maison des Elus Locaux. Dakar, July 4, 2002.

Reid, Stephen. Project manager, USAID/DGF-FELO. Dakar, October 31, 2001.

Rural Council of Diouckoul Diawrigne (Louga province). Kébémer, November 1, 2001.

Sokhanokho, Assane. Project coordinator, Ministry of Health. Dakar, July 5, 2002.

Thiam, Abdoulaye. Reporter on Governmental Affairs, *Le Soleil*. Dakar, June 14, 2002.

Village Development Committee of Swal Perl, Louga province. Swal Perl, November 1, 2001.

Village Development Committee of Thiénava, Louga Province. Thiénava, November 3, 2001.

Wambold-Liebling, Kristin. Project Manager (PADMIR), United Nations Capital Development Fund. New York, October 26, 2001.

Wané, Dieynaba Ndiaye. Technical expert, Programme Nationale d'Infrastructure Rurale. Dakar, October 30, 2001.

Wone, Ibrahima. Prefect, Kébémer, Louga Province. Kébémer, November 2, 2001.

South Africa

Abedian, Iraj. Group Chief Economist, Standard Bank SA; Former official at National Treasury. Cape Town, March 22, 2002.

Ajam, Tania. Task Force Leader, Presidential Review Commission; Member Budget Review Panel (National Treasury); Member of Intergovernmental Relations Audit panel; Director, Applied Fiscal Research Centre, University of Cape Town. Cape Town, March 11, 2002.

Bekker, Theo. Former Advisor to the Premier of Gauteng Province; Professor of Political Science, University of Pretoria. Pretoria, April 25, 2002.

Cameron, Rob. Member of the Western Cape Demarcation Board; Professor of Political Science, University of Cape Town. Cape Town, February 28, 2002.

Carrim, Yunus. Chair, Committee on Provincial and Local Relations, National Assembly. Cape Town, May 21, 2002.

Davies, Rob. Chair, Committee on Trade and Industry, National Assembly. Cape Town, May 17, 2002.

Fast, Hildegaard. Analyst/Parliamentary Liaison, Financial and Fiscal Commission. Cape Town, May 14, 2002.

Hindle, Duncan. Deputy Director-General, Education Ministry. Cape Town, May 21, 2002.

Le Roux, Ingrid. Former Advisor to the Provincial Minister of the Executive Committee (MEC) for Health, Western Cape Province. Cape Town, May 29, 2002.

Momoniat, Ismail. Head, Intergovernmental Relations Division, National Treasury. Cape Town, May 8, 2002.

Morobe, Murphy. Chairman, Financial and Fiscal Commission. Pretoria, April 25, 2002.

Murray, Christina. Legal Advisor to the Constituent National Assembly. Cape Town, April 10, 2002.

Powell, Derek. Department of Provincial and Local Government. Pretoria (via telephone), May 20, 2002.

Simkins, Charles. Advisor/Consultant, Department of Education. Johannesburg (via telephone), May 16, 2002.

Sooybryan, Bobby. Deputy Director-General for Planning and Monitoring; Department of Education. Pretoria (via telephone), May 20, 2002.

Steytler, Nico. Member of Intergovernmental Relations Audit panel, Chair of the Western Cape Constitutional Committee. Cape Town, April 16, 2002.

Surty, Mohammed Enver. ANC Chief Whip, National Council of Provinces. Cape Town, May 15, 2002.

Tapscott, Chris. Member of Intergovernmental Relations Audit panel; Dean of the School of Government, University of the Western Cape. Cape Town, March 25, 2002.

Wehner, Joachim. Analyst, IDASA Budget Service. Cape Town, April 18, 2002.

Wildeman, Russell. Analyst, IDASA Budget Service; Consultant, Department of Education. Cape Town, April 19, 2002.

Wittenberg, Martin. Consultant, Department of Education; Professor of Economics at the University of the Witwatersrand. Johannesburg (via telephone), March 19, 2002.

Zille, Helen. Former Provincial Minister of the Executive Committee (MEC) for Education, Western Cape Province. Cape Town, May 18, 2002.

REFERENCES

Abedian, Iraj, Tania Ajam, and Laura Walker. 1997. *Promises, Plans, and Priorities: South Africa's Emerging Fiscal Structures.* Cape Town: IDASA.

Abrucio, Fernando Luiz. 1998. *Os barões da federação: Os governadores e a redemocratização brasileira.* São Paulo: HUCITEC.

Adamolekun, Ladipo. 1971. "Bureaucrats and the Senegalese Political Process." *Journal of Modern African Studies* 9 (4): 543–59.

Affonso, Rui de Britto Alvares, and Pedro Luiz Barros Silva. 1996. *Descentralização e políticas sociais.* São Paulo: FUNDAP.

Afonso, José Roberto Rodrigues. 1994. *Descentralização: Um estudo de caso sobre o Brasil.* Rio de Janeiro: Banco Nacional de Desenvolvimento Econômico e Social.

———. 2002. "Responsabilidade Fiscal: Primeiros e Próximos Passos." Rio de Janeiro: Banco Nacional de Desenvolvimento Econômico e Social.

Ahmad, Junaid. 1998. "South Africa: An Intergovernmental Fiscal System in Transition." In *Fiscal Decentralization in Developing Countries,* ed. Richard Bird and François Vaillancourt, 239–70. Cambridge: Cambridge University Press.

———. 2003. "Creating Incentives for Fiscal Discipline in the New South Africa." In *Fiscal Decentralization and the Challenge of Hard Budget Constraints,* ed. Jonathan A. Rodden, Gunnar S. Eskeland, and Jennie Litvack, 325–51. Cambridge: MIT Press.

Ajam, Tania. 1998. "The Evolution of Devolution: Fiscal Decentralization in South Africa." In *Economic Globalization and Fiscal Policy,* ed. Iraj Abedian and Michael Biggs, 54–114. Cape Town: Oxford University Press.

———. 2001. "Intergovernmental Fiscal Relations in South Africa." In *Intergovernmental Relations in South Africa: The Challenges of Co-operative Government,* ed. Norman Levy and Chris Tapscott, 125–42. Cape Town: IDASA/University of the Western Cape.

Ames, Barry. 2001. *The Deadlock of Democracy in Brazil.* Ann Arbor: University of Michigan Press.

Amorim Neto, Octavio. 2002. "Presidential Cabinets, Electoral Cycles and Coalition Discipline in Brazil." In *Legislative Politics in Latin America,* ed. Scott Morgenstern and Benito Nacif, 48–78. New York: Cambridge University Press.

Amorim Neto, Octavio, Gary Cox, and Mathew McCubbins. 2003. "Agenda Power in Brazil's Câmara dos Deputados, 1989–1998." *World Politics* 55 (4): 550–78.

Araoz, Mercedes, and Roberto Urrunaga. 1996. *Finanzas municipales: Ineficiencias y excesiva dependencia del gobierno central.* Lima: Universidad del Pacifico.

Araújo, Erika Amorim, and Paulo André de Oliveira. 2001. "Receita municipal: A importância das transferências do FPM e do SUS." Working Paper no. 28 (June). Rio de Janeiro: BNDES.

Arretche, Marta. 2000. *Estado Federativa e Políticas Sociais: Determinantes da Descentralização.* São Paulo: FUNDAP.

Arretche, Marta, and Vicente Rodriguez, eds. 1999. *Descentralização das políticas sociais no Brasil.* São Paulo: FUNDAP.

Atkinson, Doreen, and Maxine Reitzes. 1998. *From a Tier to a Sphere: Local Government in the New South African Constitutional Order.* Sandton: EISA and Heinemann.

Banco Central de Reserva del Perú. 2001. *Descentralización, Estabilidad y Desarrollo Económico: La experiencia internacional.* Lima: Banco Central de Reserva del Perú/TAREA.

Barman, Roderick J. 1988. *Brazil: The Forging of a Nation, 1798–1852.* Stanford: Stanford University Press.

Bates, Robert H. 1988. "Contra-contractarianism: Some Reflections on the New Institutionalism." *Politics and Society* 16 (2–3): 387–401.

Beck, Linda J. 1997. "Senegal's 'Patrimonial Democrats': Incremental Reform and the Obstacles to the Consolidation of Democracy." *Canadian Journal of African Studies* 31 (1): 1–31.

Bird, Richard, and François Vaillancourt, eds. 1998. *Fiscal Decentralization in Developing Countries.* Cambridge: Cambridge University Press.

Boadway, Robin, Sandra Roberts, and Anwar Shah. 1994. *Fiscal Federalism Dimensions of Tax Reform in Developing Countries.* Washington, D.C.: World Bank.

Boadway, Robin, and Anwar Shah. 2009. *Fiscal Federalism: Principles and Practice of Multiorder Governance.* Cambridge: Cambridge University Press.

Boone, Catherine. 1990a. "The Making of a Rentier Class: Wealth Accumulation and Political Control in Senegal." *Journal of Development Studies* 26 (3): 425–49.

———. 1990b. "State Power and Economic Crisis in Senegal." *Comparative Politics* 22 (3): 341–57.

———. 1992. *Merchant Capital and the Roots of State Power in Senegal, 1930–1985.* Cambridge: Cambridge University Press.

———. 2003. *Political Topographies of the African State: Territorial Authority and Institutional Choice.* Cambridge: Cambridge University Press.

Bouat, Marie-Claire, and Jean-Louis Fouilland. 1983. *Les finances publiques des communes et des communautés rurales au Sénégal.* Dakar: Editions Clairafrique.

Bratton, Michael, and Nicolas van de Walle. 1997. *Democratic Experiments in Africa: Regime Transitions in Comparative Perspective.* Cambridge: Cambridge University Press.

Bresser Pereira, Luiz Carlos. 2003. "The 1995 Public Management Reform in Brazil: Reflections of a Reformer." In *Reinventing Leviathan: The Politics of Administrative Reform in Developing Countries,* ed. Ben Ross Schneider and Blanca Heredia, 89–112. Miami: North South Center Press.

Burki, Shahid Javed, Guillermo Perry, and William Dillinger. 1999. *Beyond the Center: Decentralizing the State.* Washington, D.C.: World Bank.

Burns, E. Bradford. 1980. *A History of Brazil.* New York: Columbia University Press.

Cameron, Maxwell. 1994. *Democracy and Authoritarianism in Peru: Political Coalitions and Social Change.* New York: Palgrave Macmillan.

Cameron, Robert. 1997. "South Africa's Final Constitution: The Elevation of Local Government." Paper presented at the International Association of Schools and Institutes, July 8–11.

———. 1999. *Democratisation of South African Local Government.* Pretoria: J. L. van Scheik.

———. 2001. "The Upliftment of South African Local Government?" *Local Government Studies* 27 (3): 97–118.

Cardoso, Fernando Henrique, and Enzo Faletto. 1979. *Dependency and Development in Latin America.* Berkeley and Los Angeles: University of California Press.

Carey, John, and Matthew Shugart. 1998. *Executive Decree Authority.* New York: Cambridge University Press.

Centeno, Miguel Ángel. 1994. *Democracy Within Reason: Technocratic Revolution in Mexico.* University Park: Pennsylvania State University Press.

Cheema, G. Shabbir, and Dennis A. Rondinelli, eds. 1983. *Decentralization and Development: Policy Implementation in Developing Countries.* Beverly Hills, Calif.: Sage.

Collier, Ruth Berins, and David Collier. 1991. *Shaping the Political Arena.* Princeton: Princeton University Press.

Conaghan, Catherine, and James Malloy. 1994. *Unsettling Statecraft: Democracy and Neoliberalism in the Central Andes.* Pittsburgh: University of Pittsburgh Press.

Contreras, Carlos. 2002. "El centralismo peruano en su perspectiva histórica." Working Paper no. 127. Lima: Instituto de Estudios Peruanos.

Corrales, Javier, and Michael Penfold. 2007. "Venezuela: Crowding Out the Opposition." *Journal of Democracy* 18 (2): 99–113.

Costa, Vera Lucia Cabral, ed. 1997. *Gestão educacional e descentralização.* 2nd ed. São Paulo: FUNDAP.

———. 1999. *Descentralização da educação: Novas formas de coordenação e financiamento.* São Paulo: FUNDAP.

Cotler, Julio. 1995. "Political Parties and the Problems of Democratic Consolidation in Peru." In *Building Democratic Institutions: Party Systems in Latin America,* ed. Scott Mainwaring and Timothy Scully, 323–53. Stanford: Stanford University Press.

Crook, Richard, and James Manor. 1998. *Democracy and Decentralization in South Asia and West Africa: Participation, Accountability, and Performance.* New York: Cambridge University Press.

Cruise O'Brien, Donal, Momar Coumba Diop, and Mamadou Diouf. 2002. *La construction de l'état au Sénégal.* Paris: Karthala.

Cruz, Rafael de la. 2004. "Decentralization: Key to Understanding a Changing Nation." In *The Unraveling of Representative Democracy in Venezuela,* ed. Jennifer McCoy and David Myers, 181–201. Baltimore: Johns Hopkins University Press.

Daughters, Robert, and Leslie Harper. 2007. "Fiscal and Political Decentralization Reforms." In *The State of State Reform in Latin America,* ed. Eduardo Lora, 87–121. Washington, D.C.: World Bank.

Davenport, T. R. H. 1991. *South Africa: A Modern History.* 4th ed. Toronto: University of Toronto Press.

———. 1998. *The Transfer of Power in South Africa.* Claremont: David Philip.

Diaz-Cayeros, Alberto. 2006. *Federalism, Fiscal Authority, and Centralization in Latin America.* Cambridge: Cambridge University Press.

Dickovick, J. Tyler. 2005. "The Measure and Mismeasure of Decentralization: Senegal and South Africa." *Journal of Modern African Studies* 43 (2): 183–210.

———. 2007. "Municipalization as Central Government Strategy: National-Regional-Local Relations in Peru, Brazil, and South Africa." *Publius: The Journal of Federalism* 37 (1): 1–25.

Dillinger, William, and Steven Webb. 1999. "Fiscal Management in Federal Democracies: Argentina and Brazil." Policy Research Working Paper no. 2121. Washington, D.C.: World Bank.

———. 2001. "Is Fiscal Stability Compatible with Decentralization? The Case of Latin America." Unpublished manuscript. Washington, D.C: World Bank.

Diop, Momar Coumba. 1992. *Sénégal: Trajectoires d'un État.* Paris: Karthala.

———. 2002. *Le Sénégal contemporain.* Paris: Karthala.

Diop, Momar, and Mamadou Diouf. 1990. *Le Sénégal sous Abdou Diouf.* Paris: Éditions Karthala.

———. 1997. "Pouvoir central et pouvoir local: La crise de l'institution municipale au Sénégal." In *Pouvoirs et cités d'Afrique noire: Décentralisations en questions,* ed. Sylvy Jaglin and Alain Dubresson, 101–25. Paris: Karthala.

Eaton, Kent. 2000. "Decentralization, Democratization and Liberalization: The History of Revenue Sharing in Argentina, 1934–1999." Working Paper no. 3. Princeton, N.J.: Program in Latin American Studies, Princeton University, May 2000.

———. 2001. "Political Obstacles to Decentralization: Evidence from Argentina and the Philippines." *Development and Change* 32 (1): 101–27.

———. 2002. *Politicians and Economic Reform in New Democracies: Argentina and the Philippines in the 1990s.* University Park: Pennsylvania State University Press.

———. 2004a. *Politics Beyond the Capital: The Design of Subnational Institutions in South America.* Stanford: Stanford University Press.

———. 2004b. "The Link Between Political and Fiscal Decentralization in South America." In *Decentralization and Democracy in Latin America,* ed. Alfred Montero and David Samuels, 122–54. Notre Dame: University of Notre Dame Press.

Eaton, Kent, and J. Tyler Dickovick. 2004. "The Politics of Recentralization in Argentina and Brazil." *Latin American Research Review* 39 (1): 90–122.

Evans, Peter. 1979. *Dependent Development: The Alliance of Multinational, State, and Local Capital in Brazil.* Princeton: Princeton University Press.

Falleti, Tulia. 2005. "A Sequential Theory of Decentralization: Latin American Cases in Comparative Perspective." *American Political Science Review* 100 (2): 327–46.

Fenwick, Tracy Beck. 2009. "Avoiding Governors: The Success of *Bolsa Familia.*" *Latin American Research Review* 44 (1): 102–31.

Figueiredo, Argelina, and Fernando Limongi. 2000. "Presidential Power, Legislative Organization, and Party Behavior in Brazil." *Comparative Politics* 32 (2): 151–70.

Financial and Fiscal Commission. 1995. *A Framework Document for Intergovernmental Fiscal Relations in South Africa.* Pretoria: FFC.

———. 1997. *Local Government in a System of Intergovernmental Fiscal Relations in South Africa: A Discussion Document.* Pretoria: FFC.

Fleischer, David. 1998. "The Cardoso Government's Reform Agenda: A View from the National Congress, 1995–1998." *Journal of Interamerican Studies and World Affairs* 40 (4): 119–36.

Fotsing, Jean-Baptiste. 1995. *Le pouvoir fiscal en Afrique: Essais sur la legitimité fiscale dans les états d'afrique noire francophone.* Paris: Librairie Générale de droit et de jurisprudence.

Galvan, Dennis. 2001. "Political Turnover and Social Change in Senegal." *Journal of Democracy* 12 (3): 51–62.

Garman, Christopher, Stephen Haggard, and Eliza Willis. 2001. "Fiscal Decentralization: A Political Theory with Latin American Cases." *World Politics* 53 (2): 205–36.

Garson, Sol, and Erika Araújo. 2001. "Ações sociais básicas: Descentralização ou municipalização?" Working Paper no. 23, January. Rio de Janeiro: BNDES.

Geddes, Barbara. 1994. *Politician's Dilemma: Building State Capacity in Latin America.* Berkeley and Los Angeles: University of California Press.

Gellar, Sheldon. 1976. *Structural Changes and Colonial Dependency: Senegal 1885–1945.* Beverly Hills, Calif.: SAGE Publications.

———. 1990. "State Tutelage vs. Self-Governance: The Rhetoric and Reality of Decentralization in Senegal." In *The Failure of the Centralized State,* ed. James Wunsch and Dele Olowu, 130–47. Boulder, Colo.: Westview Press.

———. 1995. *Senegal: An African State Between Islam and the West.* Boulder, Colo.: Westview Press.

Gibson, Edward. 2004. "Federalism and Democracy: Theoretical Connections and Cautionary Insights." In *Federalism and Democracy in Latin America,* ed. Edward Gibson, 1–28. Baltimore: Johns Hopkins University Press.

Gibson, Edward, and Tulia Faletti. 2004. "Unity by the Stick: The Origins of Argentine Federalism." In *Federalism and Democracy in Latin America,* ed. Edward Gibson, 226–54. Baltimore: Johns Hopkins University Press.

Gonzales de Olarte, Efraín. 1997. "La descentralización en el Perú: Diagnóstico y propuesta." In *Ajuste estructural en el Perú: Modelo económico, empleo, y descentralización,* ed. Efraín Gonzales de Olarte, 223–49. Lima: Instituto de Estudios Peruanos.

———. 2000. *Neocentralismo y Neoliberalismo en el Perú.* Lima: Instituto de Estudios Peruanos.

Gonzales de Olarte, Efraín, Teobaldo Pinzás García, and Carolina Trivelli Avila. 1994. "Descentralización Fiscal y Regionalización en el Perú." Working Paper no. 69. Lima: Instituto de Estudios Peruanos.

Graham, Carol, and Cheikh Kane. 1998. "Opportunistic Government or Sustaining Reform? Electoral Trends and Public Expenditure Patterns in Peru, 1990–1995." *Latin American Research Review* 33 (1): 71–111.

Grindle, Merilee. 1996. *Challenging the State: Crisis and Innovation in Latin America and Africa.* New York: Cambridge University Press.

———. 2000. *Audacious Reforms: Institutional Invention and Democracy in Latin America.* Baltimore: Johns Hopkins University Press.

Grompone, Romeo. 2002. "Los dilemas no resueltos de la descentralización." Working Paper no. 118. Lima: Instituto de Estudios Peruanos.

Grupo Propuesta Ciudadana. 1995. *Democracia: Descentralización y Política Social.* Lima: Grupo Propuesta Ciudadana.

Haggard, Stephan, and Robert R. Kaufman. 1992. *The Politics of Economic Adjustment.* Princeton: Princeton University Press.

———. 1995. *The Political Economy of Democratic Transitions.* Princeton: Princeton University Press.

Haggard, Stephan, and Steven B. Webb. 2004. "Political Incentives and Intergovernmental Fiscal Relations." In *Decentralization and Democracy in Latin America,* ed. Alfred P. Montero and David J. Samuels, 235–70. Notre Dame: University of Notre Dame Press.

Hagopian, Frances. 1996. *Traditional Politics and Regime Change in Brazil.* New York: Cambridge University Press.

Hagopian, Frances, Carlos Gervasoni, and Juan Andres Moraes. 2009. "From Patronage to Program: The Emergence of Party-Oriented Legislators in Brazil." *Comparative Political Studies* 42 (3): 360–91.

Heller, Patrick. 2001. "Moving the State: The Politics of Democratic Decentralization in Kerela, South Africa, and Porto Alegre." *Politics and Society* 29 (1): 131–63.

Herbst, Jeffrey. 2000. *States and Power in Africa.* Princeton: Princeton University Press.

Hesseling, Gerti. 1985. *Histoire politique du Sénégal: Institutions, droit et société.* Paris: Éditions Karthala.

Hydén, Göran, and Michael Bratton. 1992. *Governance and Politics in Africa.* London: Lynne Rienner.

International Monetary Fund. 2008. World Economic Outlook Database. Available at http://www.inf.org/externa/pubs/ft/wep/2008/01/weodata/download.aspx. Accessed August 24, 2010.

IPADEL (Instituto para la Democracia Local). 1989. *Regionalización y gobiernos locales.* Lima: TAREA/IPADEL.

Jurado Nacional de Elecciones. 2002. *Legislación Electoral 2002: Elecciones Regionales y Municipales.* Lima: Jurado Nacional de Elecciones.

Kassé, Moustapha. 1990. *Sénégal: Crise économique et ajustement structurel.* Ivry-sur-Seine: Éditions Nouvelles du Sud.

Kay, Bruce. 1996. "'Fujipopulism' and the Liberal State in Peru, 1990–95." *Journal of Interamerican Studies and World Affairs* 38 (4): 55–98.

Khosa, Meshack, and Yvonne Muthien. 1998. "Establishing Regional Governance in the New South Africa." In *Regionalism in the New South Africa,* ed. Meshack Khosa and Yvonne Muthien, 1–10. Aldershot: Ashgate.

Kim, Sung Han. 1992. "The Political Process of Decentralization in Peru." *Public Administration and Development* 12 (3): 249–65.

Kingstone, Peter. 1999. *Crafting Coalitions for Reform: Business Preferences, Political Institutions, and Neoliberal Reform in Brazil.* University Park: Penn State Press.

Kingstone, Peter, and Timothy Power, eds. 2000. *Democratic Brazil: Actors, Institutions and Processes.* Pittsburgh: University of Pittsburgh Press.

Krige, Dulcie. 1998. "The Educational Implications of the New Provinces." In *Regionalism in the New South Africa,* ed. Meshack Khosa and Yvonne Muthien, 85–109. Aldershot: Ashgate.

Levi, Margaret. 1988. *Of Rule and Revenue.* Berkeley and Los Angeles: University of California Press.

Levy, Norman, and Chris Tapscott, eds. 2001. *Intergovernmental Relations in South Africa: The Challenges of Co-operative Government.* Cape Town: IDASA/University of the Western Cape.

Lewis, W. Arthur. 1965. *Politics in West Africa.* London: Allen and Unwin.

Lieberman, Evan. 2003. *Race and Regionalism in the Politics of Taxation in Brazil and South Africa.* Cambridge: Cambridge University Press.

Lodge, Tom. 1999. *South African Politics Since 1994.* Claremont, South Africa: David Philip.

Maia Gomes, Gustavo, and Cristina MacDowell. 2000. *Descentralização Política, Feder-alismo Fiscal e Criação de Municipios: O que é Mau para o Econômico nem sempre é Bom para o Social.* Brasilia: IPEA.

Mainwaring, Scott. 1997a. "Multipartism, Robust Federalism, and Presidentialism in Brazil." In *Presidentialism and Democracy in Latin America,* ed. Scott Mainwaring and Matthew Shugart, 55–109. New York: Cambridge University Press.

———. 1997b. *Presidentialism in Brazil: The Impact of Strong Constitutional Powers, Weak Partisan Powers, and Robust Federalism.* Washington, D.C.: Woodrow Wilson International Center for Scholars.

Mainwaring, Scott, and Timothy R. Scully. 1995. *Building Democratic Institutions: Party Systems in Latin America.* Stanford: Stanford University Press.

Mainwaring, Scott, and Matthew Shugart. 1997. *Presidentialism and Democracy in Latin America.* New York: Cambridge University Press.

Mamdani, Mahmood. 1996. *Citizen and Subject: Contemporary Africa and the Legacy of Late Colonialism.* Princeton: Princeton University Press.

Manor, James. 1999. *The Political Economy of Democratic Decentralization.* Washington, D.C.: World Bank.

Marks, Christopher. 1996a. "Decentralization and the Potential for Effective Municipal Governance in Senegal." Working Paper no. 183. University of Maryland Center for Institutional Reform and the Informal Sector.

———. 1996b. "Decentralization and Municipal Governance in Senegal." Ph.D. thesis. Woodrow Wilson School, Princeton University.

Martinez-Lara, Javier. 1996. *Building Democracy in Brazil: The Politics of Constitutional Change, 1985–95.* New York: St. Martin's Press.

Mawhood, Phillip, ed. 1983. *Local Government in the Third World: The Experience of Tropical Africa.* Chichester: John Wiley and Sons.

Mejía Navarette, Julio Victor. 1990. *Estado y municipio en el Perú.* Lima: Consejo Nacional de Ciencia y Technología.

Melo, Marcus André. 1996. "Crise Federativa, Guerra Fiscal e 'Hobbesianismo Municipal': Efeitos perversos da descentralização?" *São Paulo em Perspectiva* 10 (3): 11–20.

———. 2003. "When Institutions Matter: A Comparison of the Politics of Administrative, Social Security, and Tax Reforms in Brazil." In *Reinventing Leviathan: The Politics of Administrative Reform in Developing Countries,* ed. Ben Ross Schneider and Blanca Heredia, 211–50. Miami: North South Center Press.

Meneguello, Rachel. 1998. *Partidos e Governos no Brasil Contemporâneo (1985–1997).* São Paulo: Paz e Terra.

Miranda, Sergio. 2001. *Verdades e mentiras da Lei de Responsabilidade Fiscal.* Brasilia: Camara de Deputados.

Momoniat, Ismail. 2002. "Fiscal Decentralisation in South Africa: A Practitioner's Perspective." Unpublished paper. Washington, D.C.: World Bank.

Montero, Alfred. 2000. "Devolving Democracy? Political Decentralization and the New Brazilian Federalism." In *Democratic Brazil: Actors, Institutions, and Processes,* ed. Peter Kingstone and Timothy Power, 58–76. Pittsburgh: University of Pittsburgh Press.

———. 2004. "Competitive Federalism and Distributive Conflict." In *Reforming Brazil,* ed. Mauricio A. Font and Anthony Peter Spanakos, 137–59. Lanham, Md.: Lexington Books.

Montero, Alfred, and David Samuels. 2004. "The Political Determinants of Decentralization in Latin America: Causes and Consequences." In *Democracy and Decentralization in Latin America,* ed. Alfred Montero and David Samuels, 3–32. Notre
Dame: University of Notre Dame Press.

Montinola, Gabriela, Yingyi Qian, and Barry Weingast. 1995. "Federalism, Chinese Style:
The Political Basis for Economic Success in China." *World Politics* 48 (1): 50–81.

Mora, Mônica, and Varsano, Ricardo. 2001. "Fiscal Decentralization and Subnational
Fiscal Autonomy in Brazil: Some Facts of the Nineties." Working Paper no. 854.
Brasilia: IPEA.

Murray, Christina. 2001. "The Constitutional Context of Intergovernmental Relations in
South Africa." In *Intergovernmental Relations in South Africa: The Challenges of
Co-operative Government,* ed. Norman Levy and Chris Tapscott, 66–83. Cape
Town: IDASA/University of the Western Cape.

Muthien, Yvonne G., and Meshack M. Khosa. 1995. "'The Kingdom, the Volkstaat and
the New South Africa': Drawing South Africa's New Regional Boundaries." *Journal
of Southern African Studies* 21 (2): 303–22.

Myers, David. 2009. "Venezuela: Delegative Democracy or Electoral Autocracy?" In
Constructing Democratic Governance in Latin America, ed. Jorge Dominguez and
Michael Shifter, 285–320. 3rd ed. Baltimore: Johns Hopkins University Press.

Naidoo, Kuben, and Clive Pintusewitz. 1998. "Are the Provinces Overspending? Budgeting
in the New Inter-governmental Fiscal System." *Indicator SA* 15 (1): 37–40.

Ndir, Papa Alassane, Jesper Steffensen, Svend Trollegaard, and Abdoul Wahab Ba. 1999.
*Senegal: Fiscal Decentralization and Sub-National Finance in Relation to Infra-
structure and Service Provision.* Dakar: World Bank.

Oates, Wallace. 1972. *Fiscal Federalism.* New York: Harcourt Brace Jovanovich.

O'Brien, Donal Cruise, Momar-Coumba Diop, and Mamadou Diouf. 2002. *La construction de l'état au Sénégal.* Paris: Karthala.

O'Donnell, Guillermo. 1972. *Modernization and Bureaucratic-Authoritarianism.* Berkeley, Calif.: Institute of International Studies.

Olowu, Dele, and James Wunsch, eds. 2004. *Local Governance in Africa: The Challenges
of Democratic Decentralization.* Boulder, Colo.: Lynne Rienner.

O'Neill, Kathleen. 2003. "Decentralization as an Electoral Strategy." *Comparative Political
Studies* 36 (9): 1068–91.

———. 2005. *Decentralizing the State: Elections, Parties, and Local Power in the Andes.*
Cambridge: Cambridge University Press.

Ortiz de Zevallos, Gabriel, and Pierina Pollarolo, eds. 2000a. *Educación (Task Forces
Agenda para la Primera Década).* Lima: Instituto Apoyo.

———. 2000b. *Gobiernos locales (Task Forces Agenda para la Primera Década).* Lima:
Instituto Apoyo.

———. 2000c. *Reforma del Estado: Descentralización (Task Forces Agenda para la Primera
Década).* Lima: Instituto Apoyo.

———. 2000d. *Salud (Task Forces Agenda para la Primera Década).* Lima: Instituto Apoyo.

Petiteville, Franck. 1995. "Aperçus politiques sur les processus de décentralisation subsa-
hariens." *Revue juridique et politique: Indépendance et coopération* 49 (3): 347–63.

Pierson, Paul. 1996. "The New Politics of the Welfare State." *World Politics* 48 (2): 143–79.

———. 2000. "Increasing Returns, Path Dependence, and the Study of Politics." *American
Political Science Review* 94 (2): 251–67.

Planas, Pedro. 1998. *La descentralización en el Perú republicano (1821–1998)*. Lima: Municipalidad Metropolitana de Lima.

———. 2001. *Manual del buen descentralista*. Trujillo: Nueva Norte.

Power, Timothy. 1998. "Brazilian Politicians and Neoliberalism: Mapping Support for
the Cardoso Reforms, 1995–1997." *Journal of Interamerican Studies and World Affairs*
40 (4): 51–72.

———. 2002. "Blairism Brazilian Style? Cardoso and the 'Third Way' in Brazil." *Political
Science Quarterly* 116 (4): 611–36.

———. 2008. "Centering Democracy? Ideological Cleavages and Convergence in the
Brazilian Political Class." In *Democratic Brazil Revisited*, ed. Peter Kingstone and
Timothy Power, 81–106. Pittsburgh: University of Pittsburgh Press.

Power, Timothy, and Cesar Zucco Jr. 2009. "Estimating Ideology of Brazilian Legislative
Parties, 1990–2005: A Research Communication." *Latin American Research Review*
44 (1): 218–46.

Reddy, P. S. 1996. "Local Government Restructuring in South Africa." In *Readings in
Local Government Management and Development: A Southern African Perspective*,
ed. P. S. Reddy, 49–64. Kenwyn: Juta.

Reich, Gary M. 1998. "The 1988 Constitution a Decade Later: Ugly Compromises Reconsi-
dered." *Journal of Interamerican Studies and World Affairs* 40 (4): 5–24.

Reinhart, Carmen, and Kenneth Rogoff. 2009. *This Time Is Different: Eight Centuries of
Financial Folly*. Princeton: Princeton University Press.

Riker, William. 1964. *Federalism: Origin, Operation, Significance*. Boston: Little, Brown.

Rodden, Jonathan A. 2003. "Federalism and Bailouts in Brazil." In *Fiscal Decentralization
and the Challenge of Hard Budget Constraints*, ed. Jonathan A. Rodden, Gunnar S.
Eskeland, and Jennie Litvack, 213–48. Cambridge: MIT Press.

———. 2006. *Hamilton's Paradox: The Promise and Peril of Fiscal Federalism*. Cambridge:
Cambridge University Press.

Rodden, Jonathan A., Gunnar S. Eskeland, and Jennie Litvack, eds. 2003. *Fiscal Decentralization and the Challenge of Hard Budget Constraints*. Cambridge: MIT Press.

Rodden, Jonathan A., and Susan Rose-Ackerman. 1997. "Does Federalism Preserve Markets?"
Virginia Law Review 83:1521–72.

Rodriguez, Victoria. 1997. *Decentralization in Mexico: From Reforma Municipal to Soli-
daridad to Nuevo Federalismo*. Boulder, Colo.: Westview.

Rondinelli, Dennis A., John R. Nellis, and G. Shabbir Cheema, eds. 1983. *Decentralization in Developing Countries: A Review of Recent Experience*. Washington, D.C.:
World Bank.

Rondinelli, Dennis, and Henry Minis Jr. 1990. "Administrative Restructuring for Economic
Adjustment: Decentralization Policy in Senegal." *International Review of Administrative Sciences* 56 (3): 447–66.

RP/MP (República del Perú, Ministerio de la Presidencia). 2002. *Crónica de una desac-
tivación anunciada*. Lima: República del Perú.

RS (République du Sénégal), Présidence. 2001. *Rapport du Comité Technique Sectoriel:
Décentralisation et Gouvernance Locale*. Dakar: Government Printer.

RS (République du Sénégal), Secrétariat Général du Gouvernement. 1997. *Le recueil des
des textes de la décentralisation*. Dakar: Imprimerie du Midi.

RS/MI (République du Sénégal, Ministère de l'Intérieur). 1996. *Textes de loi de la decentralization*. Dakar: Imprimerie Capital+.

———. 2001. *Manuel de procedures de contrôles et de légalité budgétaire.* Dakar: Imprimerie Saint-Paul.

RSA (Republic of South Africa), Ministry of Provincial Affairs and Constitutional Development. 1998. *The White Paper on Local Government.* Pretoria: Ministry of Provincial Affairs and Constitutional Development.

RSA/DPLG (Republic of South Africa, Department of Provincial and Local Government). 1999. *Intergovernmental Relations Audit.* Pretoria: Department of Provincial and Local Government.

RSA/NT (Republic of South Africa, National Treasury of the Republic of South Africa). 2001. *Intergovernmental Fiscal Review.* Pretoria: National Treasury.

———. 2003. *Intergovernmental Fiscal Review.* Pretoria: National Treasury.

Samuels, David J. 2003. *Ambition, Federalism, and Legislative Politics in Brazil.* New York: Cambridge University Press.

———. 2004. "The Political Logic of Decentralization in Brazil." In *Decentralization and Democracy in Latin America,* ed. Alfred P. Montero and David J. Samuels, 67–93. Notre Dame: University of Notre Dame Press.

Samuels, David J., and Fernando Luiz Abrucio. 2000. "Federalism and Democratic Transitions: The 'New' Politics of the Governors." *Publius: The Journal of Federalism* 30 (2): 43–62.

Samuels, David J., and Scott Mainwaring. 2004. "Strong Federalism, Constraints on the Central Government, and Economic Reform in Brazil." In *Federalism and Democracy in Latin America,* ed. Edward Gibson, 85–130. Baltimore: Johns Hopkins University Press.

Sartori, Giovanni. 1970. "Concept Misformation in Comparative Politics." *American Political Science Review* 64 (4): 1033–53.

Schady, Norbert. 1999. "Seeking Votes: The Political Economy of Expenditures by the Peruvian Social Fund (FONCODES), 1991–95." World Bank Working Paper. Washington, D.C.: World Bank.

Schmidt, Gregory. 1989. "Political Variables and Governmental Decentralization in Peru, 1949–1988." *Journal of Inter-American Studies and World Affairs* 31 (1–2): 193–232.

Schönwalder, Gerd. 1997. "New Democratic Spaces at the Grassroots? Popular Participation in Latin American Local Governments." *Development and Change* 28 (4): 753–70.

Selcher, Wayne. 1998. "The Politics of Decentralized Federalism, National Diversification, and Regionalism in Brazil." *Journal of Interamerican Studies and World Affairs* 40 (4): 25–50.

Serra, José. 2002. *Ampliando o Possível: A política de saúde do Brasil.* Rio de Janeiro: Campos.

Shah, Anwar. 1991. "The New Fiscal Federalism in Brazil." World Bank Discussion Papers no. 124. Washington, DC: World Bank.

———. 1998. *Fiscal Federalism and Macroeconomic Governance: For Better or for Worse?* Washington, D.C.: World Bank.

Shugart, Matthew, and John Carey. 1992. *Presidents and Assemblies: Constitutional Design and Electoral Dynamics.* New York: Cambridge University Press.

Smoke, Paul. 2001. *Fiscal Decentralization in Developing Countries: A Review of Current Concepts and Practice.* Geneva: UNRISD.

Snyder, Richard. 2001. "Scaling Down: Subnational Approaches to Comparative Politics." *Studies in Comparative International Development* 36 (1): 93–110.

Southall, Roger. 1994. "The South African Elections of 1994: The Remaking of a Dominant-Party State." *Journal of Modern African Studies* 32 (4): 629–55.

Souza, Celina. 1996. "Reinventando o Poder Local: Limites e possibilidades do federalismo e da descentralização." *São Paulo em Perspectiva* 10 (3): 103–12.

———. 1997. *Constitutional Engineering in Brazil: The Politics of Federalism and Decentralization.* New York: St. Martin's Press.

Sparks, Allister. 1994. *Tomorrow Is Another Country: The Inside Story of South Africa's
Negotiated Revolution.* Sandton: Struik Book Distributors.

Spitz, Richard, with Matthew Chaskalson. 2000. *The Politics of Transition: A Hidden
History of South Africa's Negotiated Settlement.* Johannesburg: Witwatersrand
University Press.

Stepan, Alfred. 1971. *The Military in Politics: Changing Patterns in Brazil.* Princeton:
Princeton University Press.

———. 2000. "Brazil's Decentralized Federalism: Bringing Government Closer to the
Citizens?" *Daedalus* 129 (2): 145–69.

Sulmont Haak, David. 1999. "Estrategias políticas y gobierno local en Lima Metropolitana." Working Paper no. 101. Serie Sociología y Política No. 20. Lima: Instituto de
Estudios Peruanos.

Swilling, Mark. 1996. "A Review of Local Government and Development in the Southern
African Region." In *Readings in Local Government Management and Development:
A Southern African Perspective,* ed. P. S. Reddy, 16–48. Kenwyn: Juta & Co.

Tanaka, Martin. 2002. "La dinámica de los actores regionales y el proceso de decentralización: ¿El despertar del letargo?" Working Paper no. 125. Lima: Instituto de
Estudios Peruanos.

Tendler, Judith. 1997. *Good Government in the Tropics.* Baltimore: Johns Hopkins University Press.

Ter-Minassian, Teresa, ed. 1997. *Fiscal Federalism in Theory and Practice.* Washington,
D.C.: International Monetary Fund.

Tiebout, Charles. 1956. "A Pure Theory of Local Expenditures." *Journal of Political Economy*
64 (2): 415–24.

Tinoco, Andrés. 1987. *Gobiernos regionales en un estado Aprista.* Lima: CIDEL.

Tordoff, William. 1994. "Decentralisation: Comparative Experience in Commonwealth
Africa." *Journal of Modern African Studies* 32 (4): 555–80.

Treisman, Daniel. 1999. "Political Decentralization and Economic Reform: A Game-
Theoretic Analysis." *American Journal of Political Science* 43 (4): 488–517.

Ugarte, Oscar. 2002. "Decentralización en salud." *Economía y sociedad* 47: 50–55.

Van de Walle, Nicolas. 2001. *African Economies and the Politics of Permanent Crisis: 1979–1999.*
Cambridge: Cambridge University Press.

Van Zyl, Albert. 1998. "Financing the Provinces in South Africa." *Indicator SA* 15
(1): 30–36.

Van Zyl, Albert, and Laura Walker. 1999. "Juggling Central Control and Provincial Fiscal
Autonomy in South Africa." *Development Southern Africa* 16 (2): 239–58.

Véliz, Claudio. 1980. *The Centralist Tradition of Latin America.* Princeton: Princeton
University Press.

Vengroff, Richard. 2000. "Decentralization, Democratization and Development in Senegal."
Paper prepared for the Yale Colloquium on Decentralization and Development,
January 21, 2000.

Vengroff, Richard, and Alan Johnston. 1989. *Decentralization and the Implementation of Rural Development in Senegal: The View from Below*. Lewiston, N.Y.: Edwin Mellen Press.

Villiers, Bertus de. 1997a. "Intergovernmental Relations in South Africa." *SA Public Law* 12 (1): 197–213.

———. 1997b. "Local-Provincial Intergovernmental Relations: A Comparative Analysis." Occasional Papers. Johannesburg: Konrad-Adenauer-Stiftung.

Wehner, Joachim. 2000a. "Asymmetrical Devolution." *Development Southern Africa* 17 (2): 249–62.

———. 2000b. "Fiscal Federalism in South Africa." *Publius: The Journal of Federalism* 30 (3): 47–72.

———. 2003. "The Institutional Politics of Revenue Sharing in South Africa." *Regional and Federal Studies* 13(1): 1–30.

Weingast, Barry. 1995. "The Economic Role of Political Institutions: Market-Preserving Federalism and Economic Development." *Journal of Law, Economics, and Organization* 20 (1): 1–31.

Weyland, Kurt. 1996. *Democracy Without Equity: Failures of Reform in Brazil*. Pittsburgh: University of Pittsburgh Press.

———. 1998. "The Political Fate of Market Reform in Latin America, Africa, and Eastern Europe." *International Studies Quarterly* 42 (4): 645–73.

———. 2002. *The Politics of Market Reform in Fragile Democracies: Argentina, Brazil, Peru, and Venezuela*. Princeton: Princeton University Press.

Wibbels, Erik. 2005. *Federalism and the Market*. Cambridge: Cambridge University Press.

Willis, Eliza, Christopher Garman, and Stephan Haggard. 1999. "Decentralization in Latin America." *Latin American Research Review* 34 (1): 7–56.

Wise, Carol. 2003. *Reinventing the State: Economic Strategy and Institutional Change in Peru*. Ann Arbor: University of Michigan Press.

Wittenberg, Martin. 2003. "Decentralisation in South Africa." Paper prepared for the STICERD conference, London School of Economics.

Wunsch, James, and Dele Olowu. 1990. *The Failure of the Centralized State*. Boulder, Colo.: Westview Press.

Young, Crawford. 1994. *The African Colonial State in Comparative Perspective*. New Haven: Yale University Press.

Yunes, João. 1999. "O SUS na lógica da descentralização." *Estudos Avançados* 13 (35): 65–70.

Zas Fris Burga, Johnny. 1998. *La descentralización fictícia: Perú 1821–1998*. Lima: Universidad del Pacífico.

Zolberg, Aristide. 1966. *Creating Political Order: The Party-States of West Africa*. Chicago: Rand McNally.

Newspapers and Periodicals

Brazil

O Estado de São Paulo (São Paulo)
A Folha de São Paulo (São Paulo)
O Globo (Rio de Janeiro)

Peru

El Comercio (Lima)
La Gestión (Lima)
La Republica (Lima)

Senegal

Le Soleil (Dakar)
Sud Quotidien (Dakar)
WalFadjiri (Dakar)

South Africa

Business Day (Johannesburg)
Cape Argus (Cape Town)
Cape Times (Cape Town)
Mail and Guardian (Johannesburg)

INDEX

www.ingramcontent.com/pod-product-compliance
Lightning Source LLC
Chambersburg PA
CBHW021900020426
42334CB00013B/409